Books by Author

How to Successfully Manage Real Estate—
in Your Spare Time

How You Can Become Financially Independent
by Investing in Real Estate

How You Can Become Financially Independent by Investing in Real Estate

by Albert J. Lowry, Ph.D.

SIMON AND SCHUSTER   *New York*

Contents

viii   *Contents*

Foreword

by *William Nickerson*

AUTHOR OF
*How I Turned One Thousand Dollars into Three Million
in Real Estate—in My Spare Time*

Can this book really help you?

It will help motivate and instruct two types of readers. This book
can either . . .

a. Enable you to invest modest amounts of money and time in
real estate as a practical, simple, safe, sure method of attain-
ing financial independence and security; or . . .

b. Show you exactly how to build a six- to seven-figure fortune
through repeated use of its proven formula for realty investment, if you are willing to work energetically at it for a few
years.

This book grew out of the separate but very similar experiences
of Albert J. Lowry and myself.

We both started as amateurs with very little money, learned by
trial and error how to succeed in real estate, and became millionaires. Responding to appeals from thousands of would-be investors,
we each began to write and lecture about our methods. Inevitably
we became aware of each other. When we met, we discovered that
both had followed almost exactly the same formula for quick success. We became close friends and eventually associated to fill the
growing nationwide demand for detailed information about our
formula.

This has had two results. First, this book by Albert Lowry is
based on his personal experiences in Today's Market. In it he
combines the concepts and techniques, the modern innovations and
refinements that will show you step by step how to start investing
in rent-producing income property with a modest amount of money

and how to pyramid it into an important sum. Secondly, our association resulted in the development of the internationally famous Lowry–Nickerson Real Estate Investors Seminar, a series of advanced lectures and question-and-answer sessions based on the elaboration of the formulas and guidelines in this book. The Seminar is given periodically in major cities across the country.

The unique methods and procedures developed by Al Lowry will enable readers of this book to learn and apply a wealth of practical knowledge in a short time.

Can *you* learn and follow this step-by-step method to success?

Yes! If you have average intelligence and a minimal education . . . can add, subtract, read and write . . . and really want to succeed . . . you can really do it!

I A Foolproof Formula for Financial Independence

Often I hear doleful talk from some people: "Money is tight . . . mortgages are almost impossible to get . . . sellers want huge down payments . . . taxes take away most of our profits." But I pay no attention to such talk because I know from my own current experiences that it's still possible to get favorable financing, still possible to sweep aside the down-payment roadblock, still possible to stay in a lower tax bracket when income jumps. More than ever, an alert investor can clean up in today's real estate market if he follows certain time-tested but little-known principles.

That's why it's such great fun. Once you get a firm grasp on the basic principles, you can use your imagination and ingenuity, inventing improvements in your money-getting methods with each deal you make. There's no reason why real estate shouldn't do for you what it does for me—bring in a safe and steady income for a lifetime.

In late 1963 I left home to try to get on my feet financially. I thought that jobs and opportunity might be more plentiful in California than in Canada.

I had little money and little education. I was raised in an orphanage until I was thirteen, then had worked as a butcher in A&P stores, and later had been a laborer in a steel mill. When I landed in California, the best job I could find was as a butcher. I decided not to take it, having done that kind of work for years without getting anywhere financially. I began studying real estate in my spare time. I'd heard that many people were making good money at it.

Because I was hungry, I probably studied harder than most people. I searched everywhere for legitimate shortcuts that would put me ahead of the crowds of would-be real estate millionaires. I made several astounding discoveries.

I found that it's possible to buy a modest house or duplex with little or no down payment, if you know where to look and what to do. I also found that I could resell the same property for a quick profit, by taking some simple steps to make it more salable.

Starting on a shoestring, I bought and sold small residences in my spare time, taking care to keep my shoestring safe every step of the way. Soon I discovered the magic leverage—how to buy with very little cash of my own, let other people's money do most of the work, and come out with big profits. Then I found that a small apartment house could be turned into a money machine by applying management principles I picked up from smart insiders.

As profits piled up I kept pyramiding my holdings and beefing up my income without taking any real risks. Within a few years I knew that investing in older houses and apartments was the prudent way to get the highest possible return on the smallest possible investment.

It still is. After fourteen years I'm still doing it, still making my money grow even though I attained complete financial independence about 1970.

I stopped expanding my real estate investments some years ago, in order to devote more time to another enjoyable sideline that was opening up for me: lecturing and writing. I was being asked to give courses at universities and professional associations, and to contribute articles to investors' publications. I found that I got deep satisfaction, as well as a comfortable income, from showing other people how to profit from what I'd learned.

Grateful letters kept coming in from people I helped. One man, Alan F. Hall of Santa Monica, wrote that he had dropped in at a seminar of mine by accident. "This accident was the turning point of my life," he went on. "Today [April 1975] I've retired after completing a world trip—and to think I started with only $100 in January 1972. It shows that anything is possible. I've taken your investment course three times now, in order to keep abreast of current developments. I've recommended the course to several friends who are now attaining their goals of financial independence, so I'm not alone."

Another investor, Mrs. Florence L. Prince, of Pleasanton, California, wrote me:

Starting with $1000 in savings, my husband and I added $2000 more within one month because you showed us how. With this $3000 we purchased a two-unit building.

Within another month we purchased a second duplex at the same price, although we had no cash. I did this by writing a letter of application for a loan, using my notes from your real estate course as a guide. I presented the letter to our bank. Not only did we get the $3000 loan, we also got a commitment for a new first loan of $50,000.

As you can see, we are on our way to building our pyramid, thanks to you.

I treasure such letters. Who wouldn't? It's a wonderful feeling to know that I'm enabling people with very little capital to pyramid their resources until they can settle down with ample money and no worries.

However, I'm beginning to realize that I can do much more along this line than I have done in the past. There isn't time, even in a three-day seminar, to go fully into all the possibilities that people want to know. They can be helped more by reading this book, which gives in great detail the information they can have at their fingertips— giving step-by-step instructions for spotting the right kind of property, for quickly sizing up its potential, for negotiating the purchase and the financing at money-saving terms to bring maximum profits, and eventually for converting it into the biggest possible tax-deferred capital gain.

One reason I began to think about writing this book was that Bill Nickerson and I became good friends and, eventually, business associates. Bill's life story pretty closely parallels mine. Like me, he had been a poor man with plenty of ambition, energy and curiosity. He too had seen the rich potential in real estate, had thought at first he didn't have enough money to get into it, and then had discovered that a big bankroll wasn't necessary. He had groped his way along step by step, as I had. Now we were both millionaires. We compared notes to see what principles had made our fortunes.

We were fascinated to find that, independently, we'd each worked out almost exactly the same basic methods. The more we talked about it the more we realized that our discoveries could be combined and condensed into a fairly simple formula. I'm now teaching this formula to interested people all over the country.

The book you hold in your hand is going to show you how to apply this formula in many different situations—with or without rent control regulations in force, with or without various other governmental rules that may be in effect in various areas, with or without partners, with small or large amounts available for investment, for people who want to keep expanding and for those who just want to settle down to a work-free, worry-free retirement on a steady income. Right now, to get everyone pointed quickly toward where the profits are, I might as well set forth the essentials of the formula before we go any further.

My tested, foolproof formula follows:

1. You buy income-producing rental property, if it's sound structurally and financially. (By "sound financially," I mean that within ninety days it must be bringing in more money than it costs you.)
2. You arrange monthly payments that you know you can meet, with as small a down payment as possible. (The little-known concept of loan constants, which you'll find fully explained in Chapter VII, is your key to safety here.)
3. In your spare time, you improve the property in ways that will make it worth more in resale value.
4. You pass on the detailed management of the property to others, making sure that they manage it economically and profitably. Every dollar you save increases the net income, and could be worth ten dollars in resale value.
5. You sell or exchange the property, and reinvest some or all of the gains to repeat the process with other properties.

So there's the formula in capsule form, more clearly stated than in anything I've seen elsewhere. It is an expansion of the rule that Bill Nickerson set forth in a tremendously successful book he wrote *How I Turned One Thousand Dollars into Three Million in Real Estate in My Spare Time.** His narrative shows the formula in action—before either of us realized that everything we were doing could be summed up in such a bare-bones statement.

Having just glanced at the bones, you may be wondering what's so magical about this formula. Read a few more chapters and you'll see that the magic is in the details: how to recognize the seedy-looking properties that we can turn into gold mines; how to avoid overpriced properties and other traps that could be costly; the many ways to crack the problem of too-big down payments; the creative financing

* William Nickerson, *How I Turned One Thousand Dollars into Three Million in Real Estate in My Spare Time*, Simon and Schuster, New York, 1969.

concepts that swing impossible-looking transactions when money is tight; how to generate cash from buildings while waiting for their value to skyrocket; how to use depreciation allowances and other tax breaks to switch dollars over from taxes into spendable income; how to profit from the flexibility of purchase money mortgages, wraparound mortgages, leasebacks, options, and all the other fantastic financial angles that I've tested over the years.

This book systematically blueprints the inner workings of each operation, so that you can find fast answers to problems as they arise. I have determined to make this book the most complete, easy-to-follow, foolproof guide ever written for professional as well as novice investors in residential real estate. You'll find it packed with information never before available in this form.

That's a bold statement, isn't it? I wouldn't have the nerve to make it, except for the fact that our real estate seminars in cities all over the country have produced such a flood of appreciative letters. This book will give you the essence of my course and will enable you to benefit from it equally as well as those who actually participated in it. Just let me quote a few of the many statements that investors have sent me, and have encouraged me to publish:

"This was the most informative real estate session that I have attended in my seven years in real estate, and I've missed very few such sessions in our part of the country," wrote Dick Barrett, executive vice president of the Board of Realtors of Spokane, Washington. "Your portion that dealt with creative financing was, for me, the highlight. After spending this time I feel I can help anyone who wants to overcome a financing obstacle."

Warren J. Thomason, branch manager of a Florida real estate firm, wrote: "One of my clients, a mortgage banker, told me that you had saved him thousands of dollars with only one point you made regarding title insurance. Another client made a similar remark about closing costs."

Another Floridian, Victor Nelson, wrote: "My mind works in the same vein, but I need prodding to get me moving, and the myriad of ideas which you threw out ought to do the trick."

"Your seminar was without doubt the most enlightening and positive approach to making money; thank you so much for sharing your expertise," says Bob Bartlett of Scottsdale, Arizona. A retired Army major just starting out as a real estate investor, William J. Sturm of San Jose, sent me a long letter saying in part, "I have realized an actual added profit of $3250 because I was able to determine the true worth of my home using your comparative analysis technique. Was also able to quickly and effectively negotiate the final price." And after taking the course in Salt Lake City, Bryan J. Scott sent me a Thank-U-Gram: "I hope all the students obtained as much informative knowledge as I did."

Sometimes the simplest endorsements are the most heartwarming. José Luis Gomez, who identified himself as a twenty-five-year-old journeyman construction worker in Oakland, wrote: "If you like to learn the road to financial independence take the course! If you want to learn to make it as I will, take the course. God bless you Mr. Al Lowry!"

An acquaintance of mine, reading this chapter up to this point, raised a question. "All these statements are from people in Florida or the western United States. Is it easier to make money in real estate in those parts of the country?"

"The principles I'm teaching pay off just as handsomely in any part of the country," I said. "For the benefit of any skeptics, I'd better prove that by going back into my files and pulling out endorsements from people in many different parts of the country. I've given this material in forty states."

So here's a sampling of comments from various parts of the East, Midwest, and South:

A lithographer in Michigan City, Indiana (Dwight B. Bonheur): "This course expands the knowledge of how real estate can be used as a vehicle to increase life's abundance—personally, for your family, and for the benefit of mankind."

A bookkeeper in Williamsville, New York (Mrs. Virginia C. Wild): "Can't miss this course, especially with the money situation in today's world."

A saleswoman in Tulsa, Oklahoma (Mrs. Laurie M. Wallace): "This was a most unusual opportunity to obtain the very specific and practical knowledge that is usually obtainable only by years of study and costly experience."

A school psychologist in Robbinsdale, Minnesota (Mrs. E. Jean Hosterman): "Thank you for helping to put the pieces of the jigsaw together. We recently bought two 4-plexes and have encountered some problems and were not sure of best decisions. I have better basis and knowledge for making decisions now."

An insurance underwriter in Louisville, Kentucky (Lawrence V.

Chowning): "This course shows the step-by-step method to become financially independent. I would recommend it to anyone who has this goal."

An architect in Dallas, Texas (Paul M. Terrill): "The entire picture on how to get there financially."

A salesman in Shelby, Ohio (William G. Reau): "To obtain the basic guidelines for real estate investment—plus learning the experience of professionals—a must. I drove 1,250 miles straight through to attend after missing out on two other seminars; and I don't regret it."

An educator in Washington, D.C. (Mrs. Phyllis S. Curry): "You will get a lot of information that you can use immediately to improve your financial picture."

A teacher in Arlington, Virginia (Krishan D. Mathur): "Anyone interested in entering the real estate field must attend this course, as it gives fundamental knowledge that is essential."

A real estate property manager in Wauwatosa, Wisconsin (Curtis L. Mahnke): "An outstanding course—an invaluable education and motivator to lead any person in the direction of financial independence."

What about New Englanders, traditionally the most skeptical and thriftiest of Americans? What do they think of this concept of pyramiding wealth? Here are a few statements from New Englanders who took the course:

A service engineer in Greenville, Rhode Island (William A. Corbin, Jr.): "Puts it all together. Complete, concise and cohesive."

A junior high school teacher in Cumberland, Rhode Island (Michael J. McKee): "It is as positive an educational experience as I have had."

A retail sales manager in West Warwick, Rhode Island (Robert E. Colford): "This course is of great magnitude. A course of this type can change one's whole life for the better. The course was everything I had hoped for . . ."

"If you want to make money in real estate investing, take the course!" wrote Roger E. Morril of Beverly, Massachusetts.

I could go on quoting such enthusiastic comments for many pages. But you get the idea. I realized that I was providing information that paid off quickly for people in big cities and small towns, in many different parts of the country. Their enthusiasm made me feel that I should do more. Need I limit my teaching to those who could attend a three-day lecture course? Why not put out a whole book, to be used either by itself or as reinforcement to the course?

So that's the book I set myself to write.

You'll find it strictly down-to-earth—what to do, how to do it, when and why. No cryptic financial jargon. No academic high-sounding theories. No unproven generalities. Everything as clear and simple as I could make it. Every technicality explained in non-technical words, as if you and I were face to face and neither of us had a high school diploma. Every rule illustrated with examples to show how it works in real life.

Use the table of contents as a road map, showing where to find whichever sections you need at the moment. Don't try to absorb this whole book before making your next (or your first) real estate investment. Instead, prepare for any step you're about to take by going through the chapter that deals with it. Later you can keep turning back to other sections for ready reference, looking up answers to problems as they arise, or jogging your memory about possibilities you may have overlooked.

To help you do this, I'm making the table of contents much more detailed than in most books. It is a checklist of key subtitles, grouped by subjects, so you can spot immediately the parts that will answer whatever questions come up.

Okay? All set? Then turn the page—and get ready to start using the basic formula that is making many average people wealthy!

REMEMBER THESE HIGH POINTS:

It is still possible to start investing in residential real estate with a small amount of money. Many people are doing this today, with great success.

The foolproof formula is:

1. Buy a sound, income-producing property.
2. Arrange for a small down payment, and monthly payments that you know you can meet.
3. Improve the property in your spare time.
4. Make sure that it is managed economically and profitably.

5. Sell or exchange it, and reinvest some of the gains in other properties.

To find the details of the formula, refer to this book's table of contents. Don't try to absorb the whole book at once.

II An Old-fashioned Way to Grow Richer

Our grandfathers thought they could make money multiply by buying a piece of real estate, collecting the rents, and eventually selling for a capital gain.

You may be glad to know that our grandfathers were right.

As it has been throughout history, investing in income properties is still a sound and highly profitable way of putting money to work.

When you invest in real estate you can see and control what your dollars are doing. The investment is a building you can inspect. Very little luck is involved in the profit or loss that will result; virtually all factors that will affect your investment can be examined ahead of time. So your own efforts and intelligence count heavily.

Furthermore, inflation's bite is softened, because rents and property values tend to keep rising. Rents should bring you an annual yield of 10 percent or more on your money. And there are important tax advantages, as we'll see.

Realty ventures have been making good money for countless small investors during almost every period of United States history. Here's a fairly typical example from the recent past:

A young doctor put $5,000 into an old hotel that had been converted into apartments. Within a year it was making a profit. He became fascinated with real estate as a hobby. So he took $1,000 from his apartment profits and used it as down payment on another property. Five years later he had back, tax-free, his original and only out-of-pocket investment of $5,000. Using only cash generated by rentals and sales of his various buildings, in another eleven years he found himself with an equity of $166,000 in real estate worth $1,200,000 at current market values.

"Real estate can't be lost or stolen, nor can it be carried away," Franklin D. Roosevelt once said. "Managed with reasonable care, it is about the safest investment in the world." Of course it might conceivably be damaged by fire or storm or civil commotion, but it is insurable against such risks. Few other investments can be so well protected by insurance.

Year by year the activity in real estate increases. For some people it is simply an inflation hedge. For others it ties into retirement planning; it may involve buying an apartment building for income and living in one unit, while perhaps spending part of each day as apartment manager. But most investors are in it mainly for the profits.

There aren't such big potential profits as in buying raw land—nor are there such horrendous risks. You speculate in land, but you *invest* in income real estate.

You make money by going into debt when you invest in real estate. The basic formula for profits in real estate is simple: (1) stay as deeply in debt as possible with safety; (2) make maximum use of the depreciation allowances and other tax shields; (3) upgrade your property and sell or trade it as soon as you can.

The idea of staying deep in debt sounds worrisome at first. But it's comforting to know that a big, conservative financial institution is glad to look over your shoulder, advise you, approve your borrowing and say, "Don't be afraid. We're willing to invest three or four dollars for every one of yours."

Even those gloomiest and most cautious of calculators, the life insurance companies, understand the great potential and small risk involved in owning income-producing property. That's why they make 70 or 80 percent loans on these properties. They know that rental properties rise in value, have a low foreclosure rate, and are highly profitable in the hands of anyone who takes the trouble to understand what he's doing.

This stay-in-debt principle just means that you use as little as possible of your own money and as much as possible of someone else's. In other words, you use leverage.

How leverage works can be seen in an oversimplified example. Let's say you buy a $30,000 two-family duplex to be used as a rental property. You rent each of the two units at $250 a month. This will bring you a gross income of $6,000 a year. Let's ignore (temporarily) all your expenses and mortgage charges.

You have a choice of putting up $15,000 of your own capital to buy a one-half equity in the property at the outset, or investing $6,000 for a one-fifth equity. In the first case you'll get a mortgage loan of $15,000 to finance the rest—in the second you'll go into debt for $24,000. Which will be better for you? Let's figure it out.

First-year charges on the mortgage loan of $15,000 might amount to about $1,800. On the other loan they might be as much as $2,880. So if you subtract the first from your gross income of $6,000, you'd be left with a net income of $4,200. That sounds better, doesn't it, than paying $2,880 mortgage charges and netting only $3,120 on your gross?

But wait. The important thing to an investor is yield, or percentage of capital returned. The return in these two exaggerated instances is 28 percent if you invest $15,000—or 52 percent if you choose the second proposition and put up only $6,000 of your own money.

Maybe you're thinking you'd still rather have the larger net, even if it's a lower percentage yield, because you'll need those rent dollars to keep the building heated, serviced and repaired. The cost of keeping your own home in condition often scares you, and now you're buying a bigger, older building where the maintenance costs are bound to be heavier.

The two buildings aren't comparable, taxwise. We're talking about a business property, not personal property. All operating expenses of a business property—heating, fuel, water, painting, gardening, repairs and the like—are business expenses. They are tax deductible. You subtract them from the gross rents when you report your income to the Internal Revenue Service. You do the same with the property taxes.

And there's still more you can subtract—the depreciation allowance. This is one of the most attractive features of real estate investments.

Depreciation is simply a loss in value. Every building theoretically loses part of its value each year because it is wearing out. Tax guidelines put the useful life of an average apartment building at about forty years. Uncle Sam is willing to assume that at the end of the fortieth year the building will collapse in a heap of rubble and become economically worthless.

On that assumption, the building loses one-fortieth of its value each year. So you are entitled to deduct one-fortieth of the total cost of the building each year from the gross income that the building brings in.

This depreciation allowance will be about $750 if you use the "straight-line" method (see Chapter XIII) in figuring it, or $1,125 the first year if you choose the "declining balance" method (see Chapter XIII). Let's use the latter—and watch what it does to your taxable income!

From your $6,000 gross income you subtract the following:

Interest on mortgage	$2,520
(but not payments on principal)	
Operating expenses and property taxes	2,850
Depreciation	1,125
Total deductible expenses	$6,495

Consequently your tax return shows that you operated at a paper loss of $495 for the year, although you actually paid out only the mortgage *charges,* taxes and operating expenses, totaling $5,730, leaving you with an untaxed $270 in hand, a net after-tax return of 4.5 percent on your $6,000. That's about what you'd get on a tax-exempt municipal bond. In addition, your "operating loss" of $495 can be subtracted from whatever other taxable income you receive during the year. So, depending on your tax bracket, you're ahead even further after taxes.

Such figures aren't exaggerated. They're conservative. A *Harvard Business Review* article on real estate investment points out:

A central source of profitability in real estate is the ability to use a great deal of borrowed money on a very modest equity basis.

Having realized abnormally large profits, via great leverage, in a successful real estate venture, the entrepreneur can now shield most, if not all, the earnings from income tax . . . [through] the relatively liberal allowances for depreciation and other expenses . . .

Frequently there is a loss in excess of the project cash flow which can be used to shield other profits from income taxes.

And this isn't all. The numbers can get better in following years. You take as much depreciation as you can, as quickly as you can, and then you sell the property to another investor. It's as good a buy for him as it was for you, because he'll get the same tax advantages.

The Harvard article continues:

The real estate investor can effectively have his cake and eat it too. When at the end of ten years, for instance, he has exhausted the excess depreciation on the property he holds, he can sell it to another investor . . . who can then begin to depreciate the property again, at his cost basis, thus creating his own tax shield. And he can pass it on to still another investor when he, too, has exhausted the depreciation potential.

In the example mentioned a moment ago, your property is probably not depreciating at the rate of $1,125 a year. The odds are that it's really growing more valuable each year. Countless buildings are still bringing in good rents long after their fortieth, fiftieth or sixtieth year.

The government knows this, but still considers the depreciation allowance worthwhile as an incentive to invest in real estate. So you make $1,125 of tax-free income each year, in addition to the rents. In what other investment can you get such financial advantages from small down payments, while your tenants are paying off the mortgage for you with their rents?

You can sell for less than you paid, and still make a profit. The old adage that you must buy low and sell high doesn't necessarily hold true in real estate.

Suppose that ten years ago you made a $25,000 down payment on an apartment house priced at $100,000. The other $75,000 was to be paid off by you over a twenty-year period, with interest at 7 percent. Now, after ten years, you resell the building for $90,000, thus losing $10,000, you might think.

But in those ten years you've been making payments on the $75,000 loan, you've whittled it down to $48,200 that you still owe. So the cash you receive from the sale is $41,800. In other words, you had $25,000 before you bought the property and you get $41,800 when you sell it. Meanwhile you collected rents that more than covered your expenses and monthly note payments, putting extra cash into your pocket. You're far ahead in net spendable dollars.

Such basically simple transactions are the fundamentals of realty investment. More sophisticated transactions can be even more profitable. We'll consider them in detail later in this book.

First let's clear away some misconceptions that may cloud your view of real estate as a field for you.

Real estate syndications contain many pitfalls that don't threaten a sole owner of comparatively small properties. Dangers lurk in the big limited partnership formed to build or buy a big apartment complex or similar development.

Such partnerships, once operated almost exclusively for wealthy insiders, attracted thousands of newcomers to realty investing in the early 1970's. Some 10 percent of all new security offerings in 1972 were publicly offered real estate partnerships.

Limited partnerships allow the investor to benefit from a real estate project's normal losses in its early years. He can deduct his pro rata share of the losses from his taxable income. In addition, he may sometimes receive a cash distribution from the partnership in the same year that losses are being written off.

As *Money* magazine commented in 1972:

The charms of tax avoidance, particularly when combined with title to a solid piece of American turf, are hard to overestimate. But such attractions, like paperboard walls, are often more surface than substance . . . An investor generally cannot get out of a syndicate with a positive return for some five years—if he can get out at all. There is no secondary market, like a stock exchange, through which interests in limited partnerships can readily be bought and sold.

The general partner puts together and manages the project, and is entitled to share in cash distributions, as well as to receive his fees and commissions even if there are no profits. The investors, who may put up as little as $1,000 apiece in some partnerships, are limited partners. They have no say in the management and are liable only for their investments.

Rexford Tompkins, president of New York's Dry Dock Savings Bank (and former head of the Real Estate Board of New York) told *Forbes* magazine: "I invested in a commercial syndication run by a close friend, a veteran developer. I got creamed. If I can lose in a syndication, imagine what can happen to the average guy."

Eric Bruckner, a real estate syndicator in Santa Barbara, California, takes almost as dim a view. He warned *Medical Economics* in 1970: "Leverage can be a headache if something goes wrong with your rental income. Your mortgage payments could be too high to handle, and your investors would have so little equity to fall back on they could wind up losing all their money."

Non-residential buildings are not an attractive investment vehicle for an amateur operator looking for something to buy. A store block or a shopping center may seem desirable at first, because the tenants usually provide their own heat and utilities; take care of maintenance and repairs; look after grounds' care, snow removal and other expensive chores that owners of apartment buildings must pay for themselves. A prospective buyer thinks to himself, "Owning commercial property will take less of my time than owning apartments. These tenants will pay bigger security deposits and sign longer leases. I can put a clause in the leases entitling me to higher rents as a tenant's sales grow bigger. This looks like an ideal proposition."

He seldom stops to think of how badly he can get hurt by just one vacancy. Store vacancies usually linger longer than apartment vacancies, and they hurt more because of the relatively higher rentals for stores. If business turns bad for a store lessee, the building owner is in trouble too. Remember the high mortality rate among small businesses, and beware!

Beware, too, of buying a commercial property in a neighborhood that may be declining. A thriving downtown section can turn sour in a few years because of a change in traffic patterns or consumer habits, or because of the creeping rot that afflicts the center of so many cities. Even a new shopping center can suffer from the competition of still newer centers.

Office buildings and professional buildings also look enticing at first glance. Your gross income will be high if your building is full. Professional tenants such as doctors, dentists and lawyers can afford to pay big security deposits and high rents. They are likely to stay in the building for many years. They accept tax escalation clauses in their leases. They make improvements to their own part of the premises, and keep it maintained well.

But there are built-in disadvantages. Your utility bills will be high because doctors and dentists use a lot of electricity and water. You'll have to provide more parking space than for apartment tenants. Your first tenants will ask for exclusion clauses—but if you grant these too freely, you may be unable to take on additional tenants when you need them. And when a new tenant does come in, he's likely to demand substantial renovation to suit his own professional needs. These are some of the reasons why vacancies in office buildings are hard to fill.

Again, changing conditions in the neighborhood can ruin you. A newer building in a more desirable location can lure away all the professional men as their leases expire, and you may wind up owning a white elephant.

Remember, too, that a lease is only as good as the person who signs it. If a doctor signs a fifteen-year lease but goes bankrupt in three months, there's small chance of collecting the fifteen years of rent technically owed to you.

Build your own property? Not if you're looking for a part-time investment.

The average investor does much better with already-built properties, where he doesn't have to worry about the complicated and time-consuming problems of construction. If you're building, or if your money is riding on a builder, you'll have little time to think about investment strategy. You'll be too worried about the unpleasant surprises that may come to light during excavation—underground water, for example, or soft marshy holes, or ledges of extremely hard rock. Next you may be worrying about green lumber and cracking plaster; about materials that don't arrive on time; about subcontractors who fall behind schedule, or who try to make you liable for bills they run up; about redoing work to satisfy municipal inspectors; about delays that cause the FHA to call for more and more paperwork before giving approval for low-cost FHA loans. Many a builder has run out of money when his schedule stretched.

As a rule of thumb, if you expect to build new and make it pay, no more than one-fifth of your total overall cost per unit should be the costs of land, utilities, and land developments. If you keep those costs within 20 percent of your total costs, then maybe you'll make more profit by building than by buying.

But land and utilities are seldom cheap. Unfortunately many builders apply the rule the other way, simply multiplying their land and utility costs by five to arrive at their total project budget. Sometimes this prices them out of the market; other times it brings them less rental income than their total costs.

Many people are trapped into bad investments because they think the cost of constructing a building is the yardstick for measuring its worth. Construction costs have nothing to do with the worth of a building. The value of a rental property is determined by the profit it will make, not by how much the builder spent on it.

Pride of ownership can cost you dearly, by leading you into buying property for its looks rather than its profit potential. If prestige is your objective, don't expect to make money by investing in real estate.

You'll be shocked to discover that the beautiful well-built edifice you want to put your name on has about half the actual after-tax yield of the junky-looking old place on the wrong side of town.

Usually the best path to profits in real estate is to start by buying cheap, run-down little apartment buildings. You can rejuvenate such properties and boost their value almost overnight. But here again, after you've upgraded a place so it looks fine, there's a danger that you may feel too proud to part with it.

Some owners don't realize that in using accelerated depreciation, they'll get less benefits each year from the depreciation allowance. Through pride of ownership, they hold a good-looking property until there is practically no depreciation left to charge off against income. This increases their taxable profits when they finally sell, because they must pay tax on whatever depreciation they wrote off. In other words, if you buy a property for $50,000, write off $15,000 in depreciation, then sell it for $60,000, you've made $25,000 profit—taxable profit. So don't let pride of ownership hold you back from selling early.

A realty investment is not very liquid. Don't put money into property if there's a chance that you'll suddenly need the money in a hurry—or that you might have to move to some other part of the country. You can't move real estate from place to place. Nor can you sell it with one phone call, the way you sell stocks. An emergency sale may have to be priced so low that you'll have a net loss in spendable dollars, not just a paper loss to show the tax man.

Buying property can be a way of going into business for yourself, with all the pleasures of being your own boss and taking those extra tax deductions for an office at home and other business expenses. But this business is easier than most to keep within whatever bounds of time and capital you set for yourself. You can put in all your savings and work full time on your realty operations, or you can invest a small amount of either money or time or both. Nevertheless, if you give too little time to your investment, you may get less profit than if your money was in bonds. You'll have to study real estate enough to know whether brokers and managers are offering you good advice or not. The novices who do well in real estate are those who devote some time and effort to it. Often they find it a fascinating hobby as well as a highroad to financial security.

By now you probably have read enough to know whether realty investment is a path you want to follow. Assuming that you do want to go ahead, how do you start?

You'd better start with apartment units. Apartments are in demand in every part of the country. Everyone needs a place to live, and houses are hard to find at moderate prices nowadays. The percentage of the total population living in apartments has been rising steadily for decades.

As a general rule, you'll want the greatest number of units you can buy for the money you can afford to invest. And you'll want to make as small a down payment as possible. Maybe you can afford 30 percent down, but it's still better to put up only 10 percent if this can be arranged. Your gross yield will be the same regardless of the size of your down payment, as we saw earlier, but your percentage yield will be bigger with a smaller down payment.

Within reason, the more units in your property, the better off you are (unless you plan to manage it yourself, in which case you may want to start with something like a duplex or fourplex and expand as you gain experience). The bigger apartment buildings are likely to bring you more profit per dollar of purchase price. This is because the overhead and many of the fixed expenses are proportionately lower when spread over more units. You have one boiler, one basic plumbing system, one basic wiring system, one tax bill.

You'll start with properties that you can quickly upgrade and resell. (Sometimes upgrading will just mean improving the management, so tenants will be happier and stay longer. Sometimes, with satisfied tenants, upgrading will mean finding ways to cut unnecessary expenses, thus brightening the profit-and-loss statement.)

"Buying real estate is not only the best way, the quickest way, and the safest way, but the only way to become wealthy," said Marshall Field a century ago. Maybe he exaggerated slightly. In modern terms, real estate may not be the only way to become wealthy in our high-technology civilization. But it remains one of the best and safest ways.

Whether you're aiming for a fortune or just a comfortable income, this book will tell you what you need to know as an investor in residential real estate.

REMEMBER THESE HIGH POINTS:

Use as little of your own money as possible, as much borrowed money as you can. But be sure the income from a property will cover the payments on the debt.

Take as much tax deduction for depreciation as you can, as quickly as you can, and then sell or exchange the property to another investor.

Be careful about joining a syndicate for realty investments. Most such ventures have many pitfalls.

Non-residential buildings are risky investments for inexperienced owners.

Don't build property as a part-time sideline.

Don't be seduced by the prestige of owning a beautiful building. Usually the most profitable investments are cheap, run-down little apartment buildings, which can be upgraded.

III How to Hunt for Profitable Properties

Scan first, then narrow down. Hunting can be fun, and educational. The fun is in becoming a sort of detective, scanning the field for clues, following up leads, piecing together information, drawing conclusions. The education comes in learning your way around, picking up knowledge that will help make your money grow.

But this process requires you to make efforts and spend time. Don't rush in too fast. You'll almost certainly blunder if you buy one of the first properties you see, without looking at many others. You haven't yet developed an eye for bargains, a feel for the hidden rewards and booby traps. You need the experience gained by comparing good and bad points of many different properties. This will begin to come as you look at more real estate.

The best way to start is as a hunting dog does, ranging all over the field in search of a scent—or as a radar operator does, systematically sweeping the void in all directions, studying the blips that the beam picks up. This broad preliminary scanning will give you ideas about where to look more closely.

Begin by glancing through the real estate ads in the classified section of the Sunday newspaper. See what kinds of property are being offered, for what prices, in what locations. Mark every ad that sounds like a possibility. Then clip your selection of ads and save it for use a little later on. Even in this preliminary scanning, you should keep systematic records so you can quickly refer back to any property that interested you.

One-third of all realty transactions begin with a newspaper ad. The newspaper is a central market place for real estate. Most Realtors use it—but not always to advertise their best buys. They don't want to tip off an unscrupulous rival to a hot property. So they advertise a good selection of their listings, hoping to attract prospective buyers not only for these properties but for hidden bargains too. Their business depends on keeping a steady stream of customers coming to them.

Now go out and roam around, street map in hand, sizing up various neighborhoods. For our purposes, a "neighborhood" is an area with common characteristics of population and land use. Thus it may extend for many blocks.

You can drive through some areas in your car, eliminating some in a few minutes and spending more time in others. It's also worthwhile to ride various bus routes or rail lines, getting out at points along the way to make leisurely explorations on foot.

Why do all this exploring? Because realty appraisers say the most important factor in the future value of any residence is its neighborhood. When you find a neighborhood in the path of the city's growth—a neighborhood that is attracting higher-income residents or is beginning to be developed by builders—then you stand to rake in a big profit by buying a small property there. Even if you don't improve the property, you may be able to raise rents because of the upgrading of the neighborhood. Or your location itself may become so valuable that a developer will buy the building and bulldoze it away for an apartment house or condominium. So your first objective is to learn about the "good" locations all around you.

A neighborhood isn't necessarily as "good" as it looks, or as good as a real estate agent would have you believe. Unless you ask him directly, he may not volunteer the information that the flight patterns for the nearest airport bring jumbo jets thundering over the rooftops in early morning—or that the bus system is nearly bankrupt—or that you can smell the city dump when the west wind blows.

Those quiet streets may soon be jammed with heavy traffic when an already planned access to the highway goes through, or when the new owner of a block of small shops razes them to make way for a big office building. So your eyeball inspection is just to get tentative impressions. It will tell you that some locations aren't worth considering at all. Later, when several promising neighborhoods are on your list, you'll want to investigate them more carefully. We'll consider how to do this farther along in the chapter.

You'll probably find no bargains in a luxurious high-rent district. You want low-price property that can be upgraded quickly and inexpensively. This is more likely to be found in middle-class neighborhoods. But you ought to prowl some of the better districts too, as well as some of the worst, so you'll have a mental yardstick for comparison.

Checklist for a neighborhood. Are the residences mostly neat, clean and well kept, as if the people are proud of them? Are any new stores, houses or apartment buildings going up nearby? (They often bring a rise in property values.) Is the neighborhood separated from industrial areas and from crowded commercial districts?

A better neighborhood is worth higher rents to the residents. Does a major traffic artery slash through the area, or is all traffic local, with no trucks or motorcycles? Is there enough open space for sunshine and good air?

Are there hazards nearby—abandoned lofts, or a freight yard, or a river that sometimes overflows? Do some buildings look dilapidated and vulnerable to fire? Are there nuisances such as a noisy or smoky factory, a sports arena, an all-night restaurant? If you find any of these, you'd better cross the neighborhood off your list.

How convenient is shopping? Typical apartment dwellers want a drugstore, a delicatessen, probably a bank and branch post office within walking distance. If a supermarket shopping center is only a few minutes' drive from the neighborhood, this is another plus.

Is public transportation handy? If so, where will it take people, and how often does it run, and how crowded is it? Are there churches, parks, branch libraries, movie theaters, restaurants and other amenities in the vicinity?

What about schools? How near are they, and how good is their reputation? Fine schools cost money. Houses or apartments in districts served by highly regarded public schools usually sell at a premium. Partly because of the poor reputations of most big-city school systems, housing prices often drop sharply inside the city line, even though neighborhoods may seem the same otherwise.

If an area looks interesting to you, probably you should revisit it at night by auto, to see whether streets are too dark or too glaring—and to see what sort of night crawlers, if any, inhabit the district.

Night or day, how do the pedestrians impress you? Transient drifters mean low rents and poor investment opportunities. What kinds of automobiles seem to predominate along the streets and in parking areas? It's usually a mistake to buy property located among people you wouldn't want as neighbors or tenants—even if you intend to be an absentee owner. You might change the tenants, but you can't be sure the new tenants will be much better, and you can't change the neighbors.

(However, as we'll see later, there are exceptions to the rule that you shouldn't buy in a neighborhood where the people impress you unfavorably.)

Is the neighborhood improving, worsening, or stable? Neighborhoods have different ways of aging. Some do it slowly and gracefully. Others look ravaged in their teens. The character of the neighborhood changes, or zoning is downgraded, or a cheap new building brings in a swarm of noisy people—whereupon a once-quiet district becomes undesirable to its former tenants. They move away, and the better shops follow them. Less fortunate people and cheaper stores replace them. Rents keep dropping, which pushes property values down. Year by year the buildings grow shabbier, the streets uglier. Your first glance at the people and the cityscape may tell you that this is happening. Whenever you see a neighborhood definitely on the way down, be cautious. Investing there may be too risky for you.

In rare cases a decaying neighborhood may suddenly return to health. This can happen where prosperous people take a fancy to its ancient, well-built, picturesque structures and decide to renovate the interiors; it has been happening recently in some old parts of San Francisco and Manhattan.

Or it can happen along certain run-down strips a few blocks distant from a bold big-money venture in urban development, where plazas and fountains and modern shops create an attractive new sub-city within a city: Century City and Bunker Hill in Los Angeles, for example, or Society Hill in Philadelphia, or Allegheny Center and Washington Plaza in Pittsburgh, or the Peachtree district in Atlanta, or similar transformations in a dozen other cities.

Property near these developments is usually upgraded block by block, spreading outward like ripples in a process that may take five years or more. You can see the early symptoms almost at a glance: a few new buildings being started, a few older buildings being reno-vated, a sprinkling of attractive shops and restaurants along dingy old streets. In such a neighborhood you should look closely for a chance to buy from someone who has lived there for years. He can make a good profit by selling to you—and you can profit too, by reselling to redevelopers later on.

Just because you don't see any "For Sale" signs, don't cross a neighborhood off your list. Many times an owner who hasn't thought of selling can be persuaded to do so. Later in this chapter we'll consider how to spot "problem properties" that aren't advertised but might be bought at depressed prices.

If a neighborhood seems to contain profit potentials, probably you'll want to spend considerable time there during your first or second visit. Is it the location of any of the buildings you jotted down when you scanned the ad columns, or of buildings with "For Sale" signs? Any such buildings are worth a quick look, even though you're not ready to think seriously about buying.

Does this neighborhood contain mostly furnished apartments, or unfurnished? This will give you a clue to the type of tenants you could expect. A building with furnished apartments can charge higher rents but is likely to have a high turnover of tenants—perhaps 30 percent or more a year—and high costs for maintenance. In unfurnished units, if they are well managed, the turnover rate shouldn't average more than 15 percent a year.

But here again there are exceptions to the rule. A neighborhood near a college campus may attract flocks of students, who usually want furnished studio apartments. Students can be good tenants if the manager chooses them carefully and gets them started right.

The prevailing range of rents is one of the most important pieces of information you'll need about any neighborhood you're considering. It tells you the approximate top rents you can charge. You must buy a building that is renting for less than these top rates, so you won't price yourself out of the market when you upgrade it and raise the rent.

In fact, the building you buy should be currently charging a rate near the bottom of the spread, thus giving you ample room for raises. Therefore, as soon as you see any neighborhood that interests you, make a note of the highest and lowest rents. (You can find out by asking the managers of the best-looking and worst-looking properties thereabouts.)

The rent range gives you an idea of the income you can expect from a building in the neighborhood—and the price range in which it might sell, since an apartment building is usually priced somewhere between four and nine times its annual rent roll. This range may rule out some neighborhoods without further inspection.

High-rent buildings aren't for you, obviously, because purchase prices will be more than you should prudently invest in your first venture. Nor will a very low-rent district be promising, because the income and resale potential won't be attractive unless, as we noted earlier, the district is starting to improve dramatically. As a rule of thumb, an area where monthly rents range between $120 and $220 might contain a few good buys for you.

Assuming that the district still seems worth investigating further, you might inquire into the quality of public services there: fire and police protection, street cleaning, trash collection and the like. Particularly in a suburb, you may learn that the area runs low on water during hot, dry spells. Or that the streets are full of water during rains. Maybe there are septic tanks instead of sewers. Maybe garbage collection costs extra. Something like this could explain why rents are lower than you'd expect—and why you'd be unable to get higher rents even after upgrading your property.

How do you pick up such information? One easy way is to knock on doors of a few one-family homes, if there are any, and meet residents. Another is to chat with people in a Laundromat or drugstore or supermarket. Most people are surprisingly willing to discuss the drawbacks and advantages of their neighborhood. (If you get grouchy answers, that tells you something too.)

You might ask what houses have recently been sold or rented and why. Heavy turnover is a bad sign. So is conversion of owner-occupied houses to rental. Many appraisers say that when one-fourth or more of the houses are rented, a neighborhood is likely to be on the skids.

If the area is mostly apartments, you can get a surprising torrent of information just by visiting an apartment manager and saying, "If I were to purchase this property, would you stay on?" Pick a manager whose building has few vacancies, as indicated by the mailboxes; this means he or she is probably good at the job.

The manager will probably begin by telling you what's wrong with the current owner. (This may reveal as much about the manager as the owner.) Then you can steer the talk to the neighbors, the crime rate, the public services, the shopping, the prevailing rents up and down the street, the changes in ownership of nearby buildings, and almost anything else you want to know about the scene.

When you feel fairly familiar with several promising districts—and when you have jotted down key information about them, so they won't get confused in your memory—you're ready for the next step. Start scanning for possible buys within those districts. Keep a record not only of those you might buy now, but of those you might consider later when pyramiding has given you bigger sums to invest. You should compile a fairly long list of possibilities before you start zeroing in on a few. However, if a really bright nugget catches your eye, there's no reason why you shouldn't skip ahead in this book to learn immediately how to evaluate it, and negotiate for it.

Begin your search with people you know. Just mention you're interested in buying residential property as an investment. You'll be surprised how many of them know someone who may want to sell.

Practically every accountant, attorney, banker, builder, and insurance broker knows property owners who are thinking of selling. Then too, whenever an owner of apartments is looking for a buyer, his suppliers are likely to know about it. So you can get leads from interior decorators, hardware store people, plumbers, painters, handymen, carpeting dealers, swimming pool maintenance services, and others in service industries. Your dentist and your barber often hear about real estate soon to be put on the market. So do people in your church, your PTA, and any clubs you belong to. Ask them.

Most of the possibilities they mention won't be worth pursuing. By this time you should have enough knowledge to screen them mentally. A property may be badly located for your purposes, as indicated by your scanning of neighborhoods. Or its size may indicate that you can't yet afford to buy it. Ditto for newness: if it was built within the last few years, its price is bound to be sky-high.

How much can you afford to pay? You should have some fairly definite figures in mind. Total price isn't your most important consideration. Sometimes it's good business to overpay if you get favorable terms. If you can afford the down payment and whatever repairs or improvements you plan to make, you can probably afford to buy the property, because its mortgage payments will come from your tenants. You won't go into a deal unless you're certain that the cash flow will cover the loan payments and operating expenses, with a reasonable cushion against vacancies.

To buy a fairly old and small property, the down payment will probably be 5 percent to 25 percent of the purchase price. You can occasionally get title to a small property with no down payment whatever, just by signing a personal note or giving the seller a carryback paper. You'll always be trying for a deal with maximum leverage, which means minimum down payment. And you'll need to conserve some of your cash for refurbishing whatever property you buy.

As a rough approximation, let's say that if you're starting with $2,000 you'll look first at properties priced below $30,000—although you may consider something higher priced if there's an indication that the down payment will be less than $2,000. If you have $5,000, anything up to $75,000 may be within your reach. If you have more than that, you'll be wise to spread it among several small properties; wait until you're more familiar with the field before you tackle bigger deals.

Talk to several Realtors soon after you begin asking acquaintances for leads. About eighty-five of every one hundred realty transactions are eventually handled through brokers. An owner may start with an idea of making the sale himself, but sooner or later he'll probably decide that a broker can negotiate better for him.

Many inexperienced buyers think they can save at least part of the 6 percent broker's sales fee if they deal directly with the owner. Theoretically they can, but in practice they seldom do. If there is a broker's commission the seller usually pays it. Yet a building handled by a broker is less likely to be overpriced than one that an owner himself is selling. Most owners have an exaggerated idea of what their property is worth. So even if they concede the commission to the buyer, the price may still be high.

A first-rate broker can identify the weaknesses and selling points of a building. Just remember that his business is selling—to you, the prospective buyer. When he shows you property, don't expect him to point out all its weaknesses.

A broker won't consider you a hot prospect if you simply stroll in and say something like "I'm thinking of buying property. What do you have?" A much better way to approach him is to express interest in one of the properties he is advertising.

After you've asked enough questions about one or two of his advertised properties to show that you're serious and fairly knowledgeable, you can ask, "Have you another property of the type I'm interested in?" Go on to explain exactly what you're looking for: an older building in a specified price range, located in a stable or improving neighborhood where most buildings are priced higher than the one you'll buy.

As for age, many experts believe that the best buys in today's market are buildings from seven to fifteen years old. You can see what you're buying. Unlike a newer building in which the quality of materials and workmanship may be hard to judge, these have been tested by time. Problems of plumbing, wiring, roofing, insulation and the like have usually been worked out. It may be advisable to call in a contractor or electrician to inspect a house you are seriously considering. The records of rents and expenses in past years give you solid data on which to estimate profitability. The owner of a building this old probably won't expect an outrageous price for it. And there may be an old mortgage you can take over at a low interest rate.

On the other hand, the older the building, the more money you'll probably need for repairs and maintenance. Estimate them carefully before you buy. (How to make such estimates is discussed in the next chapter.)

You can explain to a Realtor quite frankly that you're looking for basically good buildings that can be dramatically upgraded with such "cosmetic" improvements as a new paint job or fresh landscaping or attractive wallpaper. If he's experienced, he knows that one building in a drab block can be made to stand out like a new penny by spending $500 for an imaginative two-tone paint job—and that this $500 expenditure may add as much as $10,000 to the amount the next buyer is willing to pay for the building. So the Realtor begins to respect you as an astute investor.

You might also mention specific neighborhoods that interest you, and the size of the buildings you'll consider. Probably you won't want anything bigger than a fourplex for your first venture while you're learning. Depending on prices and the money you have available, a duplex may be a more promising investment. And you won't rule out a small one-family house as your first buy, even though multi-unit properties are usually more profitable for reasons explained in Chapter II.

REMEMBER THESE HIGH POINTS:

Talk to several Realtors and brokers.

Look around widely before you begin a serious search.

Check a neighborhood carefully before looking at possible buys within it.

Decide in advance what price range you can afford.

IV Investing in a Single-family House

A **single-family house** is the first property bought by most realty investors. Of all real estate investments, rental houses are probably easiest to buy and sell, and are useful for tax-deferred exchanges. With a nominal cash investment, you can often acquire one.

Most investors who own houses collect the rents themselves, and personally handle whatever problems arise with tenants. They keep the books. They write the checks for repairs and maintenance, or do these chores themselves. All this gives them part-time experience in property management, which is excellent background for more ambitious realty investments. And the money they save by doing the work adds up to a sizable increase in their spendable income as well as their resale profit.

Depending on your talents and spare time, you may or may not evaluate a house in terms of what you can do to fix it up. There are plenty of possibilities for an amateur with building-trade skills to rehabilitate houses and resell at handsome profits, if they choose neighborhoods prudently.

One college professor in California bought a sound but dilapidated house for $8,000 and spent his spare time renovating it inside and out. He sold it for a profit of more than 50 percent, and found he'd enjoyed the project so much that he retired from teaching and made a full-time business of buying and refurbishing houses for resale. In two years he was making more money than the college president.

In addition to the tax shelter—which is proportionately the same as in an apartment house—the average investor buys a single-family house chiefly for the appreciation, which comes almost automatically these days. Houses bought in Illinois for $25,000 in 1964 were typically worth $50,000 ten years later. A buyer who put down a modest 10 percent and mortgaged the rest, making the mortgage payments from the rent, was using a $2,500 lever to raise a $25,000 profit. In the New York City tri-state area, prices of homes in suburban bed-room towns went up 13 percent in one recent year. Property values seem sure to keep rising in future years, even in mediocre locations, because the building slump of the 70's has caused home shortages. (As *Business Week* put it, "1970 was the year they hid the key to the house." Since then housing costs have risen twice as fast as incomes.)

A rental house is almost a sure profit-maker if it is located in the path of future growth, or wherever housing demand is steady. Your preliminary survey of neighborhoods can pay off by enabling you to judge whether a house is in a location that should improve or at least stay the same. All experts on housing agree: Don't look at houses when you set out to buy a house. Look first at locations!

Maybe you'll hear about offerings at reasonable prices in locations you haven't yet investigated. Make a quick check with a banker or friendly Realtor to see whether the location is in a good suburb, or in a growing section of the city. Even if it isn't, maybe growth is at least moving toward it.

You're most likely to find bargains in locations that seem a little far out. Maybe the roads need widening and the shopping facilities aren't good yet; but if you know these improvements are coming, you can expect the value of property to rise. Such a location is worth study.

Remember that you'll be buying resale value, especially if you buy a one-family house. Whomever you resell it to will probably live in it —and he'll be much more concerned about the location than a renter would be. He'll want a neighborhood that's good for him and his family. Presumably you've sized up the location as "apparently good," or you wouldn't even be thinking of investing there. Now you want to make sure, by talking with people who can give you inside information.

Ask local shopkeepers whether there are rumors of big apartment or condominium developments on the way, or new office buildings going up, or industry moving in. Everything seem quiet? Fine so far. Next go to see the town clerk, if the area is suburban. If it's part of a city, go to city hall and ask for the planning department.

Municipal clerks will usually give frank, straightforward answers— and may volunteer valuable tips if you get on a friendly, chatty basis. For example, a clerk in the town hall of Mamaroneck, New York, warned one house-hunter that the town contains the Village of Larch-mont; commuters living in Larchmont can park at the rapid-transit station for $10 a month, he explained, but those living in the town of Mamaroneck must pay $80. In another town, the clerk told prospective residents about a test of the water supply, which showed 600 parts of dissolved mineral salts per million gallons of water. This meant the water was so hard that hot-water pipes would become scaly and rusty, and laundry would probably be stained.

A building's position on a map doesn't change, but everything around it may. A house next door could be honeycombed into apartments and end up as a nursing home or a seedy rooming house. An empty lot across the street could be excavated for a gas station. Those nearby acres of woods may belong to a developer whose bulldozers won't be nice neighbors. Only with the protection of strict—and strictly enforced—zoning ordinances and building codes can you be sure that a location will keep its character.

Zones vary not only from town to town but also from one block to the next within a single community. There may be four or five zones for single-family residences, each regulating land use, but in different ways. The town clerk or the planning commission can tell you about these regulations. Try to find out whether many zoning variances are being granted. If so, the area is vulnerable to quick blight.

We all remember tree-lined streets of fine old houses that are now jammed among commercial buildings. Their location changed as drastically as if they'd been jacked up and moved. A whole district with good resale potential can lose its property values if an adjacent golf course sells out to a subdivider who puts up hundreds of cheap homes. It happens often. So take a close look at areas adjacent to a neighborhood you're investigating, and ask the local planning people what changes are likely. Maybe the town engineer will tell you that a heavy-traffic route is being planned through the very area you're looking at.

Ask about taxes, too, when you talk to municipal employees. Don't rely on general "tax rates" published by the town or city. They can be terribly misleading. Real estate taxes often vary wildly among localities within the same metropolitan area, and sometimes assessments are strangely different from one house to the next. The difference could affect the value of a building by several thousand dollars. Find out the dollar amount of taxes last paid on it, and if there has been a tax boost since.

Make sure you ask about *all* local taxes and assessments, and not just real estate taxes. This is especially important in an outlying area where you could find yourself assessed extra to pay for new streets, curbs, sidewalks and sewers.

When you're sure the area is good, take closer looks at residential buildings you might buy there. How well have they stood the test of time? Your own quick once-over can tell you enough to narrow down the list; no need yet to hire an appraiser at twenty-five dollars an hour.

To learn the worst, start in the basement. That's where structural defects are most likely to meet your eye. If they're bad, figure on adding expensive repairs to the purchase cost.

Have the basement walls started to bulge inward? Then they may pose a costly problem. If you see cracks or crumbling mortar, this means dampness and weakness. If you see fresh patches, this means a recent cover-up, and you'd better beware. If you see a "high-water mark" on the walls, you know the basement has been flooded.

Look on the cellar floor as well as the walls for signs of leaks or seepage. Also look for a sump pump concealed under a wooden hatch cover. If you find one, you know it was installed to remove water, which may mean flooding problems. Even if there are no signs of water, sniff around. If you smell a dank odor, it's a danger signal. Go no further until you've consulted an expert.

You can make your own quick test for termites and rot. Take a pocketknife and probe the basement timbers called joists that support the floor above. Then probe the "sills" running flat along the top of the cellar walls. Sometimes your knife won't go in at all—a good sign. But sometimes it will crunch in easily, and uncover bugs gnawing away in the wood.

(Even if you don't find bugs, they may be at work deeper down. Always ask for a no-termite certification before you buy. But most termite and dry-rot damage can be repaired at nominal cost. Fear of termites creates bargains for people who know how to correct minor damage. Ask a licensed pest-control expert to give you an estimate of repair costs; he'll probably charge no more than forty-five dollars to inspect the property.)

In the cellar, look further at those joists. They may be rotting from water that has seeped down from the kitchen or bathrooms. Or they may be pulled away from supporting masonry, which means the foundation has shifted and the walls have moved. This could call for major rebuilding.

Have the joists been notched deeply for pipes? If notches are deeper than one-third of the depth, they've weakened the joists dangerously. If intermediate jackposts or timbers are shoring up the joists, ask an expert why.

Check the basement piping for heavy corrosion. Hot-water pipes should be copper, and should be insulated if they're long. Cold-water pipes should be copper or plastic.

Take a look at the fuse box. If you find it has only four or six circuits (which is typical in old houses) the wiring is outmoded. A house with eight to twelve rooms needs sixteen to twenty circuits and a circuit-breaker panel.

Now study the building from outside, especially if it's quite old. Line up the top ridge of the roof to be sure it's reasonably straight. Sight along the outside walls. A sagging roof or bulging walls means the frame is probably weak, and rebuilding will be costly.

See if the chimney has separated. Look for missing mortar and broken bricks. A stairstep pattern of cracks in a brick wall is evidence of a major separation. An extra-wide mortar joint in a stairstep pattern is a tip-off that such a crack has been repaired and may need further repairs as the house continues to shift its weight.

Aluminum siding is a big plus maintenancewise over shingles or paint. If the house is a frame one, look for peeling on the outside, which means the walls are poorly ventilated and are holding too much moisture. A new paint job will peel too. However, you can improve the venting at reasonable cost.

Deterioration often begins in the outside windowsills and frames. Are they freshly painted, without fresh paint on the rest of the walls? The paint may be covering rot. You'll need an expert's examination to be sure.

If everything looks okay so far, you'll want to check the roof next, or send up a professional roofer if you're getting seriously interested. Are there broken or missing shingles? If the roof is surfaced with layers of tar paper, asphalt and gravel, are there bubbles or peeling or broken patches? Look at the pieces of sheet metal that prevent leaks around chimneys and vent pipes—are they intact and watertight? They should be made of non-rusting copper, aluminum or plastic.

Do the gutters show signs of leaks or breaks? The downspouts should lead directly to storm sewers or to underground drainage at least three feet away from the house.

As a final check to make sure the roof is all right, maybe you can get into the attic or crawl space and look around with a flashlight. If there are leaks, you'll see telltale water stains.

Inside the house you'll make a quick inspection for warped doors that won't close, rattly doorknobs, creaky floors or stairs, loose tiling, inadequate plumbing and other obvious flaws. You'll look for "spiders"—plugs with many cords along the walls—betokening scanty wiring and too few electrical outlets.

You'll check on the roominess of closets and storage space. You'll look at the kitchen, and the heating equipment. The water heater should hold thirty to forty gallons if it is gas, sixty gallons if electric. If there's a fireplace, does it work?

A bad floor plan may cut the resale value of a house. Appraisers have a sharp eye for poor layout. Can you get from entry doors to other parts of the house without crossing the living room? Can you get from car to kitchen without walking clear around the house? Can you go from bedroom to bath without being seen from living areas? Modern designers say that two bathrooms are now a minimum, and one should adjoin the master bedroom.

These are all points to keep in mind. A few shortcomings won't necessarily mean you shouldn't buy, but they'll be warnings that you should get an expert appraisal, and an estimate of the cost of whatever improvements will be essential.

At this stage you should still be looking at numerous houses and apartment buildings. You're not ready yet to zero in on five or six for close study of the financial angles. Therefore the quick once-over just described needn't take much longer than you take to read about it. It's only a preliminary—a way of eliminating some properties from further consideration.

Be sure to keep notes about every house or apartment complex that seems to be a possible buy, even if the asking price is too high. In looking at many properties you'll soon find it hard to recall which was which. Your notes should include a full list of the good and bad points—and the date you looked at the property, because you may check back in a few weeks or months, and find that the price has come down into your range.

After you've had some experience with the single-family house, you'll be ready to tackle apartment buildings with multiple units.

When you're scanning other buildings, you'll look more closely for physical defects that can't be cured, but you won't be quite as fussy about location as in the case of a one-family home. Different kinds of apartment dwellers have different preferences for location. Childless people obviously won't flock into an area with two- and three-bedroom units, but families with schoolchildren may be keenly interested if it's near a good school—or even near an average school; some families don't want their children in top-quality schools because competition from bright students would be too intense. By the same token, a neighborhood far from schools may be especially attractive to childless people, and studio apartments may rent quickly there.

Take particular note of a run-down building, even if there's no indication that it is for sale. It is obviously suffering from mismanagement. Mismanaged property in a fairly good location is the golden opportunity you're seeking; a better manager should be able to turn it into a money-maker. The neglect is a clue that the owner may not even be thinking about his property. If you get him to think about it, he may jump at the chance to sell. Jot down the address for further investigation, and take a photo to jog your memory.

Another clue to a golden opportunity is a manager who seems surly or slovenly. If you buy the property, just installing a pleasant and capable manager might be enough to attract better-paying residents.

Most poorly managed property is owned by people who aren't interested in it, or aren't able to look after it. This is worth investigating. Often the owner turns out to be a widow or heir of the original owner. Sometimes the owner is an absentee landlord trying unsuccessfully to manage the property from afar. Sometimes he or she is ill—or is in financial straits, unable to pay for repairs and maintenance because the rent money is needed for other purposes.

In any of these situations, the owner probably isn't making much money from the property. His tenants surely aren't paying top rents, and probably are causing all kinds of trouble. He may be receptive to a low offer from you. (Your offer, of course, must take into account what you'll have to spend to upgrade the property and resell at a profit. In the next chapter we'll consider how to evaluate properties and how to decide what you should pay for them.)

Even if a mismanaged property is too big for you to consider now, it's worth keeping in mind for a later period when you're more experienced, can handle bigger financing, and can give more scope to your imagination. Bold and imaginative measures can attract tenants into a building that has been almost empty for years. For example, one new owner quickly filled a run-down apartment complex by advertising it as exclusively for cat-lovers. "Nobody can move in without at least one cat, female only," he proclaimed. He knew that many lonely older people like to keep cats, but that few apartments permit them. He scaled his rent according to the number of cats the tenant kept. This more than paid for whatever damage the pets did. He soon had a harmonious group of residents, since nobody complained about anyone else's cats.

Another owner's brand-new building was almost impossible to rent because it contained mostly two-bedroom units, which are seldom rented by adult-only families. There just wasn't much demand for two-bedroom apartments in that part of the city, because schools were substandard. But a resourceful manager filled the building by doing some minor remodeling, then advertising: "One bedroom with den . . . One bedroom with music room . . . Bedroom and formal dining room."

In another community, dotted with empty units, an investor converted his property's 40 percent vacancy rate into a long waiting list because he thought himself into the places of his prospects. Most of them were military families; a big military base was nearby. Reasoning that the wives of military men hated to get up early to drive their husbands to the base, he leased a bus to take the men to and fro. This didn't cut his profits, because he charged extra for his bus service. Families were glad to pay.

In Chicago the managers of many huge low-income housing developments have solved the chronic problem of juvenile mischief by finding maintenance employees who like youngsters and are willing to become leaders of Cub packs and Boy and Girl Scout troops for the residents' children. The same strategy might work for owners of smaller buildings in a district where care of children is a costly nuisance.

An owner of property in a very noisy neighborhood capitalized on this drawback by finding tenants who didn't mind noise: he advertised his apartments as "specially designed for tenants with hearing problems." He installed lights in every unit that flashed to signal that the phone or doorbell was ringing. He put amplified receivers on telephones. He provided earphones to be plugged into radios and TV sets; alarm-clock devices that awakened a sleeper by jiggling a pillow; even a shopping service for those too deaf to do their own shopping. He guaranteed that every tenant would be personally alerted in case of a fire in the building. Naturally the cost of all these extras was figured into the rent, which tenants paid willingly. The noise outside the building never bothered them.

In perhaps the strangest success story of this kind, an investor rescued a money-losing property by renting exclusively to marijuana smokers. When he bought it the building was half empty because a few tenants were smoking pot, driving away older occupants and causing complaints to the police. Instead of trying to evict the smokers, he called them together, explained his predicament, and urged them to bring in other lovers of grass to fill the vacancies. They did. Soon everyone who disliked marijuana had departed, and all units were rented to congenial souls who never complained. Sometimes single apartments were occupied by several tenants, but even this didn't dismay the owner-manager. He charged rent according to the number of people in the apartment. He had no trouble collecting, since there was a waiting list of potheads.

So you see there are countless ways to convert an undesirable property into a desirable and profitable one. Keep your imagination working whenever you look at localities or properties.

Having gone through the exploratory process suggested in this chapter, you're probably ready now to get down to analyzing and comparing several buildings that seem to be the best of those you've found in your scanning and preliminary inspecting. We'll see how to do this in the next chapter.

REMEMBER THESE HIGH POINTS:

Try to begin by buying a one-family rental house. Make a detailed inspection.

Seek out expert help, before you commit yourself to buying.

V *How to Choose Your Best Buy*

You've narrowed your list down to perhaps four or five properties. None would be a bad buy. They're the most attractive-looking investments you've seen.

Still, there may be important differences between them. One might put you much further ahead financially than others. So now you must analyze them more deeply than you did during your early explorations.

Maybe the financial terms will turn out to be the decisive difference. If the down payments, monthly payments, or other conditions set by the sellers are sharply different, at this point you may want to skip ahead in the book and familiarize yourself with the financial variables involved. First look at the final section of Chapter VII on loan constants. Then dip into the section in the middle of Chapter VIII, four variables must be negotiated. And if there seems to be plenty of leeway for reshaping the transaction by borrowing, you may want to read Chapter X. However, if all the properties are available at substantially the same terms, then you'll want to keep reading from where you are now, to see how you can analyze the properties themselves.

Don't rush it. A salesman may tell you, "Too many buyers lose deals because they take too much time trying to analyze them. While you analyze, someone else may be writing a check." What he's really saying is "Buy first, analyze later . . . leap before you look."

A broker may show you a checklist of a property's advantages and disadvantages. He may quote numbers: the "assessed value" and "projected income" of the property. But you'd better make your own checklist and figure out your own projection.

The broker gets his commission from the seller. He's a salesman. Good salesmen are optimists. It's their business to press people to buy.

If the broker is ethical he won't knowingly defraud anyone. But he may not delve deeply into defects of properties, either. It's not his worry if you get stuck with the long-term consequences of an unwise investment. That's your worry. So watch yourself.

If there's keen competition to snap up a property you're considering, it's probably not for you, especially if this is one of your first investments in real estate. Competition often bids up the price too high.

The main mistake you can make is to pay too much. The winner of a keen competition to buy a property will almost certainly pay too much. Anyhow, you don't want the kind of property that people are rushing to buy. Most buyers do little to improve a property. You can make your dimes produce more than their dollars.

You want money-losing "problem properties" that are priced low because they've been on the market a long time; unimaginative investors aren't interested in them. They can be the real bargains—if you analyze them carefully enough.

First, find out more about the current tenants of each building you're considering. This is especially important if one or more of these buildings is a one-family house.

If you own one rental house and have one vacancy, your vacancy rate will be 100 percent—forcing you to make the mortgage payments from your reserve funds. This is why you should try to find out in advance whether the present tenant is likely to stay.

If he isn't, how much cleaning, repairing, and refurbishing will you have to do when he moves out? Most tenants don't treat a house as if it were their own. You may find your empty house in bad shape, and days or weeks may pass while you're putting it in condition to be shown, and while you're finding another tenant. With no cash flow, this can be hard on your bank account.

On the other hand, a quiet steady family in the house can minimize your worries and maximize your profits. Your turnover and vacancy factors are zero—which is almost never true in an apartment property unless its rents are unprofitably low. Likewise, this quiet tenant is likely to keep your maintenance and repair bills low.

In short, unconsciously the tenant now occupying the house may give the answer to whether or not you should buy it.

Beware of a tenant who hasn't been there long, is behind in rent payments, seems to be doing considerable damage, or seems likely to move out soon. Estimate carefully whether you can afford the costs of refurbishing and/or a prolonged vacancy.

Conversely, if the tenant has lived there a long time, has paid promptly, hasn't caused much wear and tear, and seems to plan to stay indefinitely, the house is likely to be an excellent investment.

What about children? A good tenant will probably stay until the kids graduate—assuming that a school they attend isn't closed down suddenly because of a drop in enrollment, which is beginning to happen often in these days of declining birth rates—and assuming also that the character of the neighborhood doesn't change drastically, which likewise happens often and causes some families to move away.

If the house is clean and well built, in a good area, any steady tenant is likely to stay, with or without children. If he does leave he can quickly be replaced, because such houses are hard to find. A tenant may even be interested in buying the house from you.

To sum up: If you've stumbled onto a good house in a good neighborhood, and the price is within reason, you've found a good buy. This is one time you needn't check every last detail of the physical condition of the house, nor haggle over the last hundred dollars of the purchase price. You'll be investing primarily for resale. In the meantime the monthly yield on your investment will add to your security. Just be sure the mortgage payments will be significantly smaller than your income from the rent.

Tenants of a multi-family building can occasionally be just as crucial to your investment decision. Don't buy just because the building is full now, at rental rates that seem to promise you a monthly profit. After escrow closes, the building may be empty; the current tenants may be cousins, aunts, and in-laws of the builder or the seller. This happens sometimes. Make sure it can't happen to you.

Oftener it happens that residents are in the building because the owner offered several months' free rent, gifts of furniture or other inducements. When their lease expires they may either (a) demand more concessions from you, (b) look for other apartments where they *can* get concessions, or (c) slow down their rent payments until you evict them.

Concessions aren't necessarily bad. They're sometimes unavoidable in a soft rental market. But they're also a way for an unscrupulous seller to inflate (temporarily) the current rental income. Don't be misled into thinking you're acquiring a building full of tenants who are paying the full rental rates twelve months a year, if they're not.

Read their leases, and check the receipts for past rental payments. If concessions were made, or if tenants are behind in their rent, you should lower your purchase offer accordingly. The fair price of an apartment building hinges on the prospective income from rents.

You may find that most of the tenants are renting on a month-to-month basis. They may claim later that they have an oral lease—which is binding up to one year, under some state laws. Ask the owner or manager about any "oral leases"—and any commitments for future improvements of apartments—before you buy.

When you first look at a building, you may have already talked with the owner or broker. And you probably have seen some preliminary figures about its value, income, and expenses. But there's still a lot you need to know.

At this stage you can't very well ask to see the individual apartment units. Owners don't like to disturb their tenants. Until you've actually tendered an offer to buy, you probably won't be able to inspect any apartments except the vacant ones. But you can make an offer "subject to inspection of the interior." With your offer in hand, the owner will be willing to show apartments. Insist on seeing them all, without exception. The one or two that he makes excuses not to show may be just the ones that it's most important for you to see. Despite what he may tell you, all his apartments aren't alike.

In any case you'll want to allow for vacancies, bad debts and repair costs in figuring your net income from the property. How much should you allow for these expenses? It depends on the kind of tenants, and the kind of building.

What kinds of tenants are most profitable? From the standpoint of an owner, he'd much prefer a couple with no pets or children, and with both people employed and away from home most of the time.

No doubt the world needs kindly owners who accept children and pets because they love them. Such owners are rare, and seldom stay in business long. They soon learn that cats, dogs, and kids cause management problems and increase maintenance costs.

Whether a building accepts children and pets may indicate the rentability of the units, and their profit margin. If units stay vacant, owners start accepting children and pets. Pressures of competition can force concessions, and renting to less-desirable tenants is one of these concessions. The more concessions a building is making, the higher its expenses.

You're probably on the track of a high-profit investment if you find a building occupied mostly by married couples or elderly folks who have lived there for years. They'll probably stay unless you boost the rent out of sight.

Single people can be stable too if they are well established in business or one of the professions. There's a correlation between the stability of tenants and the allowance you should make for the vacancy factor, collection problems, and costs for repairs and maintenance.

Even with good management you must expect a high turnover and perhaps some skips and deadbeats if the building is full of young swingers, bearded counterculture types, carhops and fry cooks and other low-income people who tend to move often. Their ages, occupation, and places of work, as shown on their rental applications, are worth thinking about when you're comparing properties.

The type of building can tell you much about what to expect from occupants and what sort of changes will or won't pay off.

For example, if a building has a mixture of studio apartments and three-bedroom suites, you'd have a hard time making it profitable. Your tenants would be different types with different needs and desires. Ill-assorted tenants make a building hard to manage and hard to rent. The unit mix, as it is called, is a telltale factor in profitability.

As another example, maybe you're considering a building in a neighborhood where most residents are elderly retired people. The building is five floors high, it has no elevators, and all the apartments are two-bedroom units. Would it be a good investment? Almost surely not. Few elderly people would rent there, and other types of tenants might feel out of place in the neighborhood.

Suppose a building has all three-bedroom units. Can it be a good investment? Maybe. Its prospective residents would be families with children (which make up 54 percent of all metropolitan families). So you'd need to know how close the schools are, and how good. You'd also need to take into account your probable costs for frequent cleaning, painting and repairing. Children run the bills up. So the question is whether your prospective occupants could and would pay the unusually high rents you'd have to charge.

Is a building with furnished apartments a better investment than an unfurnished one? Usually this depends on market conditions in the area. As was covered in Chapter III's discussion of stable neighborhoods, if the neighborhood is full of students or transients, there's a strong market for furnished apartments. But if it's a more stable residential area, most prospects prefer to bring in their own furnishings.

Let's say you're considering two possible buys. One is furnished, in an area where furnished units seem to rent steadily. The other is unfurnished, in an area where the demand is for unfurnished. How do you choose between them?

It's a complex problem. Here are some factors you should take into account.

Furnished units tend to attract people with few household possessions, who tend to move often because they travel light. In Southern California, where there are probably more transients than in any other region, the average turnover rate in furnished units is more than 100 percent per year, while it's only 55 percent in unfurnished apartments. The rates are likely to be in roughly this proportion in other parts of the country too.

Despite the higher turnover, furnished properties have some points in their favor. Your cleaning and maintenance costs will probably be lower. Little spots that need repair or touching-up are less noticeable. Then too, if you choose your occupants carefully with a view to their job stability and ability to get along with one another, you needn't necessarily have high turnover among them. Good management can pay off even more handsomely in furnished properties than in unfurnished ones.

The unfurnished properties, as I mentioned in the paragraph above, will cost you more for cleaning and maintenance. Apartments, like homes, don't show well when they're empty. Every blemish is more noticeable than it would be if the same unit were furnished. The discoloration from gas heat is so noticeable that walls generally have to be repainted between tenants. Also, when tenants move their furniture in or out, they can hardly avoid denting walls and scarring doors.

Consequently the turnover rate becomes a crucial factor in sizing-up unfurnished property. Take a good look at the record of vacancies, and the bills for maintenance and refurbishing. If these are too high they'll eat up your rental income, and the property will be a poor investment unless you find a way to attract residents who'll stay a long time.

Another factor to think about, when choosing between furnished and unfurnished property, is how attractive (or unattractive) those furnished units look. Many people shopping for a furnished unit are more concerned with the looks of the furniture than they are with the unit itself. And they may stay for years if they feel they're getting good value for their rental dollars.

Therefore, quality furnishings can be a big plus, especially if they're almost new. Furniture in an apartment building has a useful life of three to ten years. If you plan to resell the property soon, and the furnishings are good enough now, without beginning to look shabby, you'll probably be able to keep the building filled with little difficulty. On the other hand, remember that the rents you can charge will begin to shrink as the furnishings deteriorate—so don't count on the current cash flow continuing if units are full of furniture that is wearing out noticeably.

Poor furnishings can be a big plus, too, because they constitute a so-called "valuable fault," as will be discussed later in this chapter. If you replace them with better stuff, you can charge higher rents and probably attract a better type of resident so that the building's turnover will be lower than it is now. Further, it can give you a distinct competitive edge if the other properties nearby contain old and dingy furnishings. But if you're considering upgrading a poorly furnished building, make careful calculations of the cost of the new furnishings you'll need. Retail costs needn't be your guide. You can sometimes buy wholesale, or at greatly reduced prices, through an apartment owners' association.

When you first compare furnished and unfurnished property, the former will probably seem the more enticing investment because of the higher rents that can be charged. But don't rely too heavily on its current gross income as an indicator of its quality as an investment. As we've just seen, when its furnishings begin to look scruffy, you'll have to either replace them or settle for lower rents.

To put this another way, maybe the furnished building you're considering was beautifully furnished at considerable cost, and may now be pulling in an unusually high net cash flow because of it. But some of that flow is only temporary. As soon as you have to start repairing or replacing furnishings, these costs will cut down your net. So don't base your offer to the owner primarily on this cash flow.

The most scientific way to compare the value of a furnished building with an unfurnished one is to look at each property in terms of what it would be worth empty, then consider the fair market value of the furnishings separately. What cash flow and net income could you expect from each building if you rented the units at the going rates for similar unfurnished apartments in the area? Would you be paying a higher or lower price for the rental income if you bought an unfurnished property that was otherwise the equal of the furnished one? Answers to such questions will help you judge whether the net price you'd be paying for a building is or isn't a bargain.

You should know exactly what improvements you'll make (and approximately what they'll cost) before deciding whether to buy a property. As an investor, you won't make improvements just for sheer creative joy. You'll make them only if they'll heighten the premises' attractiveness to tenants—because this should mean higher rents, which in turn mean a higher resale value. Under the Lowry formula, every dollar you spend on improvements should add at least two dollars to the property's net income, and preferably three or more dollars.

An improvement costing $100 must give at least $200 added resale value, which can be generated by $20 a year additional net income, assuming a 10 percent capitalization rate (this term is explained in Chapter VII, in case you're unfamiliar with it). To get that much additional net income per year, you need only raise one tenant's rent $1.67 per month.

Improvements that would be profitable in one property might be wasted in another. They must appeal to the kind of people likely to rent in the neighborhood. So here again you need to know about your occupants—not only current ones but prospective ones. Keep them always in mind while you're looking at property and considering possible improvements.

At this point you may be thinking, "If people are standing in line to rent these apartments anyway, why should I spend one dime remodeling? As long as I'm in a tight market with a low vacancy rate, I can just sit back and watch the big beautiful rent dollars roll in."

This thinking may put extra dollars in your pocket temporarily. But in the long run it is dangerous. If you don't keep up the property, its market value keeps sinking, because the next buyer—assuming you can find one—will subtract the cost of making those deferred improvements from the amount he'll be willing to pay.

You'll never have a better chance to make property more profitable than when you can count on its being filled. As long as you see a backlog of would-be tenants, guaranteeing full occupancy, your only question is "How much improvement shall I get them to pay for?" There always are people who will pay a better price for a better product. If the present renters can't afford to do so, there will be others who can, so long as you don't charge more than the existing top rates in the area.

In choosing a real estate investment, choose one you can upgrade. Once you're sure what its maximum potential rents will be, then do your arithmetic and see how much upgrading or remodeling these increased rents will pay for.

Now let's consider how you should analyze a prospective buy for chances to make it more attractive.

Look at the lobby and halls and other public areas: their furnishings, wallpaper, fixtures, lighting. Maybe the lobby has old wallpaper and a beat-up carpet. You could replace these quickly and inexpensively. You might put in a fine table and a lamp (which you'd bolt down so they couldn't be stolen). Maybe only a brighter carpet would be all you'd need. Or a rubber plant in the hallway. Or attractive draperies. Maybe you can hang some artwork in the halls. You can buy reproductions of fine contemporary art for a nominal sum.

(Wiseacres will warn you, "Don't buy that stuff. People will steal it right off the walls." But for fifteen or twenty dollars apiece you can buy reproductions of the finest contemporary art. Few people can distinguish them from the originals.)

First impressions are crucial. Prospective residents must be pleasantly impressed when they walk in the front entrance. If not they'll walk out again, unless there's an extreme shortage of apartments. So you should plan to make enough improvement in the lobby and halls to give you a clear competitive edge over other buildings in the neighborhood. Stay within the general level of those other buildings. If yours becomes vastly more elegant than others nearby, the prospective tenants will think it's too ritzy for them. Perhaps you should talk to tenants in similar properties, so you can get a feel for their standards.

How else can you improve the eye appeal of the property? Maybe by some fresh paint on the front door or other parts of the exterior. Probably by upgrading the grounds or landscaping, which needn't cost much.

Most older premises look unnecessarily ugly on the outside. Merely clearing away weeds and trash in a courtyard may be enough to make a property stand out. Realtors say that sprucing up an eyesore yard can increase a building's resale value, because you change the entire mood and look of the place. A buyer or appraiser usually arrives at a valuation for the building, then deducts for poor landscaping. In his book, Nickerson tells of spending $350 to plant some inexpensive young shrubs and trees on a property; because of this, an insurance company later added $12,000 to its appraised value of the place.

Is there extra outdoor space on the property? Maybe you can use it for amenities that will help hold renters. A long vacant area alongside the building might become a horseshoe pit that either young adults or senior citizens would enjoy. If horseshoes sound too noisy, how about shuffleboard or a few paddle tennis courts? One owner in Tacoma set up a canvas target on a wall, and got forty tenants competing enthusiastically in a monthly BB-gun tournament.

Looking at various garden-style courtyards, you wonder what ever happened to American know-how. Most of these yards contain only grass—plus dandelions and crabgrass. At no more cost than you'd need to keep the weeds out, you could build a flagstone walk through beds of petunias and marigolds, or a curved walkway leading around junipers to a rustic bench.

If there's an old tree in a courtyard, why not find out the cost of hanging outdoor Christmas lights in the branches? This could make the space a center of attention, and add extra security because of the lighting. (A good time to buy the lights is the twenty-sixth of December!)

If there are children among the residents, you could paint part of a courtyard or side area for hopscotch and skill ball. Walls of carports or garages might hold a basketball backboard and net. An imaginative apartment owner in Tustin, California, put a ten-foot boulder in a corner of his courtyard. It keeps children busy playing cowboy, mountain-climber, Indian and assorted other desperadoes. (The boulder cost only the trucking charge, and there are no maintenance costs.) Another owner brought in three large cement sewer pipes, painted in bright colors. The children can set them on end to climb into and out of, or lay them down to crawl through.

The point is simply this. Be glad if you can buy a basically good property with poor landscaping. It has one of those easily curable deficiencies that are so valuable.

Attractive landscaping will increase occupancy by about 5 percent on the average. A nurseryman or landscape gardener will probably be glad to make suggestions and give you an estimate of costs, if he knows you plan to buy plants from him. You may find that an adequate improvement in landscaping will cost you only a few hundred dollars, plus a monthly expense of twenty to seventy dollars for a gardener (or less, if some of your tenants happen to be green-thumb types who enjoy caring for plants themselves).

Inspecting the inside of a multi-unit property must be done more carefully than with a single unit. Remember, you can't get your money back later just because the building is in poorer condition than you thought.

An expert should check the heating, wiring, plumbing, roofs, walls and foundation of the building. (While he's at it, ask him whether rewiring the electrical system would be worthwhile. Sometimes this significantly reduces your electricity and insurance costs.) Always make your offer conditional on this expert's inspection and approval.

You and he together should work up a list of the property's faults, curable and incurable. You want the former; most of them are valuable. You dread the latter; they cut down your possible profits, and may rule out the property as a profitable investment.

Valuable faults are those that you'll profit by in correcting because you can get higher rents after correcting such deficiencies. Two of these, as already noted, are poor landscaping and an unattractive lobby.

Others are walls that badly need paint or plaster or wallpaper; seedy carpets; bad ceilings; shabby draperies; antiquated fixtures, especially in a kitchen or bathroom; inadequate heating or air conditioning; an incompetent manager; dirt.

In other words, a curable deficiency is almost anything that can be fixed up at reasonable cost and will make an apartment worth higher rent to the kind of person who lives in the area. These flaws are signs of a potentially good investment.

You can't do much about a bad floor plan, bad neighborhood, lack of parking, shoddy construction, narrow halls, small rooms, cramped closet space, sloping walls or floors. That's why these incurable defects shrink your potential profits.

You can shore up a rotten foundation but this won't make the building more inviting to tenants, so it's not a valuable defect. The same is true of a leaky roof. You'll have to fix it; occupants have a right to demand this, and can have you into court if you don't. Mending it won't justify raising the rent.

In short, whatever emergency repairs are needed must be classed as undesirable defects, and you must deduct the cost from the price you're willing to offer for the property. Broken windows, jammed locks, loose doorknobs, non-functioning light switches cost you money but don't increase the potential value. Deferred maintenance reduces the value of a property.

Inspecting the units in a multi-unit dwelling is an important part of the analyzing and comparing what you must do. Start with the vacant apartments. Later, by advance arrangements with the manager and residents, go through the occupied apartments one by one.

You might carry a small cassette recorder so that you can tape a reminder to yourself of every item you notice. Or you may prefer to jot notes on a legal pad and clipboard. However you do it, work from a checklist so you can observe and compare the same items in each place you visit.

This procedure has several purposes. One purpose, as we've seen, is to compile lists of the valuable defects in each building. Another is to start planning the possible repairs and improvements you'll make if you buy the property.

A third purpose is to make detailed comparisons of the properties you're thinking of buying. In a moment we'll consider a system you can use in comparing every aspect of the properties. But first let's continue with your quest for curable flaws in each apartment.

The kitchen and bath are the two most important areas. They are where your money can probably be spent most productively, because remodeling can show dramatic profits on improvements there. Most rental decisions are made by the ladies, and they look first at kitchens.

In most buildings more than a dozen years old, the kitchens are depressingly old-fashioned. You may find that the shelving must be doubled to bring them up to today's standards. Architects now consider sixty square feet the minimum for kitchen cupboard space, plus twenty square feet of drawer space.

So you consider ripping them out and replacing them. But maybe this would be so expensive that you couldn't raise the rent enough to pay for it. (Top rents being charged in the vicinity are your invisible ceiling. You can't raise your rents much, if at all, above this top.)

So you may consider other possibilities. You might leave the cabinets on the top and make some improvements in the counter area. You could put in a dishwasher, a range, and an attractive refrigerator. You could take the water heater out of the kitchen and put it in a closet. All these changes would be worth money to tenants.

Let's say the kitchen stove would cost $100. How much could you raise the rent because of it? Certainly five dollars a month. This would give you another $60 a year net income—which would add $600 to the value of your building, when capitalized at 10 percent.

Even assuming that you'll spend another $100 for wiring and a gas line and perhaps changing a cabinet, the improvement still makes good sense. For each dollar you'd spend, you would add at least three dollars to the resale value of the building.

This is the mental arithmetic you always do in thinking about possible improvements to an apartment. What will it be worth to you? How much return will it eventually bring on your investment dollar?

Sometimes purely cosmetic improvements in the kitchen will bring the biggest proportionate returns. Colorful wallpaper—plums and apples and cherries in a pattern, perhaps—is very smart and up-to-date on one wall. Bright cheerful semigloss paint is good too.

What about microwave ovens, indoor charcoal grills, fancy electric gadgetry? Don't get carried away. Many women won't rent electric kitchens. Too many things can go wrong with the equipment, they say.

What about a garbage disposal unit? Or a compactor? People want them, unless the units are too noisy—as many are. Something like an Insinkerator may be worth considering, despite its expense, because it is very quiet—and durable. You should know the life expectancy of whatever you put in, for appraisers will take this into account later in judging the worth of your building.

In the bathroom, if you find an ancient bathtub on spidery legs, or a stained and cracked sink, you'll have to buy replacements unless you're figuring on poverty-level rent scales. You might tear out the washbasin and install a little cabinet or chest of drawers under the new one. A built-in modern medicine cabinet and makeup bar cost little but add much to the next buyer's appraisal of the bathroom. Sometimes you can inexpensively modernize a washroom by changing individual hot and cold water faucets to mixing faucets with chrome handles. Sometimes an up-to-date adjustable showerhead over a bathtub, with sliding shower doors, will be worth another $10 a month in rent. A heater inset into a wall is another possibility.

In luxury buildings you might spend thousands of dollars to put in sunlamps, heat lamps, a fashionable new sauna unit. But in renovating older and cheaper apartments you can't do any of this without pushing your rents far through that invisible ceiling. Take a look at bathrooms in the highest-rent buildings in the neighborhood. Do they have anything that yours lack? If so, those are the appurtenances you should try to add. Without them you may not be able to boost your rents to the top of the range.

Floors and carpeting are often neglected features of an apartment. Prospective tenants are dismayed by a shabby carpet. If floors are in bad shape you should cover them with wall-to-wall carpeting. But this won't be enough if flooring is broken and creaky; you'd better get estimates for renewal from a floor contractor. Maybe the present carpeting looks okay, but you'd better find out how old it is. The average life of an apartment carpet is three to five years. You may need a reserve fund for replacement as carpets wear out.

Walls and ceiling are likely to show you possibilities—or downright necessities—for improvement. How about the electrical fixtures? Outdated switches and outdated hanging fixtures mark an apartment as archaic, so you'll probably have to replace any you find. Are there other ancient features like ornate molding or fireplace mantels? (These might be considered quaint and likable, rather than decrepit, if the rest of the apartment seems bright and convenient.) You can improve ceilings inexpensively by putting in drop ceilings. It's even cheaper to cover cracks with acoustic spray.

Depressing-looking rooms can sometimes be made cheery and inviting by your clever and tasteful uses of color. For example, a low ceiling looks higher if the walls are painted darker than the ceiling, or if wallpaper has a pattern of vertical stripes. Conversely, too-high ceilings don't seem so remote if the walls are lighter, or if horizontal bands are painted on the walls. Lighting, of course, is important, too. For example, a room with northern exposure will be dark—bright colors should be used to liven it up. Horizontal bands also broaden a small room. So do big mirrors. Papering just one wall can give an inviting, chic decorative effect. Prepasted, strippable wallpaper is moderately priced and easy to use. It's also easy to dispose of without damaging walls.

Your tentative budget for improving a property should be no more than 15 percent of your total contemplated investment. To make sure your rents will stay low enough to beat competition, you must set a budget within which you'll choose the most value-producing improvements. Your chief competitive advantage against new housing is the lower rentals you can charge while still netting a nice profit; if your costs of upgrading get too high, you'll have to charge such high rents that you'll be competing with newer buildings.

But keeping improvement costs low isn't your key objective. What you're basically trying to do is to increase the value of your property by at least 25 percent, so you can resell or exchange it for a handsome gain. When we consider the capitalization rate, later, this point will become clearer.

When estimating improvement costs, bear in mind that you may have to use your reserve cash to pay them, at least until the property's rents bring you more resources. Private lenders may be glad to make major remodeling loans at 12 to 15 percent, with repayment spread over five to ten years. But many financial institutions have cut back on lending money to improve older buildings. So you'll need hard dollars at the front end. This should change eventually, when the money shortage eases and interest rates come down.

Use as much leverage as you can—that is, use borrowed money wherever possible. Stick to the principle that each dollar you spend on improvements must add two dollars to the capitalized value of your house or apartment building.

After you've completed some changes and begun to raise rents, you may be able to borrow against the added value. Another possibility (if the current first mortgage on the property is paid down so far that you can borrow on a new first) would be to get money from this refinancing to pay for improvements.

In any case, don't overimprove your property nor go so far in debt that the cash flow won't cover your payments. One key to success will be to do the reconditioning in phases, rather than all at once.

Emergency repairs will come first, naturally, so you won't have irate residents on your hands. Then you should pretty up the exterior, and manicure the landscaping, to attract apartment hunters off the streets. At about this same time you should rejuvenate any apartments that are vacant, so you can rent them quickly at higher rates and get more cash coming in.

A little later you can rehabilitate other units one by one as residents move out, enabling you to ask higher rent from the next arrivals. And whenever you find that a desirable tenant is thinking of moving, maybe you can offer to make improvements while he's there, as an inducement to stay. Often a good tenant will do some of the work himself if you buy the materials—especially when you can also offer him a new lease at only a nominal increase.

Then you'll come to the problem of tenants who have leases with many months yet to run. You'd like to upgrade their apartments and raise their rents. One way you can arrange it is to drop in and say something like this: "You folks have been particularly good residents and I know you've been here a number of years. I'm wondering if you'd like me to go ahead and modernize your kitchen and hang new drapes here in your living room. That's what I've done for the unit down the hall. Would you like to take a look at it?"

When they've seen the apartment down the hall they're almost certain to respond, "Why, of course, we'd like to have that too." They'll put up with the inconvenience, looking forward to the nicer place they'll be getting. And they'll probably agree in advance to a rent increase.

Finally, if and when you evict undesirable tenants, you slick up their apartments too, if you haven't done so earlier.

You can keep much of this work on a pay-as-you-go basis by using some of the rental income that's left over after making mortgage payments. This net income will keep growing as you cut turnover; as you cut the vacancy rate; as you cut needless expenses; as you charge higher rents for the higher quality you're building into the place. Soon you can well afford to plow back some of the profit into renovations that will later produce a still wider profit margin.

Your schedule of priorities for improvements should take into account the logical sequence of workmanship, so that one job will follow another without letting workmen undo or mess up something that others did a little earlier. For example, if you must cut into walls for plumbing and electrical work, you'll certainly wait until this is done before you call in carpenters to install cabinets or make other changes in the woodwork. Similarly, you won't repaint a room until the plumbers, carpenters, and electricians have done whatever you planned. And of course no new draperies, carpeting, or furniture will come in until you finish whatever painting or plastering you contemplate.

Get a copy of the local building code from the city planner at City Hall before you make up your mind on any improvements—and also check with municipal authorities to be sure your plans won't violate any zoning laws. Some cities have very strict rules. Pittsburgh, for instance, won't let you close in a front porch without a zoning hearing.

Probably your building was constructed before the latest code was written. The authorities will let the building stay as it is (so long as deterioration doesn't make it dangerous), but the minute you start fixing it up they may force you to bring it into compliance with the new rules. This could cost big money. So the time to find out is before you decide on improvements and buy the building.

Permits and licenses are the contractors' responsibility, if you place contracts. If you employ a local architect or contractor he won't be likely to specify iron pipe where copper is required, or fifteen amp wiring where twenty is required. Nevertheless, he might be tempted to tell you that the code says you must do thus and so (which will inflate his bill) if he thinks you're an unfleeced innocent. Therefore, you should be able to look it up in the building code after he's gone, just to make sure it tallies with what he said.

If you do the work, or hire your unlicensed brother-in-law, or let tenants do it, the permits are your own responsibility. As a practical matter you're unlikely to need a permit if you simply paint a bedroom, add a kitchen cabinet, or put down bathroom tiles. You can do landscaping with impunity—except maybe when you cut down trees, or plant something that will block a neighbor's window. Simple repairs of plumbing or electricity or portable appliances are okay. Anything more elaborate will call for a permit.

In most places a permit is easy to get, and doesn't cost much—usually about 1 percent of the market value of the work. You'll probably pay no more than five dollars for a permit to install a water heater or stove, ten dollars for a $1,000 remodeling job. The costs merely cover the cost of inspection to make sure the work is done according to standards set to protect the safety of the tenants and the neighbors. For example, building inspectors would check the installation of a heater or bathtub to see that water, gas, and vent connections are the right size and material and are put in properly. If something is done wrong, most building inspectors will point out how to make it right so they can approve it.

Having studied each property's valuable faults and possible money-making improvements, you're still not ready to make a final choice. As an investor, you need to figure out which property will put you farthest ahead financially. In the next chapter we'll see how.

REMEMBER THESE HIGH POINTS:

Narrow your list of prospective investments to a few properties. Then compare them carefully.

Find out about each building's occupants. They can be crucial.

Look for "valuable faults" in each property. Know exactly what improvements you should make, and approximately what they would cost, as part of your comparison.

Usually remodeling kitchens and baths can pay off best.

Your budget for improvements should be no more than 15 percent of your total investment.

VI *How to Select a Good Investment*

Selecting a good investment is basically a problem of making sure you'll get good value for your investment dollar. But how do you figure value? How do you know when a buy is good, or when it's overpriced? This comes down to deciding how much a specific piece of real estate is worth.

There are three basic ways to figure the value of income property. (This reminds me of the story about the two lawyers arguing their case before a judge. The first lawyer explained his claim, and the judge said, "You're right." The other lawyer replied, and the judge ruled, "You're right." At that point, a perplexed friend of the court put in, "But, Your Honor, they can't both be right." The judge sagely replied, "You're right, too.") Anyhow, if you look at all three approaches before making up your mind, you're least likely to go wrong.

These three methods are (1) the comparison approach (2) the replacement-cost approach (3) the income approach.

Each has strengths and weaknesses. Just remember that valuing real estate is an inexact science at best. No two appraisers, even if they use the same approaches, are likely to come out with exactly the same answer. But this is the kind of situation where three heads are better than one.

The comparison approach is the best from some standpoints because you can get down to the finest details if you want to. It makes an item-by-item comparison of the good and bad features of several properties in the same general neighborhood. At least one of these properties is, naturally, a property you're thinking of buying. The idea is not to pay more for it than others are paying for nearby properties, all similarities and differences considered.

Let's say you want to use this comparison approach to value a specific property, or to choose the best buy among several. You start by choosing one property, or one kind of property, in which you might want to invest. Then you search through the neighborhood for other pieces of real estate that fit the same general description as closely as possible.

The reason I say "same general description" is that the more similar the properties are, the more easily you can compare them. There'll be fewer questions of taste and opinion. So don't try to compare single-family homes with duplexes, or a garden-court apartment house with a ten-story high-rise. If you're thinking of buying a forty- or fifty-unit apartment complex, look primarily at other apartment complexes of that size.

I've stressed that the properties you compare should all be in the same neighborhood. The neighborhood makes a big difference in property values. One apartment house in a desirable area may be a good buy at $100,000 while an identical building a few blocks away may be a white elephant at $60,000 because of a difference in surroundings. Unless you confine your comparisons to neighborhoods that appear to be about equal, you may be badly fooled.

If you're not sure whether properties you want to compare are really in the same "neighborhood," go talk to a few local real estate people or the nearest savings and loan association. They can usually give you a clear idea of the boundaries at which values change.

You can use the comparison approach to paint a broad-brush picture for yourself, or to make a sharp-pencil diagram. It depends on the number of properties you compare. As in any sampling process, the bigger the sample, the more reliable. If you get data on six or eight comparable properties, you'll see a clearer sketch of what each is worth than if you look at only two or three.

Okay, so now you've picked out a list of comparable properties. You're ready for the next big step, which is to size up the desirable and undesirable features of each. To find out what these are, walk in as a prospective renter—or even as a prospective buyer—and ask to see one or more of the units.

One building may have unusually convenient floor plans, while another with an awkward floor plan may contain the most closet space and the best kitchens. A third may be the only one with fireplaces or an intercom system. A fourth may be the only one without elevators or laundry facilities. How do you weigh all these haves and have-nots? How do you figure out which property is the best buy on balance?

Do you try to compare the good and bad points of every property against those of all the others? No. That way lies madness, or at least hopeless confusion.

Instead, you pick one property more or less at random, and measure all the others against it. You could pick the one you're most excited about, or you could pick one that was recently sold. You could close your eyes and pick one by throwing darts at a map. It doesn't matter, because we don't need a precise fix on the value of the property you choose. We're just going to estimate how much more, or less, each of the other properties is worth by comparison with the property picked as a standard.

The term we use for any property chosen as a standard against which to value others is "subject property." Maybe you think we'll be merely shadowboxing if we don't know how much this subject property is worth. But just wait. As we go along, you'll see that we're operating like a gunnery officer getting the range. All we need is a rough approximation to start with.

If the subject property has recently changed hands, you can start with its sales price (which you should be able to get from almost any broker thereabouts). If the property is listed for sale, the asking price will do nicely, and don't worry if this price tag is way out of line. Asking prices are based on personal quirks that range from greed through desperation to sheer stupidity. They may be far higher or lower than true value. But they're as good as any other figure to start from when you're using the comparison approach to valuing properties.

If the property hasn't been sold recently and isn't listed for sale, ask somebody knowledgeable to give you an offhand opinion if necessary. Just get a number—preferably reasonable, of course, but not necessarily so. You could start by saying that the subject property is worth $10,000,000, and you'd still get a good idea of which of the properties you're comparing is the most desirable investment for you.

Now it's chart-making time. We list the subject property, and all the other properties, at the top of columns on a page. On the first line under the heading, we show the asking prices of any of these properties that are up for sale. On the second line we write in the recent sales prices, if any. On the third line we show the value we've temporarily assigned to the subject property. We leave this line blank for the other properties. Why? Patience, dear reader—all will be clear in a moment.

We've said that you were walking through the various properties, sizing up the desirable and undesirable features of each. Now we list those features on our chart. We make this list as sketchy or detailed as we feel like, bearing in mind that we're interested only in features that could have a significant effect on value.

In other words, the important differences between the properties are what go into our chart. If the quality of kitchens varies sharply from one building to another, kitchens would certainly be one item on the list. Contrariwise, if all the buildings provide about the same parking facilities, you might decide not to bother listing parking as an item.

The differences you think are important should be listed down the left-hand side of our chart. Next we grade them for each property: "A" for excellent, "B" for above average, "C" for average, "D" for below average, "E" for unsatisfactory, and "F" for nonexistent.

Now we get into numbers. Dollar numbers.

That is, we make the shrewdest estimate we can as to how much each difference is worth by comparison with the subject property. Afterward we'll simply add or subtract all the value differences to get our bottom-line estimate of how much more or less each property is worth than the subject property.

To see how this works, let's take an imaginary situation and work out the analysis of comparative value. To keep things simple, we'll assume that we're comparing a subject property with only two other properties, and that all three are so much alike that we notice only five differences significant enough to jot down.

The subject property, we'll say, recently changed hands at a price of $100,000. We assume—just for purposes of our analysis—that this is its fair market value. The other two properties are currently offered for sale at $99,000 and $105,000 respectively. We write this basic information in the appropriate spaces near the top of our page.

Then we turn to the first item of major difference, which might be the bathrooms. Those in property no. 2 all have two washbasins, gorgeous ornamental tile, fancy gold-plated fixtures and faucets, and other glittering features we wouldn't expect in that neighborhood. Hard to beat. So we write an "A" after bathrooms in the column for property no. 2. By contrast, the bathrooms are about average in the subject property, so we give them a "C" in that column. In property no. 3 the bathtubs are cramped and the toilets are inconveniently placed, so we figure they rate only a "D."

Now comes the question of what these differences mean to the relative values of the three properties. To get the answer, you must estimate how much it would cost to upgrade the bathrooms in the subject property to the quality of those in no. 2. You can make your own estimate or, if you have absolutely no idea, you can consult a contractor. Just remember, you don't need to pinpoint the figure; somewhere in the ball park will be enough for our purposes.

Say you come up with an estimate of $600 each. This would mean a total of $1,800 to fix up the three bathrooms in the subject property. You write a plus $1,800 under the "A" rating you gave the bathrooms in property no. 2. Using the same reasoning, you might guess it would cost $1,550 to make the three bathrooms in property no. 3 as good as those in the subject property—so you put a minus $1,550 for the "D" bathrooms there.

Onward! Next item on our list is kitchens. Below average in the subject property? They get a "D." In property no. 2 the kitchens aren't as classy as they might be, but we'll give them a "B" because the equipment is newer. In property no. 3 they've all been remodeled lately. They rate an "A" because they're as up-to-date as any lady could reasonably expect.

Now the numbers again. How much would it cost to make the kitchens in the subject property as modern as those in properties no. 2 and no. 3 respectively?

You decide it would cost $1,900 (mainly for new equipment and cabinets) to pull the subject-property kitchens up to the quality of those in property no. 2—and about $4,000 (including extensive remodeling) to put them on a par with those "A" kitchens in no. 3.

We ran through the other items in the same way. Swimming pool? The subject property has one. The others don't. The one pool is just about average for that part of town, so it rates a "C" and the other two properties get "F," of course, on the line for swimming pools. How much would it cost to put a similar pool in the yards of no. 2 and no. 3? Maybe $6,000. So we write a minus $6,000 under those two F's.

Apartment heating system? We've noticed that the subject property's units are chilly on a cold day. But the other two buildings' heating can keep anyone cozy. So we rate the subject property "E" and the other two "A." Let's write plus $2,000 for each of the latter, because a heating-system contractor tells us it would cost about that much to bring the subject property's system up to par.

Maybe the final item on our imaginary list is storage space. Okay in the subject property, truly spacious in no. 3, woefully cramped in no. 2. But wait. There's an unfinished area in property no. 2's basement. It could be made into three good-sized storage rooms at a cost of about $2,500. So we give no. 2 an "E" and a minus $2,500. We have to award an "A" to no. 3 but we decide not to mark up the dollar value because the apartments have far more storage space than any normal resident would need. Subject property receives a "C" rating.

So now it's bottom-line time, the moment of truth. We simply add the plus and minus figures in each column. The answers tell us how much more or less properties no. 2 and no. 3 are worth than the subject property. Then we can add or subtract these amounts from whatever value we tentatively penciled in for the subject property, and the answers give us a guess at the value of the other two properties. Our hypothetical analysis sheet would look like this:

COMPARATIVE VALUE ANALYSIS

	Subject Property	Property No. 2	Property No. 3
Asking price	n/a	$99,000	$105,000
Recent sales price	$100,000	n/a	n/a
Tentative assumption of fair market value	$100,000	?	?

Major Items of Difference Between Other Properties and Subject Property:

Bathrooms	C	A	D
		+$1,800	−$1,550
Kitchens	D	B	A
		+$1,900	+$4,000
Swimming Pools	C	F	F
		−$6,000	−$6,000
Heating	E	A	A
		+$2,000	+$2,000
Storage	C	E	A
		−$2,500	-0-
Net effect of differences		−$2,800	−$1,550
Fair market value*	$100,000	$97,200	$98,450

* Relative to and assuming correctness of value assigned to the subject property.

Having done all this, we still can't be sure that the bottom-line figures for no. 2 and no. 3 are a good guide to their fair market value. They could be way off, if the subject property recently sold for much more or much less than it was really worth. Furthermore, there could be cases where your subject property hasn't been sold lately, isn't being offered for sale, and thus gives you no fix on what it might be worth. Even so, the analysis tells you that you'll probably be getting a better buy on no. 2 than no. 3 if you grab them at their respective asking prices. This is the main reason for making the comparison. No matter whether you arbitrarily assign a value of $1,000,000 to the subject property, or $1,000, you still end up with an idea whether property no. 2 or no. 3 is the better buy of the two.

If you need a more accurate reckoning of how close your figures are to fair market value, you can fine-tune them by including additional properties in your comparison—properties that have been sold lately. The more actual sales you consider, the closer you'll come to figuring fair market value.

In any real-life situation you'll surely consider more than the five categories of difference we picked out of the air for our fictitious comparisons. One important category will probably be the relative square footage of the various properties. This alone could make a surprising difference in their potential worth.

Square footage is important, because, for one thing, you'll have to heat it. For another, you rent space. People prefer spacious rooms and closets. So if one building has more usable space than the others, tenants may be willing to pay higher rents there.

Total square footage can fool you, though. Even though one building covers a bigger area than another, it doesn't necessarily contain more rentable space. Maybe the supposedly smaller building has outside patios with each apartment, or outside walkways between apartments. And maybe the "bigger" building has all inner halls, which of course must be regularly painted and cleaned and carpeted although they don't put a dollar in your cash register. In that case the "bigger" building probably has higher maintenance costs, and its actual rentable space—meaning potential for revenue—is smaller.

Step it off, use a tape measure, get the blueprints, do whatever you prefer—but know each building's square footage of rentable space. Start with its total floor space, then subtract footage that won't produce any income. That gives you the net space that will bring in all the rent money. If you know the current rentals you can compute the amount of income per square foot—a useful yardstick in comparing properties.

Some unrentable space can be made to pay off in other ways, perhaps. Maybe you can put in laundry machines if the building doesn't already have them. Or how about vending machines? Is the complex big enough to make their net revenues worthwhile after deductions for installation, servicing, repairs and depreciation? Maybe you can install a coin-operated telephone in a hall or lobby, if there seems to be demand for one. However, these possibilities are irrelevant just now. At the moment, you're trying to compare and evaluate each property's current condition. Its net rentable space is an important item for your checklist.

I wonder if you're thinking, "Wow! This is an awful lot of comparing and figuring!" Sure, you'll find it tedious the first time. But what's a few hours or even days of your time, compared with the thousands of dollars you may be able to save?

Even if you don't follow through with a purchase, making these close comparisons will give you valuable experience. Each time you do it, your analysis will be faster and easier. Soon you'll find you can get a feel for relative values of properties just by walking through.

Meanwhile, you needn't rely entirely on comparative inspections to decide which is your best buy. You can try another approach commonly used by appraisers: the "replacement cost" approach, as it's called.

The replacement-cost approach is another way of figuring the approximate current value of a property. You arrive at this by taking into account the value of the land, the age of the building and the cost of constructing it. Since costs were doubtless much lower when it was built, you go by today's costs rather than those of years ago.

You start with the total floor area of the building. You already know this figure if you've used the comparison approach described in the last few pages. Take the *total* square feet this time, not the square feet of rentable space, as you did before. Then check and see what it would cost to build that size apartment house today, using more or less the same building materials that were used originally.

To arrive at the cost you can consult several different books on cost estimating, such as *Marshall & Stevens* or *National Estimator,* or others to which your public librarian can probably steer you. Another way is to ask a few builders how much it costs per square foot to build an apartment house of the materials you name. No two builders will give exactly the same answers, of course. But they'll help you arrive at an approximation.

Other good sources are the local contractors' association, mortgage lenders, and the realty board. Best of all, you might locate the contractor who built the very apartment house you're considering, and ask him what that same structure would cost to build today.

Suppose you settle on a replacement cost of about $190,000 for the building, and it covers 10,000 square feet. Then you can use a figure of $19 per square foot. This square foot figure may be important if other buildings you're considering are different sizes.

However, for the sake of clarity, let's say we are looking at two apartment complexes: the Edifice and Sunken Heights. Let's say further that the Edifice complex would cost $190,000 to replace today, that the Sunken Heights complex would cost $200,000—and that they're the same size, and are on the market at the same price. Does this mean that the building on Sunken Heights is the better buy?

Not necessarily. What if one building is twenty years old, and the other is forty years old? Or what if one stands on much more valuable land than the other?

Obviously the replacement cost alone is only part of the equation. You must also crank in the other two factors: depreciation and land value.

Here's how you do it! Decide approximately how many years of useful life each building has, from the year it was built to the future year in which it will probably be unrentable at a profit. Here again contractors, lending institutions, and perhaps realty boards or property owners' associations should be able to guide you to a good appraiser. Maybe you'll find that both the Edifice and the Sunken Heights apartment houses have an estimated useful life of fifty years. In that case, each year they've been standing is one fiftieth of their useful life, or 2 percent. If the Edifice place is twenty years old, and the other is forty, here's how you'd figure the value of each:

	Edifice Complex	Sunken Heights Complex
Cost to build new:	$190,000	$200,000
Depreciation:	76,000	160,000
	(40% of $190,000)	(80% of $200,000)
Remaining value of building:	$114,000	$ 40,000

Finally you add the land value to these figures, to get your answer as to which property is worth more. (Note that you depreciate only the buildings, not the land. The land isn't ever "worn out" the way the building and equipment are.)

Brokers and bankers can usually tell you, rather accurately, the value of land anywhere in town. They know what prices are being paid for comparable land. Then too, similar vacant lots may be on the market, and you can price them for yourself. Or you might take data from the property tax bill to estimate the value of the lot.

The replacement-cost approach to value isn't perfect, because all the figures that go into it are estimates based on somebody's opinion. Builders have different opinions about the costs of building. Appraisers may disagree about the useful life of a building, or even about the value of land. Still, this method gives you at least a rough idea of the comparative worth of the properties you're considering.

Lenders use it in the process of deciding how much they can lend on a property. But they don't depend solely on it. They also evaluate the same property by the comparison method I described earlier, and by the "income approach," which is the third of the three common methods. If you try all three, and they all point to the same one of your prospective buys, you can be sure you're not making a mistake.

Bear in mind that the true value of a property, to you, often hinges on favorable financing or tax advantages. You might profitably buy the highest priced of three properties—or the one with the lowest intrinsic value as determined by the replacement-cost approach—if you could buy it with little or no down payment, or with exceptionally low interest rates or long mortgage term or big depreciation write-off or other unusual inducements—especially if you plan to upgrade the property and resell or trade it as I urge my students to do.

The income approach to value may be the most useful of all for you, because when you buy residential property you're buying a stream of income. Just remember that you're primarily interested in actual income, not "scheduled income." The actual income is what the units are now producing in rents (and in subsidiary income such as vending machines). The scheduled income is what the broker or seller says the total income should be when all units are rented.

For example, you may find a ten-unit building with all apartments the same. You may find that six are actually rented for $200 a month —but the four that are vacant are "scheduled" on the books at $225 or $250 a month. Those figures are merely hopeful guesses. You're unlikely to get that much until you upgrade them, since they're the same as those now rented at $200.

There are various ways of finding out a property's actual worth, as we saw earlier in this chapter. You may want to look back at those pages when you're making your final estimate of how much you can profitably pay for a property. And you'll want to allow for vacancies even if the property is 100 percent rented at the time of your offer to purchase. Gross scheduled income minus allowances for vacancies and deadbeats equals "adjusted gross income," as realty investors often call it.

Figure your prospective resale profit as a big bonus, not as your only reason for buying. Your true net monthly income is an important consideration. If it will be small, or will barely cover your mortgage payments, then you're probably speculating. Don't tie up your capital in a low-net piece of real estate, if there's any chance you may need that capital.

Many buyers, sellers, and brokers (and even some lenders) tend to think too much about the gross income a property is producing or "scheduled" to produce and too little about the in-pocket spendable money a buyer can reasonably expect to get. Scan the ads in your local newspaper. Note how often a property's "gross income" or "scheduled income" is almost the only figure given. Note, too, how often price is phrased in terms of a multiple of the gross—"five-and-a-half times," "seven times," "eight-and-a-half times," or whatever. Many people consider this the key consideration in buying or selling any property.

Sophisticated realty investors know better. The so-called magic multiplier of price times gross is a crude guide at best. A building advertised at six times gross is probably in worse condition or in a worse neighborhood than one advertised at eight-and-a-half times gross. That is all you can be reasonably sure about. Nationally, sales prices average about seven times gross income—but never choose investments on the basis of average. Don't forget the man who drowned in a river averaging only eight inches deep.

Many would-be investors also fail to realize that relative gross is absolutely no guide to relative net. Two properties with the same gross could be yielding wildly different nets. According to the magic multiplier theory, you should pay the same price for each. This would be stupid. Sometimes a property with a given gross is netting peanuts compared with another whose gross is half as big.

How can this be? Why don't grosses and nets move up or down together?

Well, sometimes taxes, insurance, and maintenance are much different for one property than another. Maybe a high-net building is well built and in tip-top shape; therefore its insurance rates are comparatively low, and its maintenance is inexpensive. Maybe a low-net property is poorly built, or in bad condition, so that virtually all the income it pulls in must be poured back into just keeping it livable.

Or sometimes the financing may be poorer and the mortgage payments much more burdensome on one of the two properties.

A third reason for the discrepancy between grosses and nets lies in what is meant by "scheduled income" and "gross income." Be sure you understand these terms.

"Scheduled income" is simply the sum of the rents the seller is asking for the various units. He could be a crazy optimist. His apartment house could be made up of ten identical units, six of which are "scheduled" and rented at $100 a month, and four of which are vacant but "scheduled" to rent at $125. Or his units could be "scheduled" to rent at a specific monthly rate although they're actually rented at a rate somewhat lower.

Gross income, to accountants, is the total dollar income that is generated from a business or investment before subtracting any expenses. But not to real estate brokers. Gross income, as brokers use the term, is an imaginary figure meaning the amount of income that would pour in during a year if a property were fully occupied for the entire year by renters who paid their rent in full. It makes no allowance whatsoever for any vacancies. It also may be inflated by unrealistically high rental schedules.

When you get down to serious consideration of a possible buy, you need to find out the true total of rent collected during the past year (or past several years, preferably). But even this is meaningless unless you know how that income was produced, and how much of it was drained away by expenses.

Let's take an extreme example. A building has been full, at impressively high rents. So it sounds like a fabulous buy at seven times the gross. But suppose the owner filled this building by putting full-page ads in the newspapers, and giving champagne parties for prospective renters. Now he keeps it full by giving free maid service, uniformed doormen, parking attendants, solicitous maintenance men, and maybe occasional gifts of steak or liquor—none of which are available in competitive buildings. These extras are costing him so much that the building is really running at a loss. Not knowing this, some would-be buyers may bid frantically for it, giving the crafty owner a fat capital gain when he sells. The next owner will probably go broke.

In older and lower-priced buildings, you run into such situations occasionally. An owner who wants to unload his property at a high price can spend money to enlarge the net income temporarily. You must know if there have been hidden expenditures, and deduct them from the property's income, to arrive at its true net income.

Or take an opposite example. A building's net income may be far below what it should be, solely because its manager is so hateful that tenants break their leases and move away, leaving the property half empty most of the time. Yet the "scheduled gross income" looks normal.

Once you know the true net income, it may point you toward a good buy. When net is abnormally low, you can harp on this in negotiating with the owner and broker, and press them to lower their asking price. Sometimes you can get them down to bargain-basement level by showing them how meaningless their statement of gross income is.

Net that's far below the gross spells lemon to most people. But you've seen how some lemons can be turned into sugary lemonade. There's a fine chance of doing this when the net is low for one invisible but simple reason such as we've just seen. If your amateur detective work (perhaps a chat with the residents, in the case we've just imagined) convinces you that you can fill the building fast and keep it nearly full by providing decent management, you've probably found a great investment.

Many intelligent brokers look at a property's operating statement and say, "This building should sell for ten times whatever the net is." Often it's a good formula. But sometimes it can be a trap for buyers.

Why? Consider another hypothetical example. A property's books may show low expenses, low vacancy rate, and comparatively high rents. So its monthly net income (as well as its gross) looks juicy. Is it worth ten times its net?

Not necessarily. As this book has kept emphasizing, your bargains in property are those where you can upgrade and raise the rent. Suppose the aforementioned property is already charging rents as high as any in the area. You may say to yourself, "So what? I'll boost my rents anyway, because I need the money." You're kidding yourself. Never forget that the competition and not the owner sets the terms. Many an owner has announced a rent increase, only to find that he can't rent his units unless he gives better terms. The law of supply and demand holds full sway in the housing business.

Coming back to this same hypothetical property we just considered, there may be entirely different reasons for its high net. You don't know. But you do know, we'll say, that its rents are lower than competition. On the surface this makes it a good buy. But look deeper. Suppose you find that the owner hasn't bought nearly enough insurance. Then you'd better add in the costs of adequate insurance, and figure what effect this has on the net income.

The "assessed valuation" of a property is another figure that brokers often mention. But its actual market value today may be much higher or lower than the tax men wrote down. When was the assessment made? If it looks suspiciously high or low, go to the county assessors and find out when they looked at the property. Maybe they came several years ago, when it was in peak condition. This is worth knowing, especially if the owners have let it deteriorate since then. After you buy, you can probably persuade the assessor to come out and look at the building again and put a lower assessment on it.

But maybe the taxes are low. Maybe the building will be valued much higher as soon as the assessor discovers that the owner has upgraded it. Or maybe the community's tax rate is due for a big boost. Or maybe the owner is a big politican with an inside track at city hall.

Take a long hard look whenever you're considering property whose taxes are less than 12 percent of its gross income, or more than 20 percent. Taxes much higher than 20 percent, unless you're sure you can get them reduced, are a clear signal that you shouldn't buy. The property will probably be a losing investment from the start.

What about insurance? It generally runs between 10 and 15 percent of the real estate taxes. Whether it does or not, look closely to see whether it's adequate and covers all basic needs. Remember, if you intend to increase the mortgage you may need additional fire insurance. Some owners don't carry nearly enough insurance against loss of rental income, which could be serious after an earthquake or tornado or any other disaster.

Incidentally, make sure that your lawyer examines any realty documents before you sign them. Ask him to insist that the tax, insurance, and utility costs be warranted by an owner from whom you're about to buy property. Your first written offer should include a statement to the effect that "I am making this offer based upon the information supplied by the broker, the statement of which information is attached to the deposit receipt." And if the broker wants a large deposit you can tell him, "I'll give you a note for that amount, promising to put the amount in your hands if the deposit receipt is accepted after the removal of the contingencies."

Deferred maintenance or deferred replacements can drastically change a property's value. If you're unaware of them, you can be fooled by attractively low expenses. Suppose the air-conditioning units (bought for $500 apiece, and built to last five years) are seven years old? Suppose the roof (which didn't leak last year, when the rains were light and infrequent) has had no maintenance for eleven years? Suppose the building contains overage carpeting, overage elevators, substandard incinerators, substandard refrigerators, toilets, dishwashers? Has the owner set aside a big enough reserve for repairs and replacements? Almost certainly he hasn't—which means he's milking the property. If you buy it you'll run into much bigger expenses than he's been paying. Insist that these anticipated expenditures be deducted from his asking price. You will find that most properties—perhaps as much as 95 percent—are not qualified as good investments; the income exaggerated and the expenses underestimated.

More data on all categories of operating expenses can be found in Service Bulletin 24 of the National Association of Building Owners and Managers at 134 La Salle Street, Chicago. For an even closer breakdown in all categories of apartments by age group, geographical region, furnished and unfurnished, send for (or borrow from somebody in the business) a copy of *Apartment Building Income/Expenses Analysis,* published by the Institute of Real Estate Management, 430 North Michigan Avenue, Chicago, Illinois 60611.

We might generalize to this extent. When you consider buying a property, if its owner or manager shows you an "operating statement" indicating that total expenses were much lower than the percentages given above, look to see if he left out some items. (You'll find a checklist in the following chapter.) If all the items are listed, including adequate reserves for vacancies, bad debts, and periodic repairs and replacements—and the percentage of gross is still lower than average—then possibly you've found a bargain.

But don't be too sure. What if the income has been grossly overstated, thereby shrinking the expense percentages? What if there are vacancies you don't know about? These are some possible pitfalls in buying property as an investment. But there are other pitfalls too, when you buy from someone of uncertain reputation. He may be deliberately trying to cheat you. In the next chapter we'll see how to protect yourself.

REMEMBER THESE HIGH POINTS:

Use three different approaches in deciding which property to buy:

1. Compare good and bad features, item by item;
2. Figure the cost of replacing each property today, taking into account its remaining years of useful life, and the value of the land;
3. Figure what net monthly income each property would bring you. Be sure to consider the *actual* income; beware of trusting figures based on *scheduled* income.

VII   How to Protect Yourself Against Fraud

To protect yourself against fraud, your offer to buy should be contingent on your right to review all leases and rent records, as well as the tax returns on the building, and to get certified copies of them before the deal is closed. If they don't tally with the alleged total income from rents, the deal should be renegotiated.

But even the rent records can fool you. As we saw earlier, they can be invisibly padded. Perhaps they show a tenant paying $150 a month rent, but they don't show that at the end of every month he gets $20 worth of groceries chargeable to the owner's credit card. In that case the true rent income is only $130—or $240 less per year.

An owner can make all sorts of "side agreements" with tenants that may or may not show up on the leases or the rent rolls. Maybe a tenant received a brand-new suit as an inducement to move in. Maybe he has an understanding that his last month's rent will be free.

All such agreements increase the risk that tenants will move out soon after a less generous owner takes possession. Ask the owner and manager specifically if there are any such agreements. You're unlikely to get lies from both of them. If you do, and you discover it after buying, you can get a court judgment against them for damages, and maybe punitive damages for fraud. But you'll still have the problem of collecting the damages. So it's important to try to detect petty deceits before you buy. Chat with as many tenants as you can. They'll probably tell you about any "special deals" they're getting from management, in hope of extracting similar bounty from you.

Sometimes an owner or manager unwittingly overstates his operating expenses, strange as this seems. He includes the costs of recarpeting apartments, replacing draperies, buying new refrigerators and the like in his total of operating expenses—rather than capitalizing them. These items are non-recurring. They really are replacements rather than repairs. Therefore, they should be figured as capital investments rather than operating expenses.

After this brief review of many ways in which costs and profits can be distorted, do you begin to see why you (or an expert adviser) must break down every item on the vague and sketchy operating statement that most owners and brokers compile? Unless you break each item down you can't tell what items have been left out altogether.

The operating statement is a sheet of paper that most realty investors use as a guide to buying. They put blind faith in the figures on the bottom lines—total monthly income minus total operating expenses, which together equal what we call the "broker's net."

The true net operating income may be terribly different from the broker's net, as we've just seen. Don't blame the broker. He merely wrote down what the seller told him, without much effort to go behind the figures or scan them for omissions. He'll go back and dig for more detail if you ask him.

The usual operating statement for a small apartment property is just one page—a standard printed form headed something like "Income Property Statement." Normally it has one short column headed "Operating Expenses," with just one line for taxes, another for insurance, another for maintenance, and a few others including one line for "other." Then there's another section for "Scheduled Income," under which each apartment gets a line to itself, with a space that contains whatever figure the owner thinks should be the rent for that apartment. Even if some apartments have been vacant for years their "scheduled rent" is added into the "total monthly income."

Maybe you looked at many of these statements during earlier phases of your search. No doubt they were helpful in a first quick scan of the market listings, enabling you to eliminate some without further investigation. But they're woefully inadequate as a tool for analyzing and comparing investments that look good on the surface. Never take a salesman's figures for granted.

As you look at these statements of operating expenses you'll almost invariably find that all items are round figures—taxes $1,400, water $100, insurance $200, and so on. This automatically signals that they are wrong. If the owner had gone through his books and added up the amounts he really paid, they wouldn't come out in round numbers.

The exact amounts may be given on the property's tax return. But even there the classifications probably aren't broken down into enough detail. Maybe the owner paid some important items out of his personal bank account, and forgot to deduct them. Maybe he spent nothing at all on various items that the next owner will have to pay for.

So it's up to you to keep asking questions until you're sure no unpleasant surprises are in store. Unless you're watching for them, it's easy to overlook omissions of figures for trash removal, exterminating, window washing and other occasional services. Do you know how much they will cost you? The cost projections almost never give you any clue. You'll have to ask for them, and find out whether or not they're included in one of those round figures. Usually they're not.

When you begin your detailed examination of a property's records, a good way to start is to check individual apartment records with the manager. Which are occupied, and which are vacant? How many were vacant last month? How many six months, a year, two years ago? What was the actual rent collected for each apartment?

Most brokers' operating statements arbitrarily deduct a standard 3 to 7 percent from the scheduled income as "vacancy factor," which may be in line with national averages. But any given building's records may show that its vacancy rate was much higher than the norm —seldom lower, or the owner would be bragging about it.

If he does show you that it hasn't had a vacancy in many months, this probably means that its rents are dirt cheap. This is good. You can probably raise them as soon as the escrow closes. On the other hand, if it has had many vacancies, the rates may have been too high.

Once you know the actual rents and true vacancy factor, you can go on to the next stage of converting the broker's financial figures into a realistic and complete projection of true net income.

Operating expenses will probably stay about the same as they are under the current ownership—unless he has been grossly negligent in keeping up the property, or unless he has been milking it and intends to cheat you. If you're on guard against these contingencies, you can soon spot them, and adjust your own projection of expenses accordingly.

(To repeat: Just because an owner hasn't paid out as much as he should for expenses, the property isn't necessarily a bad investment, even though most investors will shy away. Maybe it can be a big money-maker for you because you'll have so much scope for upgrading. But you must get an accurate idea of what your total costs will be.)

An owner may or may not provide furniture, carpeting, draperies, utilities, janitor or maid service. Each of these items can make an important difference in operating costs. The cost of each service included in the rent naturally lowers the net income. But when occupants change you can increase your net without raising the rent, simply by eliminating some of these extras.

Utilities are an item that can distort net income. Sometimes an owner understates their cost. If he represents that the costs of the heating, gas, and electricity were lower than expected per month per unit, ask for the previous year's bills, which he'll show you without resentment if he's honest.

In some states such as California it's customary for tenants to pay their own gas and/or electricity. If this is the case, of course you'll expect the owner's utility bills to be lower. His tax returns probably include an accurate statement of utility costs.

Water and sewer charges are worth checking too.

Physical features of the property sometimes give you clues to potential expenses that haven't been mentioned. For example, maybe the complex contains a swimming pool, but you see no expense item for pool maintenance. "Oh, we don't use the pool," the manager says, "so it's no expense." You notice that the diving board is gone, and there are rocks lying on the bottom. If you're going to upgrade the building you'll be operating the pool. So add an estimate for pool reconditioning.

Management is usually listed as an item on the operating statement, but you'll have to go behind the figure. Inexperienced realty investors assume that one manager is much like another. Not so. One manager will go into apartments and fix plumbing for tenants, cut the grass, keep the books, put ads in the newspapers in order to rent vacant apartments. Another may even clean the vacated apartments himself, without extra compensation. Still another won't do a thing but collect the rents and make bank deposits. If you change managers you may have to pay extra for many services that never showed up on expense sheets. Or you may have to do them yourself. If you find yourself in need of a manager, you must learn how to divide his efforts for maximum efficiency. The potential for increasing your profits through effective management techniques is so great that I have written another full-length book solely on the subject, *How to Successfully Manage Real Estate—in Your Spare Time*. It is available at $15 through Capital Printing, 50 Washington Street, Reno, Nevada 89503.

You'd better find out what the average management costs should come to. But the property you're looking at might be far from average. Ask enough questions to be sure you know exactly what is done by the present manager and every other employee, including occasional part-time ones, who are often overlooked.

You may find that the resident manager has an assistant or relief manager (one of the tenants, perhaps) and also has an arrangement with certain other tenants to do maintenance, painting, decorating or whatever. In such cases they are compensated by a rebate on their rent. Normally the resident manager gets a free apartment in lieu of part of his salary.

The net income is falsely computed when the value of the manager's apartment is shown under income and not under expense. This value should be included in the gross income, and also shown as part of the expense. Or else it should be omitted from both sections.

Ask the owner if the rental allowance for the manager includes the relief or assistant manager, too. Is there a salary for this person in addition to the rental allowance? What services are paid for by the salaries and rental allowances? Does the manager do cleaning, painting, maintenance and repair? If so, is he paid extra on a piecemeal or per-job basis for these chores? How much extra is he paid? Is it included in the payroll figures? How much of this is offset by cleaning fees and cleaning deposits, which aren't refunded?

You may find that the resident manager (who may also be the owner) does very little maintenance, cleaning, or decorating. Maybe you intend to do more. The important thing is to get all of the on-site management costs into your calculation, and be sure they are realistic and honest.

A very rough guideline for on-site management (for use only in checking your figures) is about $7 to $15 per unit per month depending on how much service the manager gives. Payroll taxes and workmen's compensation taxes should be included.

To be sure you've made allowances for every expense you're likely to run into, here's a fairly complete checklist of items you should look for.

Naturally you won't find each of these kinds of expense included in the operation of any given piece of real estate. But whenever an item does apply, you should probe to find out how much you'll need to spend for it.

Expense items may include:

Accounting	Laborers
Advertising	Landscaping
Air conditioning	Legal fees
Appliances & equipment	Licenses, permits, etc.
Assessments (special)	Maintenance supplies
Automobile expenses	Management
Cable TV	Masonry
Carpentry	Mechanical
Cleaning	Office supplies
Commissions	Oil
Draperies	Painting & decorating
Electrical systems	Parking
Electricity	Payroll & fringes
Elevator	Payroll taxes
Exterior maintenance	Personal property taxes
Fire protection	Pest control
Fixtures	Plumbing
Floor coverings	Pool service
Garbage removal	Real estate taxes
Gardening	Replacement reserve
Gas (excluding heating fuel)	Roofing
Hardware	Security patrol
Heat	Sewer
Insurance	Telephone
Interior maintenance	Television antenna
Janitorial	Trash removal
Janitorial supplies	Water
	Window washing

Make reasonable allowances for variations in income and expenses, figure out your budget for upgrading the property, and then consider the debt service—i.e., mortgage payments. You should have enough cash left over to carry the property with sizable fluctuations in income and expenses. If so, you'll have a profitable investment.

On the other hand, a fairly small miscalculation can have a heavier impact than you'd think. In one case $84 worth of expenses were left out. The cost of operating the building was really $84 more than the statement had said. To anyone buying the building for its economic value, this error meant that the property was worth $840 less because of that single error in the projection. To see why an error has a tenfold effect on value, you should understand an important concept called the capitalization rate.

Capitalization rate is an important part of the income approach to evaluating your proposed investment. It is a purely mathematical concept.

There is a formula that says that net annual income divided by the rate of yield equals estimate of value:

$$\frac{I}{R} = V$$

In using this formula, first determine the property's annual net income. Then you look at the bottom component, or divisor—that is, the yield rate, or return rate, or "capitalization rate."

There are various ways of figuring this capitalization rate. Fundamentally, the objective is to find the rate that must be paid to attract money into this kind of investment.

Not everyone will be satisfied with the same rate of return on his investment. For example, the owner's position is generally more risky than that of the second mortgage or first mortgage holder. Therefore he may expect a higher return than, say, the first mortgage holder would. If he can't anticipate this rate he won't invest his money.

But maybe he's peculiar. Maybe he will invest for a slightly lower rate of return. So the only way to figure out the proper capitalization rate is to find out what the "going rate" of capitalization is.

You can find this if you know the price for which various properties in the vicinity sold, and if you know their annual net incomes. Divide the annual net income by the price (which was the market's estimate of value) and you'll get the capitalization rate on that particular transaction.

Suppose you check five sales in your city and you find the following results:

Property	Annual Net	Sales Price	Capitalization Rate (price divided by net income)
A	$31,000	$300,000	.103 or 10.3%
B	$ 8,000	$ 90,000	.089 or 8.9%
C	$28,000	$300,000	.093 or 9.3%
D	$11,000	$120,000	.092 or 9.2%
E	$15,000	$165,000	.091 or 9.1%

This shows you that it takes a net return ranging from 8.9 percent to 10.3 percent to attract money to this kind of investment in this particular area.

There are obvious weaknesses in using only a few transactions to compute the going rate of capitalization. There may have been distorting factors in some of the deals—forced sales, high-pressure salesmanship, pride of ownership, errors in computation, and any number of other possibilities. But if you collect data on a large number of transactions, the distorting factors will offset each other and you'll see the pattern.

Since you're probably not going to take all that trouble, you may be willing to take the word of the real estate experts who are making such surveys all the time. They say that the usual capitalization rate on apartment properties in the 1970's is ten percent.

When you apply this rate you are using the process known as capitalizing income. So if a piece of property has a net income of $10,000 and the "cap rate," as it's usually called for short, is 10 percent then the property is worth $100,000—because the net income divided by cap rate equals value.

Suppose another piece of property also has a $10,000 net, but it happens to be in an area where real estate men say the cap rate is only 9 percent. Therefore its value is $111,111. When the cap rate goes down, the value goes up and vice versa.

Generally when you look at property within a given area the brokers can tell you "This particular type of property will probably capitalize at such and such a figure." Who sets the capitalization rate? The marketplace itself does—just as the stock market sets the price of a stock. The cap rate is whatever investors are demanding before they'll buy a particular kind of property.

Once you know the cap rate and understand the formula, you have another way of deciding how much a property is worth. But never forget that errors in estimating its expenses will be multiplied in their effect on the value of the property.

Loan constants are numbers that you should know about when you're considering a real estate transaction—especially one in which there'll be payments to make on outstanding loans.

Whenever you commit yourself to making regular payments on something, you must make sure it won't drain away more cash than you can afford. If it's an investment, usually you'll want it to produce a net cash inflow rather than outgo. Even if you or someone else in your family can count on a good salary from a steady job, there's at least an outside chance of losing the job. So it's nice to have the cushion of another dependable income from property you own.

One way to do this is to keep your loan constants as low as possible. A loan constant can be defined as the percentage of the total loan that must be paid out each year in principal and interest.

In other words, if you're making $100 monthly payments ($1,200 per year) on a $10,000 loan, the loan constant is 12, since the $1,200 is 12 percent of your $10,000 total debt. In the same way, if you owe $50,000 and are paying $5,000 a year toward the principal + interest, the loan constant is 10.

We've often considered leverage in this book, because leverage brings you the highest possible return on the smallest possible investment of your money. To get leverage you borrow money, of course. But, to make a profit from the leverage, you need to keep the interest rate lower than your net operating return from whatever you do with the borrowed money. If you borrow at 7 percent interest to buy a property that pulls in a net operating return of 9 percent, you'll make a profit of 2 percent per year on every dollar you've borrowed.

However, this doesn't always mean you'll be better off cashwise. That depends on your loan constant—the annual rate at which you must make payments on the loan, principal as well as interest.

So in the example above, maybe you're paying only 7 percent interest but are also paying back the principal at a rate of 2 percent yearly. Then your loan constant is 9, and you come out exactly even cashwise on your borrowing. If the loan constant is higher than 9, you're really cutting down your net cash flow. If the constant is lower, you're improving it.

This may not look important when you borrow a small amount in relation to a property's value. What's a few bucks more or less? But it might make the difference between a comfortable situation and a tight squeeze, where your mortgage debt approaches the total value of the property—when you're highly leveraged, that is.

Negotiating low loan constants on first mortgages is easier than on seconds or thirds. Aim for the lowest possible loan constant on the first, so you'll have more leeway to maneuver if you later need to take out one or more junior mortgages (see Chapter X). This will make it easier for you to keep the average loan constant for all your loans below your net operating return on the property.

Another reason to seek the lowest possible loan constants is that they don't stay the same. If you're paying $8,000 a year on an $80,000 debt, you start with a loan constant of 10. But this number creeps higher as you pay off the principal of the loan (assuming your payments remain the same) and it gets up to 20 when you've reduced the principal to $40,000, because now your yearly $8,000 is 20 percent of what you still owe.

The longer the term over which you pay off the loan, the slower the rise of the loan constant. This is one of the reasons why long-term loans are generally best. But in addition to striving for a long repayment period, there are other ways you can try to bargain for a low loan constant—especially with a lender who's less interested in a fast buck than in other considerations.

You can offer a higher total price for the property if the owner will take a purchase money mortgage (see Chapter X) with a low loan constant. You can suggest making interest-only payments for several years (to minimize your cash drain during that period) followed by bigger payments later, when you expect to have more money or to be able to refinance on better terms. Or of course you can offer a higher interest rate.

You'll almost always be better off borrowing at 8 percent interest with a loan constant of 9, rather than borrowing at only 6 percent with a loan constant of 12.

Well, we've spent some worthwhile time looking at factors to consider in realty investments. These factors can steer you to the very best of all the available choices you're considering.

So now, we'll say, you're ready to try to make a deal with whoever owns the property you've chosen. Because you're armed with plenty of facts, you're prepared to negotiate intelligently.

Negotiating is an art. The more you know about this social science, the better bargain you can strike. As you read the next chapter you'll discover a great deal about negotiating for real estate.

REMEMBER THESE HIGH POINTS:

Make your offer to buy contingent on reviewing certified copies of the building's tax records, leases and rent records.

Ask if there are any "side agreements" or "special deals" with occupants.

Never take a salesman's figures for granted. Check the operating statement carefully. Round numbers are a danger signal.

Get a detailed breakdown of all costs. Watch for omissions.

Find out how much rent was really collected for each apartment, and how many vacancies there actually were.

Find out exactly what work is done by the present manager and every other employee. Is the manager's rent considered part of his salary?

Figure capitalization rate, as a way of evaluating the investment.

Beware of high loan constants.

VIII *How to Negotiate a Good Buy*

We saw in Chapter V how to narrow down your selection to one or two properties that appear, on thorough analysis, to be the best buys for you. Now let's look at each step of the process of arranging to buy. (Some of the early steps we'll cover in this chapter may well be made before you've completed your analysis of properties. You'll see why as we go along.)

Many books have been written on selling, but buying is an art that is seldom taught. Too bad, because intelligent buying takes as much brainwork, knowledge, and persuasion as selling does. A skilled buyer tries to understand the seller's viewpoint as well as his own. It's no accident that progressive schools of business now teach marketing and purchasing together; the best preparation for buying may be knowledge of the problems and tactics of sellers. Bear in mind as you read this chapter that you too will probably be selling as well as buying later on.

A sound businessman doesn't try to skin the other party in a buying-selling transaction. It's bad business in the long run, because word gets around and people don't want to deal with anyone whose reputation is poor.

So if you're smart you'll try to strike a bargain that will be fair to both sides. All truly successful negotiation—whether it be negotiating a peace treaty or a strike settlement or a business transaction—ends with all parties convinced they have gained. If you can see the situation as the seller sees it, you'll be better able to show him why your offer is good for him.

First of all, don't set your heart on a specific building as the one and only buy for you. Many amateur buyers fall into this trap; emotions override arithmetic, causing them to pay too much. If any owner senses that you're hell-bent on buying, he'll stand pat on his asking price, and it usually will be too high.

Then, too, a few stubborn owners never come down from ridiculously high prices despite all logic and economics. You should be emotionally prepared to walk away without keen disappointment.

To minimize your disappointment, you should be tentatively angling for your second choice and perhaps your third, even while you approach the owner of your first choice. This will keep you in the right frame of mind, able to press calmly for terms that meet your standards. Owners and brokers who realize that you're considering several properties will be more anxious to keep you interested.

Moreover, you should always keep an eye open for still other buys that you haven't previously looked at. Deteriorating or mismanaged property—the kind you've been looking for—exists almost everywhere. Much of it is never advertised or publicly listed.

When a broker realizes that you'll consider such properties, he may dust off listings of "dogs" on his back shelves, and show you an even better bargain than any you've found previously. Just because you've narrowed down your shopping list is no reason to close your mind to new suggestions.

You're probably the only prospective buyer for whatever run-down buildings you ask about. When you are, brokers will try all their wiles on you—meanwhile trying to persuade owners to come down in price. When an owner doesn't sell, his broker loses a commission, or what he would call a brokerage fee.

Just keep in mind that the seller has no clear idea of what his property can sell for. You've studied it far more closely than he or his broker has. The broker may talk about "fair market value" and "assessed valuation"—but you saw in Chapter VI that these are just guesses. Unlike a bar of gold or a loaf of bread or a share of stock, where price is set daily by supply and demand, any piece of real estate has its own unique value. Its price has little to do with value. People make value. Real estate is worth whatever people will pay. It's up to you to negotiate a price. And when you're buying depressed real estate, never forget that you're in an extra strong bargaining position because there's very little demand for what you want to buy.

Before approaching the owner you should make certain preparations. They can strengthen your position by giving you still more information than you already have. The more you know, the better you can bargain.

First find out who—and where—the owner is. His name and telephone number may be displayed publicly on the premises. If you don't find it there, and there is no "For Sale" sign posted, you may be able to find out in the casual chatting you should do with neighbors, tenants and the manager as you analyze the property along the lines suggested in the previous chapter.

Quite often, in the case of run-down properties, there's an absentee owner. Quite often an absentee owner makes no effort to sell his property and doesn't even list it with Realtors. Sometimes a manager won't give information about the owner, possibly out of fear that you may be a process-server or an official investigator or someone else the owner wants to avoid.

However, an owner's name and address are usually a matter of public record if you know where to look. Ask any friend in the real estate business—or your lawyer or banker—to look it up. Or better yet, check with the tax assessor's office or an abstract or title company.

It's smart to use an expert intermediary in most real estate transactions—and in most other deals for that matter. Three centuries ago Sir Francis Bacon wrote an essay, "Of Negotiating," in which he advised: "It is generally better to deal by the mediation of a third than by a man's self. Use bold men for expostulation, fair-spoken men for persuasion, crafty men for inquiry and observation, forward and absurd men for business that doth not well bear out itself . . . In all negotiations of difficulty, a man may not look to sow and reap at once; but must prepare business, and so ripen it by degrees."

Face-to-face bargaining rarely works well in real estate. Pride of ownership can get involved. Personalities can clash. Emotion can put one of the parties into such a state that he or she makes an unwise deal—or refuses to consider any deal. But middle men with expertise in realty negotiation can keep the dickering unemotional and figure out solutions that might never occur to the principals.

Find out all you can about the owner. If you don't know who the owner is, your agent can quickly find out. Then, before getting in touch with the owner, the two of you should try to judge how badly he wants to sell.

Maybe "he" is the widow or heir of the previous owner, knows nothing about business, and has listened to a lot of bad advice. Or the owner could be a prosperous doctor or entertainer who is content to keep a money-losing investment because part of this loss can be a tax write-off he thinks he may be able to sell or exchange someday at a profit. Your negotiator may be able to show the owner why selling or exchanging would make good business sense.

On the other hand, maybe the building is already on the market. And maybe the owner secretly wants to sell quickly because he is being transferred to Alaska, or because he must move to Florida for his health. Or the owner could be some wheeler-dealer like William Zeckendorf, who used to own thousands of parcels of property scattered across the country. For a while he rejected all offers unless they were sky-high, but eventually he spread himself so thin that his only chance to avert bankruptcy was to sell properties for whatever he could get. Anyhow, your key to successful negotiations is to know as much as possible about the person you're negotiating with.

That includes knowing as much as possible about this person's property problems. Does he need the money to push through another transaction elsewhere? Is he holding the property because he has exaggerated ideas about how much its value will rise with inflation? Is he uncertain whether to sell it or keep it?

Has he sold other buildings? How long did he hold them? Answers will give you clues to his probable attitude.

Has he put this particular building up for sale several times without finding a buyer? This could tip you off that he is getting anxious to sell—or it could mean that he is merely fishing to see if he can get his price, which may be out of line. Obviously you need to know which is the case. Ask your agent to find out what prices, if any, were previously asked for this building.

How much was the property sold for when the present owner bought it? The value of the tax stamps affixed to the recorded deed may indicate the price. However, occasionally a shrewd trader puts on a surplus of tax stamps in an effort to mislead someone about the price. Therefore, your agent shouldn't rely on one source if there's any reason to be skeptical. The agent should know of other sources that can give him a fairly close idea of how much the property sold for.

How long ago did the owner buy this property? If he's had it only a short time, he's likely to insist on a higher price than he would otherwise, simply to get enough profit to cover the sales commission. Or the short period of ownership may mean that he was duped into buying a lemon and now is trying to unload it on someone else. If so, and if you're the only buyer who has nibbled, he may lower his price as soon as he realizes that you're aware of the building's shortcomings.

Does the owner have a large or small equity in the property? A small equity is usually a tip-off to a recent purchase, but it could also mean that the owner refinanced the building and pulled out cash within the last year or so. Either way, when an owner with a slim equity seems eager to sell, and willing to compromise on price, he's probably in a personal predicament that makes him desperate. Yet he may haggle stubbornly because he needs every dollar he can squeeze out.

Usually you can make a better deal with someone who has owned a property five years or more. He probably bought it when prices were lower. And his tax benefits from depreciation could now be much smaller. Moreover, he probably has a big equity, which opens up a chance for you to refinance this building and come in with a smaller down payment. So the size of the owner's equity is an important guide to your negotiation tactics.

If the owner is in business, or has been involved in previous transactions, you need to look into his reputation and history. Is he considered intelligent, ethical, and reliable—or otherwise? Find out about business ventures or deals he got into. Also try to investigate deals he failed to close. Often you can learn as much about people from their failures as from their successes. If you know why a certain deal fell through or a negotiation failed, you'll probably understand a lot about how the person thinks and operates, how flexible a bargainer he is, how he reacts to various approaches.

For example, you may discover that this owner puts on a convincing act, pretends to be disinclined to sell, demands outrageous terms, but always comes down little by little until he finds the level at which his opponent will buy. Or you may learn that he is noted for never coming in high or low, preferring to decide in advance on a fair price and stick to it. (Even so, he may come down if he finds that you and your agent are making a sincere effort to find a logical compromise, and if he is shown factual reasons why his price is higher than the property can be worth.)

When your agent approaches the owner (or when you do this yourself, if need be) the approach should be by telephone or in person—never by mail. A letter sounds impersonal, almost casual. The recipient often puts it aside, planning to write a non-committal answer, but doesn't get around to it. You may wait weeks for an answer. You may never receive one.

At your first approach to the owner, he'll expect an offer, especially if he hasn't put the property up for sale. It's a mistake for you to begin by asking "How much do you want for the property?" He can make three different responses, none of them good for you.

He may respond by setting a price on the spur of the moment. Almost invariably it will be far too high. (Sellers are notoriously prone to overestimate the value of their own property.) But having committed himself and perhaps blurted "Take it or leave it," he can't come down without losing face. Maybe you'll win the argument, but you won't make the buy.

Another possible response by the owner is "How much are you willing to pay?" This puts the burden of persuasion on you. You're in the awkward position of urging him to sell. He can easily say that you're not offering enough, even though you may be offering more than he privately thinks the property is worth.

If the owner is really shrewd he'll respond "You said you wanted to buy. I didn't say I wanted to sell." Then you're in an even worse bargaining position. You have to make a bid and coax him to consider it. Playing the role of reluctant seller, he need not even make a counterproposal. He can just shake his head and wait for you to keep raising your bid.

So you see it's smarter strategy for you to begin negotiations by dangling a figure before the owner. This is true even if he has already announced an asking price. The phrase "asking price" often is just a code for "make me an offer." The owner may have picked this asking price out of a hat. If the property is in poor shape, he probably has no idea how much he can get for it.

Even when a property is in good condition, the average seller asks a high price to begin with, planning to accept any offer within 10 percent of it—or sometimes within 25 percent.

You should know precisely what your opening offer will be, and why, before you or your representative ever pick up the phone to bargain with the owner or broker. (In a moment we'll see how you can decide on the amount of this bid.) But the figure shouldn't necessarily be your rock-bottom price.

Why? Well, suppose the conversation runs like this:

"Mr. Owner, I am an investor who is planning to buy some real estate. I might like to look at the Euphoria Apartment House, which you own. Would you consider selling it if I can pay, say, eighty thousand dollars?"

The owner may register pain and indignation, and argue a bit—and then say, "All right, you've bought yourself an apartment house."

But of course you haven't. This was merely verbal sparring. Even if there were both verbal offer and acceptance, neither would have any more legal effect than, for example, a remark that you might see him in church sometime. The courts have held that in real estate nothing is binding until it's written and signed.

When your first offer is taken up at once, it's a sign that your feeler is a pleasant surprise to the owner, and that you haven't hit bottom yet. Most buyers are too hasty in agreeing to a price after the seller makes his first concession.

Now that you know he's hot to sell, you can keep probing to find how much less he'll accept. So you respond, "Eighty thousand, eh? Well, I'll have to look at the property."

Later you can call back to say: "Now that I've looked at the Euphoria, I see that the carpeting needs replacement, which I hadn't figured on. And the kitchens are in worse condition than I realized. Under the circumstances, I wouldn't be interested unless we could talk in terms of about sixty thousand dollars at most." You may just get it for that, or for sixty-five. If not, the owner will make counterproposals. The bargaining can go on from there. But it won't go higher than eighty, because you already know he'll sell at that price.

How high should your first offer be? In the previous chapter you saw how to figure out what the property was worth to you. So you know the maximum you'll pay. But if you offer this amount in the beginning, the seller will seldom take it. He'll almost always hold out for more. The normal pattern is for the seller to keep lowering his demands, the buyer to keep coming up a bit on his offers, until eventually they meet somewhere in the middle.

You have a "top dollar" price in mind. You've determined in advance that you won't go above it, and you hope to buy for less. Usually the owner will have a "rock-bottom" price in mind. If your top dollar is at least as high as his rock bottom, there will be a deal. Otherwise, there won't. Time could be saved if the parties to the bargaining could read each other's mind, and find out at once whether there is any price that would satisfy them both. But this doesn't seem possible. Haggling is expected, and needed.

If you've never bargained for what you buy, the process may seem strange to you. But successful negotiations start every day with buyers offering less than they expect to pay, and sellers demanding more than they hope to get. The balance always tilts in favor of the better negotiator.

Coming back to the problem of setting the figure for your first offer: If you know the asking price, and you believe it to be fair market value, subtract 25 percent from it, and offer this—unless it's still above the top figure you're prepared to pay. In that case, offer about 10 percent less than you're aiming for and hope for the best. If the seller won't come down enough, there's no use in continuing the conversation.

To clarify this subtracting process, let's take an imaginary illustration. Assume that the asking price is $100,000 and you think it's a good buy at $90,000. Your first offer should be 25 percent below this target—putting it at about $67,500. That's so far below $100,000 that it wouldn't make sense in some situations. But in the case of a property that is losing money steadily, is deteriorating badly, with no other buyers in the picture, it may be an acceptable offer.

You see, maybe the owner bought the building sixteen years ago for $29,000 and owes only $4,000 on it. In such a situation he may not grab your offer but he'll come back with a price closer to it. And eventually he may accept $70,000, $75,000 or $78,900.

Consider what would have happened had you begun by offering $90,000 (your target price) and announcing "That's my firm, final offer." You would probably eventually have gotten it for that price, after the owner tried hard to bring you up to $97,500 and then to $95,000. But you would have been paying far more than he hoped to get.

When your first offer is something like $67,500 the owner may eventually come back, fancying himself an astute negotiator, and say, "Let's split the difference. I want $83,750." You could never have gotten him down into that range if you had started at $90,000.

Let's look at these hypothetical figures some more. You need to be sure that the $90,000 is a realistic target price. Maybe it's more than you should pay. Think ahead to the time when you'll resell the property. Will you make a reasonable profit then? Suppose the improvements you put in are going to cost $15,000. The broker who sells the building for you will have to be paid a commission—say $7,000. So you'll have to sell for $112,000 to break even, although your purchase price was only $90,000.

You surely won't be satisfied just to break even. You'll never attain financial security that way. (There's an old joke about a habitual horseplayer, starting out for a day at the races, who mutters, "I hope I break even today. I sure need the money.") How much profit should you figure on?

According to my formula, you should get at least two dollars back for every dollar you spend on improvements. So you want at least $30,000 for the $15,000 you will have spent. That means you should sell for $127,000 at rock bottom. Your asking price will necessarily be far above that, so the people buying from you can get the pleasure of beating you down and driving a hard bargain at about $130,000. At that price, if you can show a prospective owner a 10 percent net yield on his money from the rents coming in at your new scale, he'll have a good buy. This means that the building is a good buy for you at $90,000 right now—always providing that the improvements won't cost more than the projected $15,000, that you know where the money will be coming from to pay for them, and that rentals will more than cover taxes plus mortgage payments plus all operating expenses.

In other words, before you make an offer for a property you should know how much you'll resell it for. All that calculating you did earlier, if you followed the advice given in Chapter V, laid the mathematical foundation for the negotiations you're now entering.

Some basic rules of bargaining can help you and your representative. These have emerged from studies of the patterns of thousands of actual negotiations. If your representative is experienced, these rules may be second nature to him, but it's just as well to review them with him to make sure.

1. The largest concessions are made by the seller and the buyer early in the game. The seller will drop his price more in the first round of negotiations than he will later. As bargaining progresses, the seller usually sticks to his position longer and longer, reducing his price less and less.
2. Wherever possible, one should be prepared to concede something in early negotiations, but should not indicate that further concessions will be granted. Each offer should be phrased as a final offer, yet still be worded loosely enough to be changed without your losing face.
3. The buyer's objective is to learn all he can about the seller's problems, goals, motives, inclinations and property. Conversely, the less the seller knows about the buyer, the better, from the buyer's standpoint.
4. Whether or not it is real, competition puts pressure on a negotiator. If the seller believes that a buyer may go elsewhere and buy

other property instead, then for practical purposes, competition exists—and the seller will be more accommodating. (Likewise, if a buyer thinks that other buyers are bidding, he tends to bid higher and more hurriedly because of the real or imaginary competition.)

5. Misinformation can cause needless concessions. For example, if an owner pretends that he is in dire need of cash, and names a price as "the amount I've absolutely got to get," a buyer may be tricked into settling for this as the true rock bottom. (However, deception is more likely when an owner negotiates to sell a good-looking property. Then he can claim he is "practically forced to give it away at this bargain price," because of an urgent health problem or some other alleged emergency.) A buyer can also be deceived by false information about the property itself. For example, he may hear that a shopping center or a school is to be built nearby. If he believes this, he is willing to bid higher. If his belief is unfounded, he bids more than he should.

6. Emotion can distort the normal pattern of negotiation. Feeling elated by some happy event completely unconnected with the bargaining—a success in some other deal, perhaps, or even a trifle like winning a golf or tennis game—one party may become willing to grant surprisingly generous terms on the spur of the moment. Contrariwise, grief or anger or disappointment can cause him to refuse an offer he would normally accept. His gestures, body positions, facial expressions, tones of voice and other non-verbal communication may tell a more revealing story than anything he says. The buyer should watch for signs of emotion and act accordingly—for example, should postpone further discussion if the seller is in a bad mood.

7. The buyer should show no enthusiasm or great interest in the property he is offering to buy.

8. Without seeming contemptuous or insulting, the buyer should tactfully bring the worst defects of the property to the owner's attention. The best time to do this is as a prelude to making the first offer. But if necessary it can be done later, in explaining why the offer is so low. (A few defects can go unmentioned at first, to be brought up near the end of the negotiations as a justification for asking further reductions in price.) The buyer can walk through the property with the salesman, pointing out various unmistakable flaws. This will condition the salesman to persuade the owner that a lower price is necessary. The salesman wants to make a deal,

and if he is convinced that the asking price is too high, he will help pull it down rather than lose the sale altogether.

Maneuvers of salesmanship are common in realty negotiations. You should know these tactics so you won't be taken in by them. Sometimes a salesman will try to hustle you by implying that someone else is on the verge of making an offer. The owner may even say, "See this signed offer I've received? Look at it. Read it. This man wants to buy for a higher price than you're offering. He's even attached a big check for earnest money. Here, see it?"

After looking, you naturally ask, "Why haven't you accepted this offer?"

The owner explains, "This man wants a four-month escrow. I'd rather not wait that long. And I'm not sure he can swing the financing. So if you'll pay as much as he's offering, and take a thirty-day closing, it's yours. Otherwise I'll have to sign with him—probably tomorrow."

But the offer and the check may be phony, written by his brother-in-law for the sole purpose of pressuring you. Such wiles are part of the reason you shouldn't ever buy in haste. You must be willing to risk losing out while you wait for acceptable terms. If the phantom prospect turns out to be genuine, and he buys the building from under your nose, it's no tragedy. Better he should pay an unreasonable price than you. You're looking at other properties too, aren't you? Even if this is the very last one on your list of possibilities, don't snatch at it. You can always shop the market and find other comparable buys.

If the owner holds out for an unreasonably high price, he probably hasn't previously tried to sell the property. When he or his broker sees a dozen prospects shake their heads and turn away in the next few months, he'll become more willing to negotiate.

You can try to speed-up the softening process, if you wish, by using the reverse of the strategies described in the paragraph above. Arrange for the owner to be approached by several different people, each asking him if he'll sell—and each suggesting a lower price than you've already offered. This often convinces an owner that he's been expecting too much, and that he'd better call you back and make a deal at your terms.

Another tactic that many salespeople use is to tell you, as prospective buyer, that the seller feels you are just the type of person to whom he would like to sell his property. He or she tells you nice things the owner supposedly has been saying about you. The sales representative may work on the owner in the same way, exaggerating whatever pleasant responses you've made. Naturally, when you and the owner come together you're extremely cordial, and the final closing of the transaction is likely to go quickly and happily.

Four variables must be negotiated in any real estate deal: the price, the down payment, the interest rate on any loan involved, and the length of time in which the loan is to be repaid. As buyer, you are bargaining for the lowest possible price, smallest possible down payment, lowest possible interest rate, and the longest possible loan.

(Some buyers prefer big equities and hate to pay interest. But you know from reading this book, if you didn't already, that using borrowed money is one of the secrets of financial success. The more leverage you can safely use, the bigger your profit.)

An owner may give you favorable terms on some of these four variables in exchange for your concessions on others. He may accept a lower total price for a higher down payment. Or he may offer to arrange better loan terms on condition that you boost the total price.

Such give-and-take is part of the bargaining process. It is why sellers ask a higher price than they hope to get, and why buyers offer less than they are willing to pay. It gives you both room to negotiate.

As you and the owner make proposals and counterproposals you are inching closer to agreement. At some point one of you will yield no further—whereupon the deal either falls through or is consummated on those terms. You can usually sense when the seller has set his teeth and absolutely isn't going to give another nickel.

When the owner accepts your terms, he'll expect you to clinch the deal with a deposit—sometimes called "earnest money" or a "binder" or simply a "deposit," for which he'll give you a Deposit Receipt. A little carelessness here can put you into big legal trouble. Don't be too quick with your checkbook.

Let's suppose that you give the owner $500 as earnest money, writing on the check: "Deposit toward purchase of Euphoria Apartment House at 1850 Wright Way for $99,750." A day or two later you tell your attorney that you've just about decided to buy the property. He asks, "Are you sure there are no claims against it, or easements on it?"

"I asked the owner," you answer, "and he assured me there wouldn't be any difficulty."

But the lawyer looks into it, and reports that the Flood Control District has the right to flood the property to a depth of ten feet. (Such an easement actually existed in Florida, as a horrified buyer found out too late, and a nearby river was diverted to rise across his property.) In addition, the lawyer says, the owner of the Euphoria hasn't paid his taxes for years, so the government is threatening to seize and sell the property.

So you hurry back to the owner and explain that you don't want the property after all. "A deal's a deal," he growls.

You go home to tell your family that you've forfeited a $500 deposit. But later you discover this isn't what the owner meant. His lawyer points out to your lawyer that you are going to buy the property whether you like it or not. The notation on your check was as binding as a ten-page contract.

REMEMBER THESE HIGH POINTS:

Seek terms that will be fair to both buyer and seller.

Don't set your heart on a specific deal being the only one for you. Keep looking.

Before approaching an owner, find out as much as you can about the owner himself and the property. Then send an expert intermediary to negotiate.

Know the maximum you'll pay, but offer 10 to 25 percent less.

Wait for acceptable terms, even if this means not buying.

Consider offering adjustments in four variables as part of the negotiating process:

1. the total purchase price;
2. the down payment;
3. the interest rate on the loan;
4. the length of time over which the loan will be repaid.

The written purchase agreement should include certain requirements for the seller, and escape clauses for you.

IX *How to Avoid Legal Booby Traps*

Legal booby traps, such as that mentioned in the previous chapter, are all over the place when you buy or sell real estate. Here are a few others.

Some previous owner may have granted easements allowing the electric company to run power lines over a corner of your premises; the telephone company to put poles on your land; and the water company to dig a pipe through your patio. It could happen that the companies never exercised these rights—but suddenly, after you become owner, they decide to do so. The worst of it might be that the swimming pool in the patio will have to be taken out at your expense, since it comes across the water company's surveyed path.

Maybe the balconies of some of your apartments extend a few inches beyond your property line, above the right-of-way marked by the alley. Maybe the eaves of your garages stick out over a neighbor's land. Maybe your hedge on your driveway is slightly outside your boundary. These encroachments, as the law calls them, might have to be removed and "the land restored to its original condition," under the law. This could be expensive for you.

Maybe your newly bought building burns to the ground after you've signed a sales agreement, and you discover the fire insurance had automatically lapsed because of the change in ownership. You could be stuck with an ironclad agreement to buy a blackened ruin.

Agreements, deeds, and contracts drawn to your attorney's satisfaction can protect you against most misfortunes and mistakes, by giving you the right to withdraw under certain conditions or by providing compensation for damage or loss. Your legal fees should be figured in as part of your cost of buying a piece of real estate.

The first paper you sign may be a standard printed form that the broker pulls out of his desk. It may be called a Deposit Receipt, a Sales Agreement, a Real Estate Purchase Contract, or an Earnest

Money Agreement. Such forms are all right if you make sure that your attorney inserts certain clauses to protect you, and if he checks the fine print.

What protective clauses should be inserted? One should be that the sale is "subject to inspections and approval of property and contract by—" whatever expert on realty investment is going to advise you. Having read this far in the book, you surely realize how dangerous it is to invest in property without inspecting every square foot carefully or having it inspected by an expert.

Also make the sale subject to getting estimates "satisfactory to Buyer" on the cost of whatever remodeling or improvements you plan to make, as discussed in Chapter V.

With these provisos you have tied the property down so you can buy it if the owner signs this same form. But you're still free to withdraw and get your deposit back if you decide the deal would be unsatisfactory for any reason. You won't even need to give a reason, except that your adviser disapproves or the remodeling estimates weren't satisfactory. Some investors have two or three offers floating around, all with contingencies that must be filled before the agreement is binding.

The agreement should also specifically state that the sale is subject to your obtaining whatever terms of proposed financing are specified. Never leave your financing to chance, no matter how easy the broker or seller says it will be. Without this escape clause, if you find you can't get the loan you're counting on, you may forfeit your deposit. In any case, if you're going in for a new loan, allow yourself ninety days to close the escrow. If the deal depends on the sale or exchange of another piece of property you own, give yourself six months.

The escrow account, incidentally, need not be placed in a bank in most states, and usually should not be. Use an independent escrow instead. Bank escrows are slow, independent and indifferent. The bank escrow people really don't care about you, since this isn't an important part of their business. But it is 100 percent of the business of an independent escrow agent, so you'll be better served. (The word "escrow" is not used in some states; "closing" or "settlement" is used instead.)

A good source of financing is likely to be the owner himself. He and his broker try much harder to arrange financing when a sale depends on it, and often will take a second mortgage to make up the difference between sales price and funds provided by the down payment and other financing.

Many mortgage loans have clauses that hook you for costly penalties if you pay off ahead of time. Try for one with no prepayment penalties or mild ones. It's likely you'll want to pay off before the full course of years runs; most people do. Prepayment is worthwhile if you take out a mortgage at a high rate of interest, and interest rates drop later, because then you can refinance the property at lower interest charges.

Also try to get a loan that allows you to make your own arrangements for paying taxes and insurance, rather than impounding them into the monthly mortgage payment. Beware of so-called package deals that make furnishings, appliances and other short-lived articles part of a long-lived mortgage. Such a package makes you pay interest on the stuff long after it's worn out and discarded.

Another good clause to try for is one stipulating that you can let someone else assume the mortgage if and when you are ready to resell the property. It means that the new buyer can take over the balance of the payments on your mortgage, after paying you what you would get in cash. This clause can be attractive to him, because it saves him the expense of arranging a new loan—and because a new mortgage might call for higher interest than the existing one.

Avoid the so-called "balloon payment" clause. Such a payment is an inflated final installment, perhaps several hundred times as big as the payments you've been making monthly. This clause could make it impossible for you to complete the contract. It may sound fine in the beginning, because you figure that you'll either be much wealthier by the time the balloon comes due, or will have resold the property by then. Meanwhile those low, low installment payments sound seductive. And maybe the money men assure you that you can easily negotiate a new loan if necessary when the balloon comes due. But this isn't necessarily true. You may not be able to refinance the loan if the money market becomes too tight or the cost of refinancing may be prohibitively high. And if you don't have the money for the balloon payment and can't raise it, the lender can foreclose and take the property. So make sure that the sneaky balloon clause isn't included in any agreement you sign. In fact, your preliminary sales agreement should spell out the financing terms in enough detail to preclude any balloon clause being proposed. (Balloon payments get into the picture because of the practice of writing second mortgages for relatively short terms—usually three to five years. Such short-term borrowing makes it hard for a borrower to take on payments that will fully amortize the loan before the due date.)

A requirement for a guaranteed title to the property is now standard in most realty agreements. Title insurance companies can search the records to make sure that the seller has a clear right to sell, and then will issue a policy guaranteeing to reimburse the purchaser if the title doesn't stand up under challenge. In some parts of the country the buyer customarily pays the premium on this policy, in other areas the seller does. It's a matter for negotiation. As buyer, you'll press for a clause requiring the seller to pay the premium, and you're in a good position to get what you ask. Just make sure the policy equals the full purchase amount.

The standard forms of purchase agreement (many of them prepared by Realtors themselves) usually include a clause: "Title is to be free of liens, encumbrances, easements, restrictions, rights and conditions of record or known to Seller." Fine. Make sure this clause or the equivalent is included in any form you're asked to sign.

This protects you if claims against the property are filed by an electrician or plumber or anyone else who has done work on the property but hasn't been paid. Such a claim, called a workman's or mechanic's lien, is often filed just a day or two before the closing, when an unpaid contractor hears that the building is being sold. By paying the bill, the Seller can clear up the claim at the closing.

But suppose the elevator or the air conditioning suddenly breaks down and can't be put in working order by the time of closing? In that case you may be entitled to hold back part of the purchase price, depositing it in the escrow account. Your attorney, or the seller's attorney, can pay the money to the contractor when the equipment is satisfactorily repaired. If this doesn't happen by a stipulated date, you get back the money that is in escrow. This sort of arrangement is useful if work is in progress on the property when it is sold—maybe the roof is being mended, or the driveway is being paved. Putting the money in escrow is simpler than postponing the closing.

Some people besieged by creditors try to make a quick sale of real estate to keep it out of the clutches of their creditors. If the law finds that you bought from such a seller, it may declare the sale null and void. Then you're entitled to get your money back from the seller—if you can find him. Otherwise you've lost the property as well as your money. However, you haven't lost your money after all if your title insurance policy was properly drawn; the title company will pay you. Just make sure you're protected. Some policies protect only the lender of the mortgage money. This is one more reason you need a good attorney's advice in every step of a realty transaction.

What happens if the property is damaged by earthquake, hurricane, fire or other calamity between the time you sign the deposit receipt and the time you become the official owner? Either you or the seller stands to lose heavily. It needn't be you, if the sales agreement says the premises will be turned over "in the same condition as they are now, reasonable wear and tear excepted," or that "this contract shall at Buyer's election immediately become null and void" if any part of the property is destroyed or materially damaged.

It's a good idea to take photographs of the property as it looks when the agreement is signed. Have the date certified and keep copies. This gives you conclusive evidence if there's a dispute later—if, for example, the diving board disappears from the swimming pool, or the beautiful trees you thought you were getting are gone when you take title.

Even with protective clauses, there might be a lawsuit in case of accidental damage. Courts in some states have held that once the buyer takes legal control over the property, he is the one who takes the risk of accidents.

The best way to protect both parties is to arrange for adequate insurance to cover the premises from the time of signing until the closing. The agreement should specify the types of insurance, amounts of coverage, and who is to carry it. The seller's existing policies may not be valid after he signs a sale agreement; most homeowner policies lapse when there is any change in title to the property. So the buyer and seller ought to have all insurance policies amended to protect both parties at the time the sales agreement is signed. Often this can be arranged by a telephone call.

The agreement should also include other financial adjustments to be made between the parties—usually at the closing—for such things as insurance premiums prepaid to a future date, fuel oil left in the tanks, interest on any loan taken over, real estate taxes, and rents. All such items of income and continuing expense are customarily prorated between the buyer and seller. For example, if the owner has paid a year's real estate taxes in advance, but sells the property in the middle of a tax period, the buyer would normally give him half of the tax money he has paid.

Does the owner or manager live on the property? If so, the agreement should specifically fix the date on which you take possession, such as "Possession to be given thirty days following close of escrow," or "Possession to be given immediately on closing of escrow." A portion of the sale money should be held in escrow until this is done. Otherwise the ex-owner or ex-manager may continue to occupy his apartment until he is good and ready to leave.

In Chapter VII we noted why you should get the seller to certify the correctness of the records of income and expenses for the past several years. Sometimes there may be no chance to ask for these until you've gotten well into the negotiations. And sometimes negotiations don't really start until you plunk down a deposit and make an offer in writing. You needn't hesitate to make an offer early, even in cases where you don't know much about the property, if your written offer includes such escape clauses as I suggested a few pages ago. Anyhow, be sure to insert a clause saying something like "Expense and income statements to be provided and certified by Seller and approved by Buyer before close of escrow," if you haven't already seen such statements.

Likewise, there may have been no chance yet to ask the owner to certify that the building is free of termites and rot. When you apply for a mortgage the lender may demand such a certificate. Therefore you should be sure the sale agreement contains a clause to the effect that "Sale is subject to inspection by a licensed and bonded pest control company showing no visible rot, infestation from fungi, or damage by insects. Any such damage will be repaired at cost of Seller."

Time is a weapon in negotiations. Make sure that it is used for you, not against you. Never give a broker an offer that says "good until accepted." This would permit him to comb the city for other potential buyers, and to show them your offer as a lever to pry higher bids out of them. It would also give the owner freedom to hold your offer to fall back upon, while he waited for other brokers to bring in other prospects with better offers.

Even if an owner and broker are sure there'll be no other offers, they may not feel any urgency about saying yes to you if your offer is good indefinitely. They may give priority to other businesses, and get around to this transaction when they have nothing better to do. Meanwhile you'd be losing the interest that you might have drawn on the money you put up as a deposit.

(If you're operating on slender capital you can give a promissory note as a deposit—or even the ownership certificate for your automobile if it is free and clear. But there are advantages to giving a sizable check. It's impressive. It might give the broker that little extra urge he needs to put the sale together.)

If you've discovered that the owner is eager to sell, your offer can include a statement to the effect that the offer must be either accepted or rejected upon the broker's presentation of the offer. Even if you're not sure he wants to sell, you can speed up his response by dating the offer and stipulating a limited time for acceptance.

How much time? One week should be enough, except in unusual circumstances, such as an owner living faraway. You may find a printed line in the agreement form, "Time is of the essence of this contract," with space after it for a time to be specified. Overriding the broker's automatic suggestion that this line be crossed out, you should keep it in, and write after it something like: "The Agent is granted 7 days to obtain the acceptance of the Seller. If this offer is not accepted within said 7 days, the deposit will be refunded to the buyer."

Finally, when the offer is worded to your satisfaction, you sign it. The broker must give you a copy of this offer. Sometimes a broker overlooks this. You must be sure to insist on it, because the offer isn't quite foolproof otherwise. You might get back a signed copy that looks like the same document but contains some changes. Or the owner could change his mind and squirm out by "losing" the only copy of the document.

When the owner accepts your offer, and complies with all the protective clauses you've inserted, the attorney can draw up the deed. This is usually a fairly simple step, because you and the seller have already agreed to the basic provisions of the sale. These were settled when the seller signed the section headed ACCEPTANCE on the deposit receipt or purchase contract.

In whose name is the property being bought? This is an important question to consider when the deed is being drawn. But no real estate broker or layman can properly advise you how to take title; for them to do so is illegal in most states. So see your attorney about this.

A husband and wife often buy property together. When they do, they usually take title as either "joint tenants" or "tenants-in-common," although there are certain other ways they could do so, varying from state to state.

"Joint tenancy" is by far the most widely used form of ownership. Under joint tenancy, all joint tenants have equal ownership interests in the property with "right of survivorship." This means that if any tenant dies, his interest in the property passes immediately to the surviving tenants, regardless of the terms of the deceased's will, or whether he or she happens to die without a will. Thus the property doesn't become involved in probate procedures and isn't tied up during settlement of the estate. However, joint tenancy may mean higher estate taxes. And these taxes can take a needlessly big bite out of your estate.

"Tenancy-in-common" is a form of ownership in which two or more parties can have either equal or unequal undivided interests in a property without right of survivorship. Each tenant-in-common has some designated proportionate interest in the property as a whole but no clear title to any part of it. Each can sell, transfer, or assign his interest to anyone he wishes, or pass it on by will to his heirs at his death, without affecting the interests of the others.

If you want to keep full control of the property yourself, with the right to leave it to anyone you wish, you should be sure you are named sole owner in the deed. This probably won't do you much good, however, if you're married and live in a community-property state. The community-property laws will probably defeat your purpose. This is because generally under these laws all property acquired by a husband and wife during marriage is considered to belong equally to the two marriage partners, regardless of the name in which title is taken. See your lawyer for exceptions that may apply in your particular case.

Whatever you decide after discussing it with your attorney and your family, make sure that the names of the buyer or buyers and type of ownership are set forth unmistakably in the deed, because it may be hard to change the type of ownership after you have received and recorded the deed.

The closing is the awesome ceremony that marks the instant when your purchase is completed, the deed is usually transferred to you, and ownership passes from the seller to you.

Two steps must be taken before the deed can change hands at the closing: "execution" and "delivery." Execution occurs when the seller fills in the appropriate blank spaces in the deed and then signs it. Delivery takes place when he turns the deed over to you. This gives you ownership and possession of the property.

You and the seller won't be alone at the closing. It is a solemn ritual attended by numerous participants, some of whom bring legal documents. You probably won't understand everything that is done at the closing unless you hold graduate degrees in law, accounting, and mathematics. You will have to sign your name to a number of papers that may be almost incomprehensible to you. Just so you won't feel uneasy, we might consider here the underlying import of what is happening.

The papers that are passed around, perused, discussed and perhaps signed may include the contract of sale, the deed, the seller's insurance policies, his receipted utility and fuel bills for the past several years, his mortgage documents, a survey or plan showing the boundaries of the property, the abstract of title, a title insurance policy, maybe a bill of sale for personal property, and documents certifying that the seller has cleared up any defects in the title or liens against it. All this may take place in the office of the lending institution or the title company, or in the office of the seller's attorney.

Closing costs may be negotiable before the closing, especially under the new Real Estate Settlement Procedures Act which took effect in June 1975. "Closing costs" can include the title-recording fee, your loan application fee, a bank service charge, a state mortgage tax, an escrow fee, a fee to the bank attorney for drawing up the mortgage, the fee for recording it, document stamps, the cost of a credit report on you by the mortgage lender, the cost of surveying property lines, the cost of the title insurance policy that protects the bank, life insurance to cover the mortgage payments in case you die before paying, loan discount points, inspection and appraisal fees, and various other obscure items.

A 1971 survey showed that these costs ran from a low of $165 to a high of $1,189. Purchasers of property were often caught short by bills presented to them at the closing. The new law was passed to bring all this under better control. The law requires that you be told in writing, to the penny, how much the closing costs will be, exactly what each item means, and usually what the previous buyer paid for the property if he or she owned it less than two years. It also puts ceilings on the monthly payment set aside for tax and insurance impound accounts.

Under this new law, you can have at least twelve days before you sign the final papers to look over a standard settlement-cost itemization of all fees and prepaid charges. If you don't like any of them, you have the right to cancel the whole transaction. Consequently you may be able to shop around for the best settlement charges, just as you shop around for the best terms on your mortgage.

However, if you sign a sales contract to take effect on a certain date, then go to a lender for financing and are unhappy with the closing costs, you may not have enough time to find another lender. If possible, try to make the sales contract contingent on your approval of the advance disclosure statement. (If you and the person selling the property both agree to waive the twelve-day requirement, this disclosure statement can be given to you a shorter time before the sale is to close.)

To help you understand the terms by which various closing costs are called, you can get a free booklet, "Settlement Costs and You," published by the American Bankers Association, available at any savings bank or lending institution. Any federally chartered lender will give you a copy. It's in non-technical language and well worth having.

The new law prohibits kickbacks or referral fees that some lawyers, brokers, and insurance people used to receive when referring clients to one another. It also forbids sellers and lenders from requiring buyers to purchase insurance from any particular company. People in business are being careful to abide by the new law, because penalties can run up to a year in prison and a $10,000 fine.

Nevertheless, the law may be something of a nuisance if you're in a hurry to complete a transaction. Some bankers say the law has increased their paperwork on mortgage loans by 30 percent or more, and that sales formerly closed in seven days may now take two or three weeks. Then too, some sellers just don't want to disclose what they paid for the property they are selling, and this can cause difficulties.

Anyhow, the days of costly surprises at the closings are gone. Closings now tend to be brief and brisk. Sometimes you and the seller may never meet face to face. The recorder's office may simply mail you the signed deed.

Get your deed recorded immediately if it hasn't already gone through the recorder's office. You may not be fully protected until the deed is on file. The vast majority of people in real estate are honest, but a shady operator could conceivably sell the same property to you and someone else at about the same time. If the other owner gets his deed recorded first, he'll probably be adjudged the legal owner.

Evidence that you received your deed first could help you. But the best evidence is likely to be the public record. So don't delay a minute in taking your deed to your County Recorder's Office or County Clerk's Office, whichever it is called in your area.

Once this is done, the long search and negotiations that we've covered in these past several chapters have come to an end. You've bought a piece of real estate. All the rights and profits of ownership are now yours.

REMEMBER THESE HIGH POINTS:

Find out if any easements were granted by previous owners.

The first paper you sign should contain protective clauses making the sale subject to:

1. Approval by whatever expert is going to advise you;
2. Satisfactory estimates of the cost of improvements you plan to make;
3. Satisfactory financing;
4. Your approval of certified income and expense statements.

Try for a mortgage loan with clauses favorable to you. Don't commit yourself to a balloon payment.

The agreement should promise that the premises will be turned over to you in the same condition they are now. Or else insurance should cover the property from the time of signing. Take photos of the property as it looks when the agreement is signed.

Never give a broker an offer that says "good until accepted."

Decide how title of ownership is to read.

Take a hard look at closing costs. They are negotiable.

X *Ways to Borrow on Real Estate*

Chapter II discussed the value of debt. Now you're almost ready to learn some seemingly magical uses of leverage. Creative financing will enable you to buy properties that you'd thought were beyond your reach, and to reap your share of the fortunes being made in real estate.

But truly creative financing is more than just borrowing big. It involves fairly sophisticated transactions. Before getting into them, you'd better make sure you understand the fundamental techniques of real estate financing. That's what this chapter will be about.

Mortgages and trust deeds are the two most common arrangements for borrowing money on real estate. They are different from other loans. The lender is much more concerned about the piece of property offered as collateral than about the character and quality of the people who borrow the money. The security is mainly the land and the building, not the future income of the owner of them. Therefore as you become an owner of property, your borrowing power increases.

In some states mortgages are more common than trust deeds; in others the reverse is true. Whichever type of paper is used, it enables someone either to borrow money against property he already owns or to pay the seller less cash down payment for property he is buying. The borrower signs an agreement that he will pay back the borrowed money, together with interest at a specified rate, either in a lump sum or (more commonly nowadays) in installments due on specified dates. Usually the agreement gives the lender the right to foreclose—that is, force a sale of the property to satisfy the debt—if payments aren't made as agreed.

The biggest difference between the two kinds of paper is that there are only two parties to a mortgage, and three parties to a trust deed.

If you take out a mortgage you are called the mortgagor, and you owe money to the lender, called the mortgagee.

If you take out a trust deed you are called the trustor. The lender is called the beneficiary. The third party, who holds naked title to the property, is called the trustee.

This difference becomes important only if you fall behind in payments. Foreclosure can usually be faster if you signed a trust deed. Foreclosure on a mortgage could take up to a year. The lender must first declare a default, and then he must usually file a foreclosure action. The court then orders an auction sale. But the successful bidder doesn't always get clear title to the property immediately. Instead he may get a sheriff's Certificate of Sale. Possibly for a year after the foreclosure, you (as the original borrower) can come back and take over the property again by paying up all the past-due payments, penalties, interest and costs.

Foreclosure on a trust deed is simpler. In the beginning, when you made the transaction, you signed a trust deed to the property, and gave it to the trustee. The deed empowers the trustee to sell the property if you default on your loan, and to deliver a trustee's deed to anyone who buys it at foreclosure. Under a trust deed, as soon as the lender tells the trustee to record a "notice of default"—meaning that you're behind in payments—you'll usually have only three months to make up the overdue payments plus penalties and costs. At the end of the three months, the trustee advertises the property for sale for at least three weeks. You can still reclaim it during those three weeks but only by paying off the full amount of the loan, if the lender insists on it; sometimes a lender will settle for all back payments and the penalties and costs. Anyhow, after three weeks the trustee can auction off the property. Whoever buys it will receive a Trustee's Deed. You've lost the property, in a period of less than four months.

To a lender, the main advantage of a mortgage is that if the property isn't resold for enough to pay off all you owe him, he can get a "deficiency judgment" giving him the right to claim against other property you may have (except where laws prohibit this under certain conditions).

Most lenders prefer trust deeds—because these usually give a lender the choice of foreclosing as either a mortgage or a trust deed. If he wants a quick and easy foreclosure, he can go the trust deed route. But he can go the long route and foreclose as a mortgage if he figures that an immediate sale won't bring in enough to cover the amount of money lent against the property. (This is rare in our era of inflation and rising realty values, but if the property has gone badly to seed, maybe he'll prefer the chance to get back the rest of his money through a deficiency judgment.)

Junior mortgages and junior trust deeds play a key role in many real estate transactions. Some studies indicate that three-fourths of all property transactions include some form of junior financing.

This kind of financing gives the lender a subordinate claim against the property. It means that if you can't repay what you've borrowed, the holder of the first mortgage or trust deed can foreclose and get paid off first, after which the holders of junior claims are entitled to leftover proceeds from the foreclosure sale. If there aren't enough proceeds to pay off all the lenders, too bad for the subordinate ones!

A subordinate (junior) claim on property may be a second, third, or lesser one. Nobody can tell just by looking at the paper whether or not it gives the holder first claim. It doesn't say "first mortgage" or "second trust deed" or whatever. Normally the priority depends on the date when each was recorded with the county recorder. One of the purposes of the "title search" done by an abstract or title company, before the signing of a mortgage or trust deed, is to find out what priority claims, if any, are on record.

Sooner or later, if you keep on making real estate transactions, you're bound to take a junior mortgage or trust deed on a piece of property. Here is what you should know when you go into such a deal:

As soon as you accept the paper, you should file a "Request for Notice of Default" with the county recorder. This means that you'll be notified when there is a default on a higher-priority loan. You may have the right to make the payments on that other loan yourself, thus preserving your claim on the property. Then you can start your own foreclosure action if you decide it will bring you out ahead.

Most junior mortgages are short term—typically three to five years. Longer than five years is unusual. Quite often the regular payments aren't big enough to pay off the whole debt during the term of the loan. Instead, the mortgage or trust deed is written to require a sizable balloon payment on the last payment due.

Purchase-money mortgages or trust deeds are simply ordinary mortgages or trust deeds issued by a buyer in favor of a seller instead of some third-party lender. They may be either first or junior. Often a buyer of property doesn't have enough cash to close the gap between the full purchase price and other loans outstanding. To make the sale possible, the seller accepts a mortgage from the buyer as security for the buyer's future payment of the difference. No money changes hands. But the seller is in effect "lending" the difference to the buyer in return for the mortgage.

Suppose you want to buy my house, and I agree to sell for $25,000. You give me a down payment of $2,500 and the bank agrees to lend you $17,500 (70 percent of the purchase price) in return for a first mortgage on the property. But this still leaves you $5,000 short. Because I'm in a hurry to sell my house, I may accept a second mortgage as security for the $5,000 you'll still owe me. You sign a note promising to repay the $5,000 plus interest at an agreed rate. And we have a deal.

A seller who accepts a purchase-money mortgage may be saddled with the chores of checking up on the buyer's insurance and tax payments as well as keeping after him for the monthly payments on principal and interest. If you take such a mortgage, you may want to put it in the hands of a mortgage company, for management on a fee basis, to spare yourself these chores.

Hard-money mortgages or trust deeds are those where money really does change hands. For example, let's say you own property that has gone up in value. Maybe it's worth $50,000 now, although you paid far less for it, and you've given a mortgage on it in the amount of $30,000 as security for a loan. You should be able to borrow much more on the property by executing a second mortgage. This will free some of your capital for other transactions. Similarly, if your property is on the market but you're having trouble selling it, a second mortgage will give you extra cash until you make the sale.

The money you borrow in this way needn't be part of a real estate transaction. You can do whatever you want with it—make an investment, start a business, buy a car, take a vacation. You simply put up your property as collateral for a loan. That's why a hard-money mortgage is sometimes called a collateral-security mortgage. Like the purchase-money mortgage, it can be either a first mortgage or a junior one.

Most successful real estate investors borrow as much money as possible on their properties. We've already seen why in a previous chapter: leverage can multiply their profits. But let's consider one more example here, to make the point more vivid. An owner of vacant land, appraised at $100,000, says to you: "I'll sell you the land for $10,000 down, and subordinate a balance of $90,000." This means he'll let you owe him $90,000 on a trust deed or mortgage whose claim against the property he agrees to make secondary (see Chapter XI) to some other mortgage loan you take out later. You decide to do this. You go to an insurance company and get its written commitment for a $300,000 loan to put a building on the land. Then you go to a bank and get a construction or interim loan (a type that will be explained in Chapter XI). When you start building, you have a $400,000 project going—yet you've put in only $10,000 cash! Do you begin to see why some builder–developers grow rich?

Some builder–developers go broke, because costs keep rising beyond what they've figured. Or they get greedy and borrow more than they're certain they can repay; bankers aren't supposed to take any undue risks because bankers are lending other folks' money, but they haven't always stuck to this principle in recent years. In fact, some have shown genius at lending money without asking many questions. A retired bank president recently expressed his admiration for "all those young men from the Harvard Business School who are wizards, just wizards, at making loans. Not quite so good at collecting them." (If you're curious about the underlying economic changes that have caused lending officers to become money salesmen, you'll find a brilliantly clear explanation in Martin Mayer's book *The Bankers.**)

If you've taken to heart the principles already laid down in this book, you know how to use leverage scientifically and safely. Before you go into any transaction you'll analyze it so thoroughly that there will be very little risk of any lender foreclosing on you. Your financing will be structured in such a way that there'll always be more than enough cash flowing in to meet whatever debt payments you've signed up for.

The very word "mortgage" still sounds scary. It comes from the legal French the Normans brought to England many centuries ago. Its original meaning was "dead pledge" or "dead hand," which certainly sounds unpleasant. And in the old-time stage plays the heroine was always at the mercy of the villain because he held a mortgage on her family farm; if she didn't pay by the due date—which she couldn't, of course, or there'd be no suspense in the melodrama—he would foreclose and turn the family out into the snow.

Many farmers did lose their farms in the 1920's and 1930's because mortgage holders foreclosed. In those days a mortgage was

* Martin Mayer, *The Bankers*, Weybright & Talley, Inc., New York, 1975.

simply a loan with a fixed term; at the end of the term it had to be paid off in a lump sum, or renewed. If the interest rate had soared in the meantime, or if the due date fell during a money panic, an owner could lose his property simply because he couldn't find anyone willing to lend. The situation got so bad that Minnesota passed a law forcing mortgage holders to renew their loans—and the United States Supreme Court upheld it, against a storm of arguments that the law was unconstitutional.

This chronic problem of mortgage foreclosures was solved in the 1930's with the invention of the self-amortizing mortgage and a government guarantee that certain classes of mortgages would eventually be paid. Instead of paying only the interest and renewing the loan each time it came due, the property owner would make a monthly payment big enough to cover not only interest but also the complete repayment of the loan over the life of the mortgage.

The best way to minimize mortgage costs is to buy property when interest rates are low. But if you buy when rates are soaring, shop for a clause that will permit you to "refinance" the mortgage—in other words, to pay it off ahead of time by taking a new mortgage for the purpose—when interest rates go down. Or ask for an agreement that one year later you can pay the current "going rate" or the original rate, whichever is lower.

Contrariwise, if you're borrowing on a mortgage when interest rates are low, try to get advance agreement from the lender that anyone who buys your property can take over your mortgage. Naturally this will make the property more attractive to prospective buyers when current interest rates become high. By the same token, if you're buying older property with a low-interest mortgage, try to persuade the owner to let you take over the mortgage if the lender will permit it.

It costs money to borrow against real estate—not just the interest, but various one-time charges that can add up.

There will be costs for title search and/or title insurance. This shows the lender that you have a right to pledge the property as security for the loan, so that his claim against it will be what he thinks it will be. If the lender isn't sure how much the property is worth, he may expect you to pay for an appraisal.

Also, he may have someone investigate your credit, and charge you for this. There'll be charges for drafting documents, forwarding them, and recording them; for insurance-policy endorsements; tax service contracts; probably for the services of an escrow or settlement company, whose main service is to hold the documents until the conditions of the purchase and sale have been met.

Sometimes you have to pay a commission to some third party for arranging the loan. And the lender may ask a special fee for what he says were his trouble and expenses in working out details of the loan and setting it up on his books. This sort of a loan fee is sometimes called "points." A point is 1 percent. If the fee is "three points," it is 3 percent of the total loan amount. It has been known to run as high as 20 percent, particularly on junior loans. In effect it is a one-time charge that comes out of the money before the borrower gets it. This is true of the other charges mentioned above: they'll cut down the net proceeds that the borrower receives. Therefore the amount you get will be smaller than you expected, if you didn't know about all these extra charges.

The longer the mortgage, the better. It's to your advantage to stretch out the period of repayment. The longer you can take in paying back the loan, the more of the principal you'll have for your own use during any given year of the repayment period. Isn't it obvious when the point is stated this way?

"But what about those hefty interest charges?" you may be asking. "The longer the term of the loan, the bigger the total interest I'll be paying."

If total costs over a long period are your chief worry, you probably shouldn't be thinking about borrowing at all. It makes no sense to borrow unless you use the borrowed money to bring in bigger earnings, profits, and/or other benefits than the borrowing will cost you. One of the best reasons for borrowing is to invest the borrowed money at a return that will be higher than the interest you pay. There's nothing wrong with paying high interest if your return is higher still.

Money is a commodity to be rented, like a U-drive car. It is a means to an end. How you're going to use the money is the important question. Just as you wouldn't squander your savings without thinking about whether you really need the sports car or fur coat you want to buy, you won't use up your borrowing power just because you possess it.

Your borrowing power is as much a financial asset as the money in your savings account. The more intelligently you use it, the stronger your financial position—and the more secure your future. People who keep all their reserve funds in a low-interest savings account, and never borrow for the purpose of making sound investments, really grow poorer year by year as inflation eats away the buying power of their savings.

Successful real estate investors don't pay cash for property they buy. They use other people's money—borrowed money, mostly.

Finding the best mortgage is a matter of shopping around, comparing terms, and knowing what to look for. Each lender is slightly different. The less institutionalized the lender, the more variety and flexibility. (You can often come out ahead by arranging mortgages and other credit with a property owner rather than with a savings institution.)

Some mortgages are less attractive than they seem at first thought. Sometimes you'll be offered terms whereby your installments are so small that they won't repay the loan in full before its term is up. Sounds wonderful, doesn't it? But the catch is that you'll be committing yourself to make a painfully large lump-sum payment (the balloon payment mentioned in previous chapters) to retire the loan at its expiration date.

A lender may even offer you an interest-only loan, with the entire principal due in one payment at the end. This really is fine if you know exactly where to get the money for the balloon payment. But balloon payments have a way of sneaking up and falling due at inconvenient times. Don't get trapped into having to borrow money for the balloon—money might be extremely costly and hard to get at the time you need it.

Instead of a loan with very small installments and a balloon at the end, you'll usually be better off to spread the installments over a longer period while keeping them big enough to amortize the loan. You can often get a lender to agree to this if you offer something in return. He might go for a higher interest rate, a slightly higher price for the property he is selling, a higher loan fee or whatever other sweetener your imagination suggests.

The interest rate on your mortgage loan will depend on supply and demand. As you know if you've been reading the financial pages, banks and other lenders change their rates from time to time, adjusting to the supply of money and the demand for loans. Whatever rate happens to be in effect when you take out the mortgage will normally be the rate you'll pay throughout the term of the mortgage.

However, lending institutions have more than one interest rate. The lowest is their "prime rate"—the rate they charge their biggest, strongest corporate borrowers. Individuals pay higher. But the exact rate charged any individual will depend on the property against which he's borrowing, the size of the loan he wants, the term of the mortgage, and sometimes his personal credit rating. As we saw earlier, second mortgages and other "subordinate" paper usually carry higher interest rates.

When you've figured out the exact terms of the mortgage loan you're going to ask for, don't assume that any two lending institutions will quote you the same interest rates for that loan. Some have more money to lend than others, and are more eager to get it working for them. Some are trying to attract more loan business in the area where your property is located. Some won't quote at all, but simply refuse to make the loan—maybe because they have no money to lend, or don't want to make any more loans in your area, or are prohibited by external regulators or internal policies from making loans against your kind of property.

The lender who quotes you the lowest interest rate isn't always offering the best deal. We've noted this before, but it's worth repeating. Other provisions in the mortgage are important too. Some are good for you, some are to be avoided. You should take these into consideration before you sign a formal loan application. Here are some of the provisions that are harmful or helpful:

"Due-on-sale" acceleration clauses are bad for you. Avoid them if you possibly can. Acceleration clauses commit you to pay off the entire unpaid balance immediately if certain stated events occur. What events? Falling behind on payments, for one. Failing to pay insurance and property tax bills for a second, selling or transferring the property for another. Taking out another loan on your property for still another.

The first contingency—falling behind on payments—isn't so bad. If you're the prudent type for whom this book is written, you'll make sure in advance that the money to meet your payments will always be available. Moreover, the laws of most states allow a borrower to "cure" the default and reinstate the loan by bringing his payment up to date and reimbursing the lender for any costs incurred.

However, some lending officers like to keep a borrower on a tight leash—retaining a right to demand payment in full whenever the borrower sells, transfers, or even makes major changes in his property.

Sometimes they want the privilege of raising the interest on a borrower who does any of these things. Whenever you run into such lenders, try to get them to liberalize the clauses before you sign. For instance, you might get them to agree that they'll permit a buyer of the property to assume your loan if the buyer meets certain credit standards.

Anyhow, when you're shopping for a loan—making telephone inquiries and the like—try to find out whether a prospective lender expects to include an acceleration clause. If he does, you may be able to get him to soften the terms or even drop the clause entirely through negotiation.

Ask for a prepayment clause permitting you to pay off part or all of the mortgage before it is due, without being charged a special fee for the privilege. Prepayment is a way you can make a nice saving if interest rates drop after you've taken out the mortgage—you can then refinance the property at lower interest. Likewise, there may be times when you want to resell property without a mortgage on it, or a buyer wants to refinance himself.

FHA and VA loans all have clauses allowing prepayment. Different lenders have different rules about this sort of thing. Some don't allow refinancing for the first three or five years, then allow prepayment without penalty. Others charge a percentage of the balance—six months' interest is common—as a penalty for prepayment. Some mortgage notes say the borrower can make the specified payments "or more." If the note and the mortgage or trust deed say nothing about prepayment penalties, you may be able to negotiate with the lender, but he'll have the option of refusing to let you pay the loan off at a faster rate. So try to get a definite prepayment clause written in.

An open-end provision would also be helpful to you. It lets you borrow more money in the future under the same mortgage agreement, without going to the trouble and expense of refinancing or taking out a second mortgage. This could be especially helpful if interest rates go up. However, if they do, the lender may ask for a higher rate of interest.

Package provisions allow you to include in the mortgage the cost of large appliances that will be permanently installed in the property.

Assumption and release agreements mean that the transfer of your mortgage to anyone who buys your property "will not unreasonably be refused." In effect, they let you do the very things that "due-on-sale" clauses are intended to prevent. In other words, someone else can "assume the mortgage" when you decide to sell the property. The new buyer thereby takes over the balance of the principal owing on your mortgage, after paying you your equity.

This provision can be a help to you in selling the property, for it saves the prospective buyer much of the trouble of negotiating a new mortgage, and may set him up with a mortgage at an economical rate. (An old mortgage at a low rate is something to be cherished. It makes the property attractive to buyers when you choose to sell.)

Lenders prefer not to make such agreements. They'd rather be free to make a new mortgage with the buyer if rates have gone higher in the meantime. Still, it's worth a try.

When you buy property that already carries a mortgage, you may want that mortgage to continue in effect—and sometimes the mortgagee (the lending institution) will insist on it. Maybe the mortgage company won't let the original owner prepay the balance of the mortgage loan. In that case the property will remain subject to the terms of the original mortgage. Or maybe you want to assume the balance of an original mortgage loan issued at lower interest rates than the current ones. When interest rates are going down, lenders are less likely to allow prepayment. When rates are going up, they may insist on it.

Anyway, for whatever reason, you may decide to buy the property "subject to the mortgage," or to "assume the mortgage." In either case, if you should fall behind in payments, the lender (the original mortgagee) could foreclose the mortgage or trust deed in the normal way and sell your property to recover the money that was lent. Technically, the responsibility for repaying the loan remains with the original owner even after he has sold the property to you—unless the lender has agreed in writing to accept you in his place. Even if you assume the mortgage, this merely establishes a contract between you and the lender and doesn't take away the rights of the lending institution to make claim against both you and the seller.

From all the foregoing, you can see that a mortgage or trust deed agreement can be complex. Read every word. Ask your attorney to read it too—and your real estate counselor, if you have one. They may be able to help you fix the loan document so some of its clauses are more favorable to you.

Now that you know about these various kinds of borrowing arrangements, you're ready to look for a lender. Some lenders are better than others. It depends on the situation. We'll see in Chapter XI.

REMEMBER THESE HIGH POINTS:

A junior loan is a handy tool. You may want to use it either as borrower or as lender.

Find out what extra charges will be involved before you borrow against real estate.

Try for the longest possible repayment period.

Shop around before you borrow. Each lender is slightly different.

Avoid "due-on-sale" acceleration clauses.

Ask for a clause letting you make prepayment without penalty.

XI Selecting the Best Lender

What kind of lender is your best prospect? This depends on how big the property is, where it's located, how much you want to borrow, and the kind of loan you want. The terms will depend mostly on the kind of lender you approach.

The main sources of real estate loans are commercial banks, savings and loan associations, insurance companies, real estate trusts (REIT's), pension funds, trust funds, credit unions, mortgage companies, finance companies, private investors, and sellers of properties.

Commercial banks specialize in short-term loans, but they also make fairly long-term loans on improved real estate. Federal and state laws and regulations generally prohibit them from lending more than 80 percent of the appraised value, and from making loans for longer than twenty-five years. Usually they prefer to stay well below these legal limits. Just how far they'll go depends on the current condition of the money market, the quality of the property you'll put up as security, and their own internal rules and policies.

We all know how conservative bankers are supposed to be. The old joke used to be that they would lend money only to people who didn't need it. But there are many degrees of conservatism, and nearly all banks have loosened up somewhat in recent years. When they do make real estate loans, their loan fees are usually low. In fact, sometimes they charge no loan fee—no "points"—at all. Their interest rates are usually lower than what you'll be charged at a savings and loan, but higher than those at insurance companies. They usually don't put prepayment provisions in their loan documents—but they seldom charge prepayment penalties either.

Most of today's bank lending officers pride themselves on being good judges of character, and shrewd evaluators of personal credit risks. Consequently they like to keep close tabs on a borrower—which means that they want the right to approve or disapprove any arrangement you want to make with someone else to take over your mortgage. Moreover, they hate to get stuck with a low-interest loan if rates go up. For all these reasons, bankers almost always insist on putting acceleration or alienation clauses into a mortgage agreement, on charging assumption fees, and on increasing the interest rates, if a new borrower takes over your property and your mortgage.

Savings and loan associations (sometimes known as savings associations or as building and loan associations) may seem like banks, but they aren't. They are associations of people who pool funds and lend the money to other people who want to build or buy homes. The S & L's, as they are often called, are legally prohibited from offering most of the usual banking services. But they are popular places for savings because they generally pay higher interest rates than commercial banks. And they do a lot of urban mortgage banking, naturally, since they were created for this purpose. In fact, they are the biggest source of loans for single-family homes and smaller multiple-family dwellings.

S & L's can be organized under either federal or state charters. Federally chartered S & L's can legally lend up to 90 percent of the first $35,000 of appraised value of single-family homes—but wait! Before you rush downtown to apply for a loan, you should know that this law applies only to homes that are to be occupied by the owner. When you're buying and selling property as investments, you can't get quite such liberal terms: if the property is anything up to a fourplex, 80 percent of the appraised value is the most they can lend. On larger apartment property, 75 percent is their limit. (Remember that "appraised value" may be quite different from the asking price.) State-chartered S & L's have different limits, set by laws in their particular state.

Unlike bankers, S & L lending officers figure that if the property is good enough security, they needn't delve deeply into the background of the borrower. They'll usually make bigger loans than banks. And they may give you a longer-term mortgage than a bank will. (This can be a profitable advantage to an investor, as we've seen.)

However, you'll probably have to pay higher interest for an S & L mortgage, and your loan fee may be fat. If you want to pay off the mortgage early or sell the property, you'll almost always be charged a penalty, unless the buyer is taking out a new loan with the same S & L.

Due-on-sale alienation clauses are about the same as those used by banks.

Insurance companies aren't making many home loans at this writing—but by the time you read this, they may be a good source again. Look into it, because when they have extra cash they are likely to charge the lowest interest. Another advantage: they seldom write an acceleration clause into their documents, which means you can sell the property later and let the new buyer assume the mortgage without paying extra for the privilege.

Every type of lender has disadvantages as well as advantages. Here are the less joyful aspects of borrowing from an insurance company. Processing your loan may take weeks. That's partly because the companies usually work through mortgage bankers, and partly because the loan may have to be okayed by an office outside the state. Generally the property must be good quality, and in a good area. The borrower's income and credit standing must also be good. Prepayment penalties usually are high, especially in the first few years. Sometimes there is a "lock-in" that prohibits you from making any prepayments at all in those years. Also, an insurance company seldom will lend as high a percentage of the value of the property. The kind of transaction it usually prefers is a really big one—a large high-grade apartment complex, shopping center, office building, or industrial property.

Real estate investment trusts, too, look mostly at big developments in the million-dollar class. They will lend against an attractive property, and may accept a slightly higher risk than the other types of lenders mentioned above. Naturally they'll want a higher interest rate because of the risk. They work primarily through mortgage bankers, as insurance companies do.

Pension and endowment funds are a fast-growing source of realty loans. Mortgage brokers steer them to most of their investments. Since they're not regulated by governmental watchdogs, they can use more discretion on kinds of property, location, types of loan, and mortgage terms. Here again, they may ask for slightly higher loan fees and interest rates than the more conservative lending institutions.

Trust funds are legal arrangements by which a trustee (often a bank's trust officer) manages somebody else's money. A wealthy person often puts a large chunk of money into trust; the trustee will invest the proceeds and pay them out in installments to the heirs or beneficiaries. It's a way for a rich man to provide for the financial security of himself and/or his widow, children, and grandchildren for a long period of time. If his money were paid to inheritors in a lump sum or over a few years, they might squander it all and end up broke.

Many trusts make real estate loans. The terms depend on the judgment of the money manager who is handling the trust, and on whatever restrictions were laid down by the person who put the money into trust. You can't be sure until you ask, just as in dealing with managers of pension and endowment funds. (Technically the man who manages a highly paid entertainer's money may not be managing a trust fund, but for our purposes he likewise can be considered a potential lender.)

Because of the unpredictable difference in personalities and purposes, it's hard to generalize about any real estate loan you might get from the administrator of a trust. However, trust officers of banks usually charge somewhat stiffer interest rates than other loan sources, and prefer shorter-term mortgages or trust deeds. Loan fees are usually competitive.

Credit unions, especially the bigger ones, make real estate loans—both firsts and seconds. Loan fees, if any, are usually nominal. Prepayment penalties don't exist. Interest rates are likely to be quite competitive. Credit unions are generally more promising sources for second mortgages than firsts.

"This all sounds wonderful," you're probably thinking as you ponder the above paragraph. "There must be some drawbacks. What are they?"

Well, credit unions make smaller loans in relation to the property's value. And they want their money paid back faster, which of course means your installment payments must be bigger. But the biggest drawback is that you have to be a member of the credit union in order to borrow from it.

Credit unions (like S & L's) are associations of people who pool their savings. But in this case membership is open only to people with some common bond or interest—such as employees of a certain corporation or members of a church, labor union or fraternal society, or even of professional groups like actors or writers. Members with extra money deposit it with their credit union and are paid interest on their savings. These funds are then used to make loans to other members—at low rates.

Still, you're likely to find that a credit union will take a longer-term second mortgage than most other institutions will, especially if it is secured by a reasonable amount of equity. So if you're negotiating with a prospective buyer who hasn't enough cash, always ask him if he belongs to a credit union. He may be surprised to learn that the credit union can solve his borrowing problem. By the same token, if you happen to belong to one of these credit unions, or have an opportunity to join one, it may turn out to be a big help in your own investment program. Credit unions receive only about 4 percent of America's total savings deposits, yet they are collecting on more than a tenth of all installment debt owed by individuals.

Mortgage companies (sometimes called mortgage brokers or mortgage bankers) are always worth checking when you want a real estate loan. They are listed in the Yellow Pages of the telephone book.

Their business is to keep in constant touch with a great multitude of lenders, so they know who has money to lend at what rates and terms. Therefore they can often arrange a much better loan for you than you might find on your own. Naturally they charge you a fee for their services in bringing you and the lender together. So if you're able to ferret out the same lender on your own—which is a big if—you may sometimes pay even less for your borrowing.

Finance companies (also known as small-loan companies, personal finance companies or consumer finance organizations) used to do almost all their business in small cash loans from $25 up to about $1,500. But lately they've been branching out. Many of them now make loans secured by junior mortgages or trust deeds, for periods up to ten years. The rates are high—as much as 1½ percent per month on the unpaid balance, or 18 percent a year—and there may be loan fees of as much as five points. Leave no stone unturned before dealing with a finance company.

Private individuals may be the largest single source of money for higher-risk junior loans. Obviously they are more flexible than institutions. But they usually want a higher return on their money.

An inexperienced borrower seeking a loan thinks that money is money wherever he finds it, and that the important thing is to find a lender—any lender—who will say yes. Unfortunately there are some people in the business of lending money who are all too eager to say yes to almost anyone. Be wary of the stranger who identifies himself only as "investor" or "businessman" and offers you a loan with no questions asked. It may seem temptingly easy to borrow a few thousand at only 6 percent—until you study the note you're asked to sign, and realize that it's 6 percent a month, which is 72 percent a year. The smiling stranger may turn out to be an underworld character, with friends ready to break your arm or worse if you don't make payments on the dot.

The law tries to protect borrowers against such loans by setting limits on what interest rate may legally be charged. Any financial institution can tell you what the legal limits are in your state.

Your rich uncle may be just as willing to lend you money as the Mafia. And there are plenty of highly reputable private individuals, from the Rockefellers on down, who make loans against real estate. The terms will be whatever you can negotiate. If you know somebody who's sitting on a comfortable investment portfolio, he might be the first source of funds you should approach.

Even if you don't know any private investors, you can find them through mortgage companies or real estate brokers. Many of these moneyed people also put small ads in the classified or financial pages, or watch for ads of would-be borrowers. A well-worded ad, describing the property and its location and the loan you want, might bring you some worthwhile phone calls. Just be sure you know whom you're dealing with, and read every word of the loan agreement carefully even if you write it yourself. Again, it's wise to have your lawyer go over any financial agreement before you sign it.

The seller of a property you're buying should be the very first person you consider when thinking about financing. Not only is he an excellent prospect for carrying back a sizable second trust deed or mortgage, but he might make a very attractive deal on a first.

Why is he such a good prospect? For one thing, selling is likely to be more important to him than to any other lender. It's to his advantage to work something out with you, especially if you're the only prospective buyer. If you walk away from the transaction because you can't arrange the financing you want, there's no cash coming to him until he finds another buyer. Probably he'd rather take a lower interest rate than lose the sale entirely. Ditto for the down payment, alienation and prepayment clauses, and other terms. (Before you begin negotiations to borrow from him, go back and read this book's Chapter VIII, on negotiating.)

Another reason why it's to your advantage to borrow from the seller is that he won't charge you a loan fee. Still another is that he probably would hate the thought of taking his property back by foreclosing; so if you ever want to readjust the mortgage payments, he's likely to lean over backward to work something out with you.

How favorable a mortgage you can negotiate with a seller will depend on how much you know about his needs and motives. If he needs a lot of cash in a hurry, you can take one approach. If he mainly wants a steady income for his retirement years, you can take another. His tax position will also be an important angle. We'll examine various propositions you might make in different buyer-seller situations when we get into the chapters on creative finance.

Primary and secondary are two words you'll hear often in real estate dealings. Each is used in two different senses.

When realty people talk about financing, "primary financing" means loans secured by first trust deeds or mortgages, and "secondary financing" is a loan that has a secondary or subordinate claim against the property.

But when they talk about the real estate market, the "primary market" means the sources from which investors can get loans directly. There is also a "secondary market," which buys and sells mortgages, borrows against them, and trades in them.

The secondary market does an important job for all of us in the realty field. It stabilizes the primary market. That is, it helps protect us from sharp ups and downs, scarcities and surpluses of loan funds. If there's a shortage of mortgage money anywhere in the country, the secondary market almost automatically sends surplus money flowing in that direction. More lenders and more funds are attracted to any area where there's a need for them.

The leading secondary market for existing primary loans is the Federal National Mortgage Association. It started out as a government agency created by the National Housing Act, but now is an enterprise that anybody can buy into, because its stock is traded on the New York Stock Exchange. You'll often hear it mentioned as "Fanny Mae," a nickname bestowed because of its initials, FNMA.

Fanny Mae buys existing trust deeds and mortgages. It may not ever be important to you directly, unless you soar into the upper regions of wheeling and dealing in blue-chip real estate, but it's worth knowing about in case you wonder about changes in ownership of a mortgage you're interested in.

You may also hear mention of Ginnie Mae, the Government National Mortgage Association. It is a government agency that also does its bit in stabilizing the market, especially for FHA-insured loans on low-income housing, and redevelopment projects. It also guarantees payment on certain private mortgages backed by the FHA or VA, or owned by FNMA.

The secondary market includes private investors who buy and sell mortgages between themselves. Some of them also act as intermediaries for other investors who want to buy or sell. Escrow companies and real estate brokers get into this act occasionally. These are the channels through which second trust deeds and second mortgages are usually bought by investors.

If you're a veteran of the United States Armed Forces, you may be able to borrow money under especially favorable terms. A GI loan, for which you may be eligible, is simply a loan on which the government guarantees to repay the lender in case the borrower defaults or dies. Such a loan can be used only to buy a home or farm that you, the borrower, will occupy. However, you needn't occupy it indefinitely. You can move out later, and sell or rent the property. So it may be a useful investment tool for you.

To get a certificate of eligibility for a loan guarantee, apply to your regional Veterans Administration office. Then you can take this certificate to any bank, S & L, insurance company, or mortgage company, and apply for a loan on the property you want to buy. You won't necessarily get the loan, however. There's no law forcing any lender to grant a loan on VA terms. And some lenders simply won't make such loans under any circumstances, although they'll generally be able to steer you to someone who will.

VA loan terms and conditions are fixed by the government, which also sets ceilings on the interest rates that can be charged. These ceilings are generally lower than the going rates for similar loans from conventional lenders.

This brings up a question. Suppose you were a lending officer at a bank or S & L. Would you grant VA loans at, say, 8 percent when you could pump out money through conventional loans at 9 percent or more, with takers for all the money available?

Sure you would. Lenders still make VA loans. They bring their returns on these mortgages into line by charging a discount, or points.

In money-tight periods, sellers may be socked as much as eight points (8 percent of the total amount of the loan) for a VA mortgage. The result is about the same as if they were paying the going interest rate.

Because the loan is so safe, lenders sometimes write a VA mortgage with little or no down payment. And the term of the mortgage, under the protecting law, can be as long as thirty years. So you'll want to look into the possibility of getting one. Just be prepared for some red tape. A VA appraiser must go out and evaluate the property, then issue a "Certificate of Reasonable Value" (unlike conventional mortgages, a VA mortgage can be for 100 percent of the VA's appraised value. This is how you sometimes get a no-money-down buy). But government offices aren't always fast-moving.

In some rural areas, if there is no lender available, the VA will make the loan directly to you.

Even if you're not a veteran, the government may help with your real estate investment. Here's one way it can help: maybe you want to sell some property to a would-be buyer. In order to make the buy he needs a mortgage, as ninety-nine of every one hundred buyers do. But this buyer hasn't established a credit rating that looks good to lending officers, and his savings aren't big enough for the usual-size down payment. If he's a veteran, a VA mortgage may solve his and your problem. You, not he, may have to pay the points or loan fee, but it can still be a good deal for both of you. Remember that a lending institution doesn't have to worry about the credit of the borrower when it grants a VA mortgage; the loan is almost risk-free (although the VA itself wants to know something about the credit-worthiness of the borrower, and his ability to repay).

Another way you may be able to use Uncle Sam's help is by assuming someone else's VA mortgage when you buy property from him. This is almost sure to be a good deal for you, because of the low interest rate on the mortgage. GI loans can be readily assumed by a purchaser, even if he couldn't qualify for the loan himself. No okay is needed from either the VA or the lending institution. (However, the veteran remains personally liable for repaying the loan in case you default. If he's worried about this, you can ask the VA to investigate your income and credit standing. Having investigated, the VA can agree to release the original borrower from his liability.)

A Federal Housing Administration mortgage is still another way the government may be able to help you borrow on real estate, whether you're a veteran or not. FHA loans, like GI loans, are not made by the government. Private lenders put up the money, and the FHA insures them against loss.

Interest rates on FHA loans vary with market conditions, but can't go above ceilings set by the FHA. Loan terms are up to thirty years, or three-fourths of the estimated remaining life of the property, whichever is less.

The chief advantage of the FHA over conventional loans is that the down payment may be lower. In this protected situation, where he knows he can't lose, a lending officer may let you borrow up to 97 percent of the FHA's appraised value of the property.

FHA appraisers have upgraded standards of design and construction all over the country—not because they can dictate to builders, but because the standards the FHA set up to protect itself against loss have been copied by many local governments and private lenders. An FHA appraisal is universally respected as a shrewd estimate of what the property is really worth. An FHA agreement to insure a loan convinces lenders that the property used as collateral for the loan is well built and in good condition.

Because of the guarantee against loss, FHA-insured mortgages are readily salable in the mortgage market. This has helped to pull mortgage money from have to have-not areas, since lenders know they'll be able to convert their mortgages back into cash at any time.

FHA mortgages can be paid off in full at any time without penalty, provided proper notice is given to the lender. They don't contain due-on-sale or other alienation clauses. Therefore, if you want to buy property from someone who has an FHA mortgage on it, you can either take title "subject to" the loan or "assume" the loan without getting an okay from either the lender or the FHA. Lenders aren't legally allowed to charge you more than fifty dollars for their trouble in changing the records.

Taking title to a property "subject to" a loan leaves you with no responsibility for paying the loan. "Assuming" a loan means taking over the primary liability. However, the seller still has secondary liability—which means he isn't completely off the hook, but will not be asked to pay unless you, the buyer, fail to pay the lender. Thus you're much better off as buyer when you take title subject to the existing loan. As a seller, you're better off if the buyer assumes the debt that was previously your sole responsibility. But these technicalities are academic, since we assume you'll be a solid investor who won't ever skip a payment.

FHA loans can also be used for building purposes. If you follow the Lowry–Nickerson system of investment you won't be doing much building. But you conceivably may want to improve a property by building an addition. And there's always the outside chance that a property you own might be damaged or destroyed, and you'd want to rebuild. Here's the information you'd need under such conditions.

Construction loans are different from the so-called permanent loans we've been considering in this chapter. If you're constructing a building, you need money to pay construction bills as you incur them. What do you do? You get a construction loan, sometimes called an interim loan, to provide temporary funds solely for this purpose.

The odd part about this procedure is that you don't start by going to the short-term lender from whom you'll borrow the money. First you get the plans drawn up for whatever building you want to do. Then you take these architect's plans to contractors, and get written bids. Next you take all these papers to a long-term lender—any of the organizations mentioned in this chapter that lend on mortgages and deeds of trust. You ask this long-term lender (let's say it's an insurance company) for a letter of commitment.

Now at last you're ready to go to a short-term lender—which may be a mortgage company, REIT, pension fund, bank or S & L. You tell this lender that you have an insurance company that will lend money on the building if you can build it and get it into use.

The bank, or whoever it is, will ask to see the loan commitment in writing. You show it. The bank will then lend you the money on a temporary or interim basis. It's a pretty safe loan because of the "take-out" commitment from the long-term lender. Therefore the short-term lender is usually willing to advance more money, and give better terms, than he otherwise would. (To make the loan even safer, you'll probably have to post a bond, guaranteeing that the building will be completed as specified and that there'll be no liens against it from contractors whose bills haven't been paid.)

Construction lenders all insist that their loans must have first claim against the property. So if any part of it is already mortgaged, you must get written agreement from the mortgage holder that he'll subordinate his claim to the construction loan. So if you're buying property on which you plan to do some building, try to negotiate this provision into the purchase and sale agreement.

As we've seen throughout this book, part of the simple formula for big profits in real estate is to stay deeply in debt. You use as little as possible of your own money and as much as possible of someone else's. This chapter has shown you who all those someones might be.

When you are buying through a real estate broker, he may offer to arrange financing for you. This can be a useful and timesaving service. But don't say yes in a hurry. Thank him and tell him you'll let him know shortly. Then make inquiries of your own to see whether better terms are available.

A Land Contract is the standard document for transferring ownership of real estate in most states. It can be a flexible and worthwhile tool for buying and selling, as we'll see when we get into Chapter XVIII on such creative financing.

On the other hand, in states where it isn't standard, a few lenders have used it to skin a careless buyer, by rigging it so that if he misses a payment for any reason whatsoever, he loses all he has paid and has no deed or equity. A California court outlawed this kind of contract a few years ago, but there are some states where it might stand up in court. Just be sure to get your attorney's help in writing up the transaction.

Here's a sample document which I often use in my own dealings:

LAND CONTRACT

THIS AGREEMENT, made and executed on the ___ day of _____, 19___, by and between _____ and _____, his wife, hereinafter called "Sellers," and _____ and _____, his wife, hereinafter called "Buyers," evidences that, whereas: Sellers are the owners of that certain improved real property, commonly known as _____,

> (include here the commonly known street address of property and the parcel, lot and tract numbers as described in the County Recorder's office)

Sellers desire to sell and Buyers desire to purchase the Subject Property on the terms and conditions herein described:

1. The purchase price of the Subject real and personal Property shall be the sum of Six Hundred Thousand Dollars ($600,000.00).
2. The said purchase price shall be payable as follows:
   a. The cash down payment shall be a sum of Thirty Thousand Dollars ($30,000.00). Payable on or before the close of escrow.
   b. The balance of the purchase price in the sum of Five Hundred Seventy Thousand Dollars ($570,000.00), bearing interest at the rate of 8% per annum on the unpaid balance, shall be payable as follows:

(1) Four Thousand Five Hundred Fifty Dollars ($4,550.00) or more per month beginning October 1, 1976, and continuing for each successive month thereafter, all due September 1, 1982. Said monthly payments shall be reduced by an amount equal to the amount of monthly payment made by Seller on encumbrances specified in paragraph four (4) which are to be assumed by the Buyers under the provisions for the release of properties as provided in paragraph six (6).

(2) Additional payments shall be paid as follows:
January 1, 1977—Six Thousand Dollars ($6,000.00)
January 1, 1978—Six Thousand Dollars ($6,000.00)
January 1, 1979—Six Thousand Dollars ($6,000.00)
January 1, 1980—Six Thousand Dollars ($6,000.00)
January 1, 1981—Six Thousand Dollars ($6,000.00)
(Many contracts do not reflect a balloon payment. A prudent investor will always total his principal set payments over the years to determine the remaining balance due at maturity of contract.)

(3) All payments shall be credited first to interest and then principal.

(4) A late fee of 10% of the monthly payment will be charged for all payments remaining unpaid after the tenth of the month in which due.

(5) It is understood that final payment of this contract is due on or before September 1, 1982. Buyers may extend the contract by notifying the Sellers in writing at least sixty (60) days prior to September 1, 1982, of their intention to extend the contract. If Buyers extend the contract, additional payments shall be made as follows:
September 1, 1982—Fifteen Thousand Dollars
($15,000.00)
September 1, 1983—Fifteen Thousand Dollars
($15,000.00)
Such payments shall apply to and reduce the contract balance as of the date of payment. It is also agreed that the amount of the monthly payments made by the Buyers shall be increased Five Hundred Dollars ($500.00) beginning with the October 1, 1982 payment.

3. If Sellers fail to discharge monthly obligations or encumbrances on the Subject Properties, taxes or other assessments for which monies have been collected, Buyers have the right to make any and all payments that will correct any arrearage. Buyers shall receive credit for such payment. Such credit shall reduce the immediate succeeding monthly obligations until such credit is exhausted.

4. Said properties are subject to the following encumbrances, which are

outstanding at the date of this agreement and will be paid by Seller according to their terms and as otherwise provided herein:

. . .

5. It is further agreed that after Buyers assume possession of the Subject Property, if the Buyers shall fail, for a period of thirty (30) days after the same shall have become due under the terms of this agreement, to pay the Seller any of the sums herein agreed to be paid monthly by Buyer, either as installments on account of principal, interest, or taxes and insurance, the Sellers, except for provisions for the release of properties described in paragraph six (6), shall be released from any further obligations in law or equity to convey Subject Properties and the Buyers shall quit all rights thereto and any and all payments theretofore made by the Buyer under this agreement shall be considered as rent and compensation for the use and occupancy of said premises and be retained by the Seller.

6. It is agreed that Buyers have the right to request and obtain deeded title to individual duplexes under the following terms and conditions:

  a. The "value" of the duplex released less the current balance of the applicable encumbrance described in paragraph four (4) will equal the amount of Buyers' equity required for and applied to the release of the specific duplex.

  b. It is agreed that the "value" of certain duplexes for release purposes is as follows:

    (1) One bedroom duplexes—Twenty Five Thousand Dollars ($25,000.00) more particularly described as Lots 4, 18, 41, 50, and 51.

    (2) Two bedroom duplexes—Thirty Five Thousand Dollars ($35,000.00) more particularly described as Lots 8, 9, 22, 23, and 24.

  c. At the date of release:

    (1) The Buyers shall assume or take "subject to" the applicable encumbrances on the property being released. The Buyers shall pay any assumption charges, and any title insurance charges shall be shared by Buyers and Sellers as specified in paragraph 20.

    (2) The contract balance shall be credited with an amount equal to the balance of the encumbrance. Interest as provided in paragraph 2(b) shall then cease on the credited amount. Prorations for accrued interest, if necessary, shall be provided.

  d. A release shall be permitted only if interest payments under the contract are current and principal payments under the contract have created Buyers' equity in an amount which:

    (1) Permits a reserve of Buyers' equity in the contract to no less than Fifteen Thousand Dollars ($15,000.00).

(2) Exceeds any Buyers' equity applied to any previously released duplexes and,

(3) Exceeds the Buyers' equity required for the current release as specified in paragraph 6(a).

e. Principal payments shall be all amounts paid by the Buyers (including down payment) that are credited to the original sales price but not including amounts credited representing encumbrances assumed as described in paragraph 6(c).

f. Buyers are allowed the right to make extra principal payments without penalty to permit release under the provisions of paragraph 6(d).

7. Sellers shall deposit Grant Deeds to said properties with a mutually agreed-upon trustee holder. Said Deeds shall be recorded when Buyers have performed according to the provisions of this agreement. Any costs of holding documents are to be incurred by the Buyers.

8. Seller warrants that all payments due under encumbrances specified in paragraph four (4) are current and that there are no additional liens against the property. Seller, after the date of this contract, shall not, in any manner, further encumber the Subject Property without the prior written consent of Buyers. Sellers shall be required to remove within a reasonable period of time any additional encumbrances upon the Subject Property that may arise without the written consent of the Buyer. Any damages incurred by the Buyer as result of such an encumbrance shall be the obligation of the Sellers.

9. Seller shall discharge, when due, all real and personal property taxes and all assessments levied directly against or upon the Subject Properties. Buyer shall pay to Seller monthly, at the time the aforementioned installment payments are made, a sum equal to a pro rata share of such taxes and assessments prorated on the basis of twelve (12) thirty- (30) day months per annum, commencing with the date of this contract.

10. Buyers during the continuance of this agreement shall insure and maintain at their own cost and expense a minimum of ($600,000.00) Six Hundred Thousand Dollars fire, and One Million Dollars ($1,000,000.00) liability insurance covering the building and improvements located on the Subject Property against loss by, but not limited to, fire or the elements, with loss payable to the following in this order: First lien holder of record, and Buyers. Buyers agree to continue in force insurance as is required by the existing lenders of record of the type and amount they require and in the name of the Sellers. In the event of a loss, and the insurance proceeds exceed the then existing loan balance of said contract of sale, Seller agrees to pay over to Buyers all additional proceeds. If Sellers' existing insurance policies are maintained Buyers shall pay to Sellers monthly, at the time the aforementioned installment payments are made, a

sum equal to a pro rata share of such insurance prorated on the basis of twelve (12) thirty- (30) day months per annum. Sellers in turn shall discharge the annual insurance obligations.

11. At close of escrow, any trust account balances are to be prorated with Seller receiving credit for any balances in the trust account. After initial prorating, trust account balances will be deemed to belong to Buyers.

12. Sellers, by the close of escrow, will execute a Bill of Sale, in Buyers' favor, for all furniture and personal property used in the operation of and located upon the Subject Property, and hereby warrant that they hold marketable title to said property, free and clear of any liens in favor of third parties. No furniture may be removed for a period of three years.

13. Upon the close of escrow, all prepaid rents, security payments and security deposits and any other concessions to current tenants then being held by or for Sellers shall be credited to Buyers in escrow. All prepaid expenses shall be prorated in escrow as of the close of escrow.

14. Sellers shall, upon the close of escrow, execute an assignment of rents of then-current tenants of the Subject Property to Buyers.

15. Buyers will cause, at their own cost and expense, the Subject Property to be inspected by a duly licensed pest control operator to determine the presence or absence of termites or other required corrective work. Sellers shall pay for or complete corrective measures of work required as a result of such inspection. Exceptions, if any, are to be approved in writing by Buyers prior to close of escrow.

16. Buyers shall not make any major alterations or additions to Subject Property during the term of this agreement without the prior written consent of Sellers, which consent shall not be unreasonably withheld.

17. Buyers shall, at their own cost and expense, keep this Subject Property and all its improvements located thereon in good repair and condition. Said condition shall be comparable with the condition of the property as of the date of this contract of sale.

18. Buyers shall indemnify and hold Sellers and the property of Sellers free and harmless from liability for any and all mechanic liens or other expenses or damages resulting from any renovations, alterations, repairs or other work placed on the Subject Property by or at the direction of Buyers.

19. During the term hereof, Buyers shall comply with any and all State, County, City or other governmental statutes, ordinances, rules and regulations of the use and occupancy of the Subject Property.

20. Upon the delivery of the deeds to the Subject Property to the Buyers, evidence of title is to be in the standard form, American Land Association, title insurance policy for the full purchase price from an insurer of Buyers' choice. Any actual Title Insurance costs incurred by the Buyers are to be shared by the Buyer and Sellers.

21. Buyers shall be entitled to possession of the Subject Property upon the close of escrow.
22. None of the rights and remedies provided herein shall be construed as a waiver of other rights or remedies as provided by law or equity.
23. In the event Sellers bring suit to enforce this agreement for damages resulting from any breach hereof, Sellers shall be entitled, in addition to other relief as may be granted, to a reasonable attorney's fee and costs for bringing such action.
24. This agreement shall be binding upon and shall inure to the benefits of the heirs, executors, administrators and assigns of the respective parties hereto.
25. Time is expressly declared to be of the essence of this contract.
26. Waiver of any breach of this agreement by Sellers shall not constitute a continuing waiver or a waiver of any subsequent breach, either of the same or of another provision of this agreement.
27. The date of the close of escrow shall be the First of September, 1982.
28. Buyers are fully aware of the contractual relationship with the Sellers, Buyers agree to avoid any comment, act, or statement that will jeopardize the existing financing.
29. Seller shall have the right to fully assign this contract of sale.
30. Buyers and Sellers agree that this agreement constitutes the sole and complete agreement between them respecting the Subject Property and correctly sets forth their rights and obligations to each other.

EXECUTED on the ___th day of August, 19___, at _____

(State)

_____

(Seller)

(Official Seal)

_____

(Seller)

On _____, 19___, before me _____ personally appeared _____, known to me to be the persons whose names are subscribed to the within instrument, and acknowledged that they executed the same.

_____

(Buyer)

(Official Seal)

_____

(Buyer)

On _____, 19___, before me _____ personally appeared _____, known to me to be the persons whose names are subscribed to the within instrument, and acknowledged that they executed the same.

REMEMBER THESE HIGH POINTS:

The seller may be your best source of financing. Feel him out.

When selling to, or buying from, a veteran, see if he can get government-insured financing.

Construction loans and FHA-insured mortgages have desirable features. Watch for possibilities of getting one.

XII *Tax Breaks in Real Estate Investing*

Few kinds of quality investment offer more tax advantages than real estate. You needn't be a tax expert to use these advantages for your own financial benefit. This chapter should give you most of the basic information you need. You can plan your buying, selling, and exchanging of property accordingly. (However, in complicated transactions, you'll probably want to doublecheck your thinking with a tax expert.)

The Internal Revenue Service got after a friend of mine when an article in *Time* magazine reported that he had netted a million dollars' profit in real estate, virtually tax free. The IRS didn't think this could be done legally.

The tax agents put him through a full audit, back to the first house he ever bought. Finally they conceded he was clean. Everything he had done to minimize or defer his taxes was perfectly legal. He had simply planned each transaction to use tax breaks that the law offered him. If he hadn't done this, his spendable profits might have been so much smaller that he would never have felt safe in giving up the regular paycheck he was getting.

We briefly considered, earlier in this book, how to cut taxes by using the depreciation allowance. We'll get down to more details on depreciation later, since it offers so many goodies. But first you need to understand the basic principles determining how income from real estate is computed and taxed.

The tax consequences of a realty investment begin with the purchase. How much did you pay for the property? The tax collector will want to know. Your cost includes not only the actual purchase price but most of the other costs involved in obtaining title. This amount (also called book value) is the starting point for determining the property's tax basis. And the same amount is likewise the starting point for computing your depreciation deduction, as well as your profit or loss when you sell the property.

So sharpen up your pencil and keep accurate records when you buy. Forget the stated purchase price except as a part of your actual outlay in buying the property. IRS Document 5447 says:

. . . items which are charged to you at settlement or closing are added to the cost . . . and are part of your original basis. These items include attorney fees, abstract fees, utility connection charges, surveys, transfer taxes, title insurance, and any amounts that may be owed by the seller but which you agreed to pay, such as back taxes.

You can also add, as part of your cost basis, various expenditures that may come later. You can add money you spend for improving the property (but not what you spend for normal repairs and maintenance). Blacktopping what had been a gravel driveway, putting a light in the backyard, landscaping, adding a fence, putting in tennis courts or a swimming pool—all such outlays add to the permanent value of the property. Therefore they should be included in your cost basis. You "capitalize" them, as money men say.

If the city assesses you for street improvements, save the bills and canceled checks—because special assessments also are improvements. If you pay a lawyer to get an assessment reduced, you can add his fee to your cost basis.

If you're following my formula, buying houses and apartment buildings and improving them for resale, you'll net a profit each time you sell. But the higher your cost basis, the smaller your taxable profit will be on the sale. (In passing, it's also well to remember that your cost basis—not your purchase price—determines how much loss you can claim on your tax return if the property should be partially or totally destroyed by fire, earthquake or any other casualty.)

On the other hand, your cost basis shrinks as you claim the depreciation the tax authorities allow you to take (since you are telling them, when you record this depreciation, that the property has shrunk in value).

Ordinary income or capital gain: all taxable income falls basically into one of these two categories. The bite of federal income taxation cuts most deeply into ordinary income. Taxes usually are lighter on the other kind, so you need to be very clear about which is which.

Ordinary income is the kind most of us are quite familiar with: The compensation someone pays us for our services, whether in salaries, wages, tips, fees, commissions, or even prizes we win in a contest. The interest and dividends credited to us, even if we don't cash them or draw them out of the account. Our net profits from our business or profession. Anything we may win by gambling. Rents we collect from property we own less deductions for expenses. We must pay taxes on all such income at so-called ordinary income tax rates. These rates usually range from a low of 14 percent to a high of 70 percent.

Capital gain is income too, at least on paper. But it is the special kind of income that we get by selling a capital asset for more than it cost us.

What is a capital asset? There are many kinds. In general, they include all properties that you own if you're not in the business of buying and selling such properties. Thus stocks and bonds are capital assets in the hands of a doctor, a housewife, or anyone else holding them for investment. But a stock broker can't consider the securities he owns as capital assets, if they are simply inventory items held for sale in the ordinary course of his business.

Likewise, real estate you own but don't use in your trade or business is a capital asset unless you're a dealer in real estate—as distinguished from an *investor* in real estate. Who is a dealer? Are you? The question could ultimately go to the tax court, in case the Internal Revenue Service disputes your answer. But if you follow the general guidelines set down by the IRS, there'll probably be no disputes.

If you don't buy and sell real estate continually, but just do it occasionally, you're generally not classed as a dealer. However, if you buy and sell too frequently, hold properties for too short a time, or get too big a share of your income from real estate transactions, you could become a dealer in the eyes of the law. Then your realty profits would have to be reported as ordinary income, not capital gain. Therefore, if you become so active that you feel you're getting close to the borderline, consult a tax attorney.

The difference is important because the tax rules are different for capital gains. The tax you'll have to pay will depend on how long you've owned the property—whether the gain was "short term" or "long term."

If it is short term, you'll have to pay taxes on the full amount at ordinary income tax rates. But if it is long term, you get a break: you'll generally have to pay on only half the amount (subject to certain considerations for other provisions of the tax laws).

The Tax Reform Act of 1976 lengthened the period that can legally be classed as "long" term. The act says that capital assets must have been held for more than nine months to qualify the gain (or loss) as long term if the property is sold or exchanged in 1977. In later years this period becomes twelve months instead of nine. (The holding period was more than six months before 1977.)

In other words, the gain (or loss) will be short term if the holding period for a sale or exchange in 1977 was nine months or less; in later years it is twelve months or less.

This means that when you contemplate a sale or taxable exchange at a profit, you'll want to consider carefully whether better timing might give you a substantial tax break.

The treatment of capital losses isn't very sympathetic. If you suffer a net loss from sale of capital assets, you'll at best get a tax credit for the loss on the same basis you'd have to pay taxes on a gain. (If the loss is a long-term one, you'll get credit for only half of it—in line with the philosophy that lets you pay taxes on only half a long-term gain.) At worst, you'll get no tax benefit at all (as when the loss is sustained on property used as a personal residence).

Furthermore, no matter how big your net capital loss is in any particular year, there's a definite limit to how much of it you can use to offset ordinary income in that year. The maximum you'll be able to deduct is $2,000 in 1977, but will be $3,000 in 1978 and thereafter. There's one small consolation: you can carry forward the rest of the loss as an offset against future net capital gains plus not more than the stipulated amounts of ordinary income in each future year.

Fortunately, the kind of property you'll usually buy when you invest in rental income real estate isn't likely to be classed as a capital asset. It falls into a different category—"real property and property subject to depreciation used by a taxpayer in his trade or business." This means that it is regarded as a noncapital asset rather than a capital asset, and gets more favorable tax treatment. As with capital assets, you pay taxes on only half your gain when you sell it at a profit after the minimum holding period. But, unlike capital assets, your losses on such sales can be deducted from other income in full and without limit, regardless of how long the property is held. This makes the red ink quite useful sometimes.

By timing the sales of several properties, you may save yourself many tax dollars, if you don't mind incurring losses on some of the sales. By making the profitable sales in one year and the loss sales in another year, you can get capital gain treatment on the profitable sales and take full ordinary income deductions on the losses. This is because all your long-term sales made during the year are combined for tax purposes. If the combination adds up to a net profit, it is taxed at capital gain rates. If it adds up to a net loss, the loss is fully deductible against other income. Therefore you come out ahead if you don't take your losses in the same year in which you take your profits. Contrariwise, if you have a very prosperous year and want to cut your tax on ordinary income, it may be advisable to sell enough of your loss property to at least partially offset it.

Be careful about the holding period, because IRS auditors draw the line very sharply. An error of one day can make all the difference between short term and long term. The holding period for real property normally begins the day after title passes. From that date, the number of months is figured by the calendar. So if you buy on February 2, the nine months end on November 2, even though some of these months are shorter than others. If you want the gain to be treated as long term, you must wait until November to transfer the title.

If you take possession of property before title passes, your holding period begins the day after you take possession. But if you, as owner, let someone else move in under an option-to-purchase agreement, your holding period doesn't end until you actually sell the property.

If you're making a sale close to the borderline and there's any doubt about the length of the holding period, check with a tax consultant in advance.

When you sell your home at a profit, you can defer or avoid any capital gains tax if, within eighteen months, you buy and live in another house costing as much or more than the price you got for the old house.

Furthermore, if you see a house you'd like to move into, you needn't wait to buy until after you sell. You can purchase the new house (or co-op or condominium) any time within eighteen months before you sell—and still sidestep any gains tax.

You get the same tax break if you build a new house. However, you must start building it within eighteen months before or after you sell your old home. And you must occupy it as your principal residence not later than two years after the sale.

Notice the words "principal residence." They're vital. If either the old home or the new one is a secondary residence, such as a beach cottage or a mountain cabin that you occupy only now and then, you'll be taxed on any profit.

If you're over sixty-five, you get another tax break in selling your home. You can move to a rental unit, or move in with relatives (making no new buy) and still pay no capital gains tax on any gain attributable to the first $35,000 of the sale price less selling costs. If the net amount of the sale is greater than $35,000, part of the gain is still excluded from income for tax purposes, depending on the actual net sales price.

While you're under sixty-five, the capital gains tax on any profits from sale of your home (or a series of profits on a series of sales) has only been postponed. Many people sell one house only to turn around and buy another; their capital gains are paper profits instead of cash in the bank. They must report the capital gain but needn't pay the tax until they sell the final house in what might be a chain of ever-more-expensive homes. Each one adds its bit to the total of the potentially taxable gain that is adding up.

What happens if you sell a house and don't buy another at an equal or higher price? Then you'll be taxed on your accumulated gains to the extent the purchase price of the new residence is less than the sales price of the old.

At death, however, if you still own a home, it passes to your heirs at a minimum of its fair market value as of December 31, 1976, with no liability or potential liability to either you or them for any previously untaxed gains to that point. If your heirs should later sell the home at this value, there would be no gain for income tax purposes— and therefore no tax on the sale! (Special rules apply that will increase the tax basis at which your heirs inherit your home if your estate is valued at less than $60,000.) Other capital assets you leave to your heirs at your death are subject to essentially the same income tax rules.

Here are a couple of fine points worth remembering about the over-sixty-five rule. In order to get this tax break, the seller must have owned the property and used it as his principal residence for at least five of the eight years before the sale. The property needn't be the owner's principal residence on the date of sale, and the five years needn't be consecutive. Moreover, short absences for vacations and the like won't count, even if the place is rented during the absences; what counts is the period during which the house was the owner's "principal residence."

However, a seller can get this benefit only once in a lifetime. If you're over sixty-five and expect to switch homes a few more times before you die, you can bypass the exemption for age, saving it for a later sale. You'll still be deferring all tax for capital gain, under the other rule mentioned—the replacement-of-residence rule.

An installment sale is a way to spread the taxability of a gain over a period of years—usually cutting your taxes at the same time you're deferring them. You'll generally be much better off taxwise if you don't have to report more than a small fraction of a big gain in any one year. Moreover, picking up the full profit—and paying the full tax —in the year of sale might confront you with a bigger tax bill than the down payment you'd be receiving.

Letting a buyer pay you in installments lets you spread your profit over the installment payments you receive. You report each year only that percentage of your gain that principal payments received bear to the whole amount of principal being paid. In other words, each installment on principal is reported as a separate capital gain. This is one of the most common methods of postponing the taxability of capital gains on realty sales.

But you must make sure you follow the rules. A slight deviation and you're disqualified.

A transaction qualifies as an installment sale *only* when the buyer is indebted directly to you for all or part of the selling price. If he finances the purchase through a third party such as a bank, you can't report it to the IRS as an installment sale.

Therefore, if the buyer can't get financing from an outside source, and you're willing to extend credit to him over two or more years, an installment sale is logical. However, even where a buyer can finance the purchase, you may want to arrange an installment sale. You can do this by taking back a mortgage yourself, payable over more than one tax year.

The main requirement for installment reporting of sales has to do with the amount of the down payment, and any other payments received in the year of sale. All these payments, called "initial payments," must not exceed 30 percent of the total selling price.

"Selling price" is usually the gross contract price. Commissions and other selling expenses are not deducted, even though these do reduce your net profit.

Payments in the year of sale include all payments made by the buyer that year. You include all cash and property received from him during the year. You also include any option payment made in an earlier year, if it becomes part of the down payment according to the terms of the contract. If the buyer pays off any liens on the property during the year of sale, these payments are included too.

You must also include a buyer's note payable on demand or payable during the first year, even if he never actually makes these payments. But you don't include as initial payments his notes or other evidence of indebtedness that come due in a later year, because the law regards these as merely promises, not payments.

Amounts put in escrow aren't considered initial payments, if they are out of your control and not due to be paid to you until a following year. Nor is an existing mortgage taken over by the buyer classed as an initial payment if it is in an amount that does not exceed the seller's tax basis.

However, part of an existing mortgage will be included in the initial payments if the mortgage is for more than the tax basis of the property (that is, your cost basis as seller). For example, suppose you've reported that your total cost of acquiring the property, for tax purposes, is $30,000 but there is a $35,000 mortgage on it. If the buyer assumes this mortgage, he'll be considered as adding $5,000 to his initial payments to you.

To be sure the sale will qualify for installment treatment under the 30 percent rule, you'd better allow for some margin of error in your calculations. This is why we often see down payments advertised at 29 percent or less.

If you do make an error and take more than 30 percent, try to return the excess to the buyer before the end of the tax year. Tax courts have held that such a correction to the original transaction can still qualify it as an installment sale.

One error in your calculations might be charging no interest, or interest of less than 6 percent on payments due in more than one year in an installment sale where the sales price is more than $3,000. The United States Treasury assumes that unless an interest rate of at least 6 percent is stipulated, all payments you are to receive on your installment note more than six months after the sale in realty include interest at a discount rate of 7 percent compounded semiannually. It figures money paid in installments is worth that much to most people these days. Therefore, it arbitrarily "imputes" this interest into your installment contract. The new rate will reduce the sales price of the contract as viewed by the tax man, because it means that part of the principal due on the contract is considered to be interest. The lower sales price may mean that your initial payments are bigger than the

30 percent limit, and the transaction is disqualified for installment treatment.

You can also be disqualified if the buyer unexpectedly chooses to pay off more than 30 percent of his debt to you in the year of sale. You'd better write it into the sales contract that he can't do this—or that if he does the money is to be paid into a trust account that you can't touch until at least the following year. If you overlook this provision, and the buyer tries to prepay, return the money.

If you want more cash than you'll get from initial payments of 30 percent, is there any way to qualify the deal for tax treatment as an installment sale? Yes, there is.

Ask the buyer to give you notes, payable in later years, for part of what he owes you. Then you can sell these notes, or pledge them as security for a loan. Even if you do this the very next day after the sale, you're still within the law because these notes—or the cash into which you convert them—are not legally considered as part of the initial payments.

Of course you'll pay taxes at capital gains rates on the amount you realize by selling the notes. Therefore it's usually better to put them up as collateral for a loan for some third party. You don't pay tax on money you borrow, even though you do pay interest—which is tax-deductible.

Be careful in your computations if the buyer takes over an existing mortgage and gives you a second mortgage. Any excess of the old mortgage over your cost basis will be treated the same as cash. Adding this to the initial payments might run them up over 30 percent. No installment sale.

Also be careful if a buyer wants to throw in some bonds or other securities, counting them as part of the payment that will be due in the second year or later. If you accept them in the first year, their fair market value is counted as part of the initial payment, regardless of whether or not you sell them. (This situation often comes up when you sell property to a corporation. The company may offer to sweeten the deal with debentures, corporate bonds, or other paper that is evidence of its indebtedness. If they're readily tradable in an established securities market, the IRS treats them as payments made in the year of sale.)

However, you can accept the bonds or whatever they are, and still qualify the transaction as an installment sale. Here's how. Suppose the securities are worth $15,000 and the buyer wants to give you a

$60,000 promissory note for the balance due. Just have him write his note for $75,000, secured in part by the pledged securities. Then the tax man can't consider them as part of the initial payments.

Sometimes, instead of reporting a sale on the installment basis, you may be better off taking the whole gain in the year of sale. Maybe your income that year is much lower than in other years, so that you're temporarily in a low enough tax bracket to bring your tax on the gains down to a nominal level.

Another way to postpone taxes is through a deferred-payment sale. You can use this type of transaction when the initial payments are more than 30 percent.

Although payments are deferred over a period of years, you must report the entire capital gain in the year of sale. However, the gain you report that year may not be the full amount you hope to gain later, if the market value of whatever the buyer gives you is less than face value.

The buyer may give you notes, contracts, personal property or evidence of personal obligations. These are included in the initial payments, at their fair market value. If their face value is more than this, the excess is what you defer.

Of course this usually doesn't give you as big a tax break as an installment sale, because it increases the percentage of the total profit that will be taxed in the year of sale. But if there's no way to figure the fair market value of the buyer's obligations, the transaction is considered open and continuing, and you don't pay tax until you convert the paper into an actual profit.

How is fair market value determined? Obviously this is the sticky question on which the whole transaction turns, for tax purposes.

The IRS will challenge a claim that the buyer's notes or other consideration have little or no market value. It presumes that you have received full value. So it's up to you to prove the actual market value —or lack of value—of what you've received. In one case when a seller reported that the second mortgage he took back was worth less than it promised to pay, he brought in no evidence of this, and was required to report it at face value.

If the buyer is solvent and his promise to pay is unconditional, and if it is the kind of promise that is frequently transferred to lenders at a normal discount, then the courts consider that his promise to pay is equivalent to actual payment to the extent of the discounted value.

However, here are some cases in which the courts held that the buyer's obligations were unsalable and therefore had no market value:

1. The buyer gave non-negotiable promissory notes; no bank would buy them, even at a discount, nor accept them as collateral for a loan.
2. The buyer deposited notes in escrow for future payment to the seller.
3. The only evidence of the buyer's debt was the contract of sale; he gave no notes, bonds, or other evidence of indebtedness.
4. The contract of sale didn't commit the buyer to make any payments after the initial payment; the only penalty for non-payment was forfeiture of the payments already made.

And here are some cases in which the IRS (or the courts) agreed that the seller could defer reporting income until payment was actually received, because the buyer's obligations depended on outside factors that couldn't be valued:

1. The buyer promised to make payments out of the future earnings of his company.
2. The buyer promised to pay in shares of a mining company; he would pay a share each time the mines produced a certain number of tons of ore.
3. The promise was to pay out of future royalties on patented machinery.
4. Payments went into escrow until the purchasing company made enough profits to retire its preferred stock.
5. Second mortgages bought at a discount were highly speculative, and full payment was always uncertain. In such a deal, you pay no tax until the mortgage payments (or their sale) bring you more money than your cost basis.

When you do get the IRS to agree that the paper you've accepted is worth less than its face value, you'll later pay tax at ordinary income rates (instead of the lower capital gains rate) if you eventually convert the paper into more money than you said it was worth. That is, you'll be taxed at full rates on the excess above the figure agreed upon by the IRS of what you received over what you estimated as the fair market value.

But this holds true only if an individual signed the promise to pay.

If a corporation gave you evidence of its indebtedness, you'll be taxed only at capital gains rates if you hold the paper more than six months and if it wasn't originally issued to you at a discount. (This would mean that you hadn't undervalued the paper, or reported it as worth less than its face value, when you reported the price at which you sold the property.)

Tax-deferred exchanges of real estate are becoming more common, as brokers and investors awaken to the advantages. In Chapter XX, we'll take a long, detailed look at them. For now, let's just consider their tax aspects.

Under section 1031 of the Internal Revenue Code, you neither incur liability for taxes on gain nor receive tax credit for loss if property held for productive use in a trade or business or for investment is exchanged "solely" for property "of like kind." The potential tax on the gain is postponed until you sell the new property at a price exceeding your tax basis. Moreover, as with a personal residence, you and your heirs escape any income taxes on the gain if you die while still holding title to the property, and they get to figure gain on a tax basis stepped up at least to its fair market value on December 31, 1976, if they subsequently sell.

The definition of "like kind" is broad. An owner of a commercial building trading his building for an apartment complex, a corporation trading industrial property for unimproved land, and an apartment house owner exchanging his apartments for a farm would all qualify. It makes no difference whether the real estate is productive or unproductive, improved or unimproved, or whether it is residential, commercial, industrial, or agricultural. It can't be a property "held primarily for resale" (dealer property), and it can't be a personal residence, since these are not considered properties "held for investment."

Whether an exchange that otherwise meets the requirements will be completely tax-free or not depends on whether either party receives any consideration other than the property "of like kind" that is being acquired. If in a "like kind" exchange you receive cash, securities, or any property of a different kind in addition to the property "of like kind," you've received "boot" and will be taxed on your gain to the extent of such "boot." If you trade mortgaged property, the mortgage released is treated as boot—whether or not the other party assumes it or takes the property subject to it. When there are mortgages on both properties, one is netted against the other, and the party relieved of the larger mortgage in favor of the smaller must report this benefit as boot.

Boot is often given or received to equalize matters in exchanges. One party may have to pay some tax even though the other gets off tax-free. There are ways of minimizing boot, however, and the tax liability that goes along with it, as we'll see in Chapter XX on exchanges.

REMEMBER THESE HIGH POINTS:

For tax purposes, the cost of a property includes all costs involved in obtaining title. This amount is also the starting point for computing your depreciation deduction.

You can also add, as part of your cost basis, various expenditures you make to improve the property.

The higher your cost basis, the smaller your taxable profit.

You can save taxes by timing sales properly. Make sure you have held it more than nine months if you sell at a profit before January 1, 1978, and twelve months if you sell thereafter.

An installment sale can spread your profit over several years, and probably spread your taxes too. To qualify, make sure the down payment is less than 30 percent.

When the down payment is more than 30 percent, you may still get a tax break by accepting notes or contracts from the buyer.

One of the best ways to save on taxes is to exchange property rather than sell it.

XIII Mortgages Can Be Tax Shelters

Mortgages can be tax shelters, if you use them protectively. Or they can add to your tax bill if you don't know how to use them.

There are no immediate tax consequences when you negotiate a mortgage, as either borrower or lender. The consequences come when you sell a mortgage or sell property.

You pay no tax when you borrow money, of course. You may be able to borrow $80,000 on property for which your cost basis is only $20,000. Thereby you would realize $60,000 more than your cost—and you wouldn't be liable for any tax on the $60,000.

You could then take the full $60,000 (minus processing costs) and invest it in another rental property. So you would have two properties working for you instead of one. You've acquired a property with tax-free money! Furthermore, it could be a property worth far more than the $60,000 you've unfrozen. With this amount for a down payment, you might buy a $500,000 apartment complex.

Obviously you're much farther ahead than if you had simply sold your first building to get capital for further investment. You would have parted with the property and would be facing a substantial tax bill for the capital gain.

Mortgages are a handy multi-purpose tool for acquiring more property. You can acquire the property either by giving the seller a purchase-money mortgage, or by assuming an existing mortgage, or by taking the property subject to an existing mortgage. Whichever way you arrange it, the amount represented by the mortgage becomes a part of your cost basis for the property you're buying.

This rule applies even in figuring depreciation, as we saw earlier. It's one of the many tax advantages you get by investing in real estate. When you buy a building for little or no down payment, giving a big mortgage for the balance, you take a big tax deduction for depreciation on the total value of the building.

When you sell a mortgaged property, there's a different way to shelter your profit from heavy taxes: pay off the mortgage first. It's easier than you might think, and more advantageous. Let's look at the difference in tax consequences.

Remember that when you sell a mortgaged property, and the buyer takes the mortgage off your hands, you must figure the mortgage into your sales price when reporting your capital gain (or loss). So if you sell a building having a cost basis of $10,000 for $90,000 with the buyer assuming your $60,000 mortgage and giving you $10,000 in cash plus a $20,000 purchase-money mortgage, you'll have an $80,000 gain to report and pay tax on in the year of sale. This is because the IRS would consider that you received initial payments totaling more than 30 percent of the sales price. These initial payments would be deemed to consist not only of the $10,000 in cash, but also the $50,000 difference between the $60,000 mortgage assumed by the buyer and your $10,000 cost basis. You would have disqualified yourself from reporting the gain on an installment basis and might very well end up having to pay a capital gains tax that would be far bigger than the down payment you'd be getting.

But now look what happens if you pay off that $60,000 mortgage and take back an $80,000 purchase mortgage from the buyer.

It's all the same to him, because he's borrowing $80,000 either way. But it's very different for you. Because this way you qualify the transaction as an installment sale. (Just be sure not to collect more than 30 percent of the $90,000 in the year you sell.) If you collect only the $10,000 down payment, you pay tax on only one-ninth of your $80,000 gain that year! The remainder of your tax liability on the gain will be put off to future years—and will be taxed each year only to the extent you receive additional payments on the principal.

"But wait!" you may be mentally protesting as you read this. "You said it would be easy to pay off my $60,000 mortgage. Where am I going to find that much cash?"

Borrow it. You'll probably have no trouble doing so. You're receiving a new $80,000 mortgage, remember? It's good security for a long-term bank loan. If you pledge it as collateral (hypothecate it, as bankers say), you can probably get most if not all the $60,000 you will need to pay off the mortgage you are replacing. Naturally, you'd work out the details in advance with the bank and the buyer. Then the whole transaction could be handled in escrow without a hitch.

If you do set things up this way, try to get the borrower to agree to an interest rate on the purchase-money mortgage higher than the rate you must pay on your loan at the bank. Then his mortgage payments will more than cover your payments on the bank loan, leaving you with a sweet little surplus. Banks are generally happy to handle all the details of collection, accounting, and payment in such matters, and credit the surplus to a seller's account.

To repeat, you pay no tax on money you acquire by borrowing. Borrowing against a mortgage (that is, hypothecating it or turning it over to the bank to hold as security against your debt) has no more tax consequence than any other kind of borrowing. Do you begin to see what a useful financial tool a mortgage can be?

However, you must be sure to understand that a mortgage can make you liable for taxes if you sell it, or trade it for something else. The fair market value of whatever you get for the mortgage, minus the cost basis of the mortgage itself, is taxable as capital gain.

This means you can't make a tax-free exchange of a mortgage for real estate. Mortgages and real property are not "of like kind" in the eyes of the revenuers.

Depreciation means big tax savings too, as mentioned earlier, in Chapter II. And it involves no cash outlay. Having read this far, you probably feel familiar enough with real estate investment concepts to take a closer look at various tax benefits available through depreciation—that is, through the tax deductions you're allowed to take for the theoretical or actual depreciation of your property.

Depreciation is simply a loss in value. However, depreciation in the tax sense is different (and more imaginary, sometimes) from depreciation in the physical or economic sense. Economic depreciation is a drop in value because some outside change has caused a drop in the demand for a property. If a glue factory were built across the street from your apartment building, you might have to lower your rents or lose tenants. This would be a case of economic depreciation. Physical depreciation is easier to measure. It happens as your property becomes less valuable because of wear and tear, the actions of the weather, structural aging such as cracks in the plaster, or whatever.

The tax people generally do not take account of economic depreciation, unless you can prove that it will shorten the "useful life" of your property. However, they do recognize that all structures and fixtures are bound to deteriorate physically as time passes. So they allow a tax deduction for physical depreciation.

They figure that the useful life of a new apartment building is about forty years; of a house, about forty-five. At the end of that period of time, in theory, your building will collapse into rubble and become worthless.

Therefore they allow you to take an annual deduction from your taxes to compensate you for losing part of the value of your building. If your apartment building is estimated to have a life of forty years, you can recover a minimum of one-fortieth of your total cost (including the mortgage) each year as a "depreciation allowance."

We all know of apartment buildings that are still useful and profitable after much more than forty years. That's okay. Congress has said that you can nevertheless charge off your building investment in its entirety, over whatever is its estimated useful life. For example, you might prove that your property isn't as well built as others of similar nature, and will therefore wear out sooner. Or you might convince the IRS that the property will be rentable at a profit for only a few more years because the neighborhood has been rezoned and factories are being built around it. If the tax men agree that the building can be operated profitably for only fifteen years, they'll let you take an annual depreciation deduction of at least one-fifteenth of your cost basis. Or they'll let you compute the deduction in certain other ways if you wish. We'll get to these in a moment.

It makes no difference how large or small a down payment you make to acquire the property. The only important figure is your cost basis. You can take the same depreciation allowance even if you made no down payment at all.

Depreciation is considered a business expense. So you can take the deduction only on property held for use in your trade or business or for the production of income. You can't claim depreciation on property bought for your personal use, such as your residence (although an office in your home and whatever else you use for your income-producing activities can be depreciated).

To be depreciable, property must have a prospective limited useful life. Land, because of its essentially unlimited life, doesn't qualify for depreciation. This is logical enough. If your apartment building becomes worthless, you can always use the land for a parking lot or some other purpose, or simply hold it as an investment for possible sale at a later date.

However, the cost of landscaping may be a depreciable item. If you cover the land with paved walks or tennis courts, if you dig it out for sewers or for a swimming pool, if you plant trees on it—all these improvements to the land have a limited life, so you claim depreciation allowances on them if you know their cost. Just be ready to prove, if challenged, that they add to the value of the property. And be ready with a sensible estimate of their life expectancy.

Maybe you've bought property and you don't know how much of the price was for the structure, how much for the land under it. You can get an idea from the property tax assessor, or from an independent appraiser, or from real estate people who know the values established by sales of similar property nearby. Or in some areas you can simply prorate your cost basis of the property as per the tax assessor's ratio of land and improvement values.

Making maximum use of depreciation allowances is one of the important keys to profits in real estate investment. Many investors judge a deal heavily on its possibilities for depreciation deductions.

There are three basic methods that are commonly used to compute depreciation deduction on real estate: straight-line, declining-balance, and sum of the years' digits. You can choose among them within certain limits. And you needn't use the same method for all your realty assets. Let's consider them one at a time.

The straight-line method of depreciation. You write off the depreciation in equal amounts over the useful life of the asset. This method may be used for any new or used tangible, depreciable property, regardless of when it was acquired or the length of its useful life.

To use the method, you take an annual deduction for your tax basis after subtracting the property's estimated salvage value, if any. Thus the formula looks like this:

$$\text{Depreciation deduction} = \frac{\text{Cost minus salvage value}}{\text{Estimated life}}$$

For example, if you paid a total of $27,000 for a property and decided by looking at the life of similar property that yours would be usable for 25 years, and if you estimated that it would bring $2,000 at the end of that time, the difference is $25,000. You simply divide this by 25 years. And then you know that you can take a $1,000 deduction per year, each and every year until 25 years have elapsed.

If you want to think of this in terms of a percentage, just divide the 25 years into 100 percent. The total value of your property less its salvage value represents the 100 percent. Divide it by 25 years, and you find that you're writing off 4 percent of your property's value every year. It's the same thing, because 4 percent of $25,000 is $1,000. Or if you prefer fractions, you can say that you're depreciating $\frac{1}{25}$ of the value per year.

This straight-line method is just an accounting concept. It depends mostly on a guess that the property will depreciate at a steady rate throughout its estimated life. This may not be very scientific. But the IRS says it's fair enough, and many taxpayers use it because of its simplicity.

We mentioned salvage value. Maybe you're wondering how you can estimate your property's future worth at the end of its usable life. You need a crystal ball to look twenty-five years ahead and figure the salvage value. Since this seems so difficult, many people just shrug and say there will be no salvage value. The IRS probably won't object unless your cost basis is up in six figures, or the estimated life is usually short.

In fact, when a building is no longer usable, you may have to pay money to get it torn down. You're entitled to figure this in, if you're putting salvage value on the property. For example, you may guess that the junk men will pay $3,000 for the materials in the hypothetical building mentioned above, but that the wreckers will charge $1,000 to knock it apart. Subtracting $1,000 from $3,000 gives the $2,000 salvage value used in our formula.

The declining-balance method permits you to take larger depreciation deductions in the earlier years in which you own a property. The deductions steadily dwindle, however, until eventually the amount of depreciation that can be taken is smaller than you could take under the straight-line method. For this reason, the taxpayer who selects declining balance may want to switch in a later year to the straight-line method.

Declining-balance depreciation can be at double the straight-line rate, 150%, or 125%, depending on the kind of property, whether it has previously been used, and certain other considerations laid down by the tax laws. Since this method never fully depreciates the property, salvage value usually does not have to be considered.

Under the declining-balance method, the first year's depreciation is the straight-line rate multiplied by 200%, 150%, or 125%, whichever rate you select among those for which the property qualifies. To compute the second year's depreciation, however, is a bit more complicated. You must first adjust your tax basis by subtracting from the original basis of the asset the first year's depreciation. The result multiplied by the depreciation rate is the deduction you take for the second year.

Confused? Well, here's an example. Assume we have a property with a tax basis of $25,000 to be depreciated over twenty-five years at a rate of double the straight-line rate. (The same basic principle would apply if either the 150% or 125% declining-balance rate were used.)

The first year we'll claim twice the 4% rate of depreciation we would be able to claim on a straight-line basis, or $2,000 instead of $1,000. This would reduce our tax basis for the next year's computation to $23,000. That year we would again take twice the straight-line rate of depreciation (instead of 4%) but this time on $23,000 instead of $25,000. This would result in a depreciation deduction of $1,840 the second year and reduce our basis to $21,160 for the third-year computation.

We would then continue doing this year after year, with steadily decreasing amounts of depreciation being allowed, unless and until we decide to switch to a straight-line basis for the remaining undepreciated value of the asset.

The sum-of-the-years'-digits method is another method for accelerating depreciation. It gives you bigger deductions in the earlier years than the straight-line and 125% and 150% declining-balance methods but not as big as the 200% declining balance.

To use this method, you add up the total of the digits for the number of years in the asset's useful life. If its life is 10 years, for example, you add the digits 1 through 10, for a total of 55. Each year your depreciation deduction bears the same relationship to your original depreciable cost as the remaining years of useful life at the beginning of the year bear to the sum of the years' digits. (Steady, now, I'll untangle that with an example.)

In the case of a 10-year useful life, you start out with 10 years to go. So your depreciation the first year is 10 divided by the sum of the years' digits (55), times the cost basis of the asset (less its salvage value). The next year you have only nine years left. So your depreciation goes down to $\frac{9}{55}$ of this same cost-less-salvage-value figure. The year after that it would be $\frac{8}{55}$, and so on until the end of the 10th year, when the asset value would be written down to its salvage value and no further depreciation could be taken.

If you own several different properties for which you wish to use this method, here's a quick way to figure what the denominator of your fraction (the sum of the years' digits) will be for each. Just multiply the number of separate digits by the middle number in the series. For example, if you want to depreciate the property over five years, you'll have five numbers in the series, and the middle digit is 3. So you multiply 3 × 5. It equals 15. So does 1 + 2 + 3 + 4 + 5. Or if you're using ten years, there are ten separate digits, and their middle point is halfway between 5 and 6 or 5.5. So you multiply 5.5 × 10 = 55. When you have a long series this saves a lot of tiresome addition. To find the denominator for 25 years, you can then compute to find that the middle number in the series is 13. Therefore 13 × 25 gives you 325, which is the same as the total of all numbers in the series from 1 through 25.

Using sum-of-the-years'-digits depreciation on a property with a 10-year life, you get approximately ten times as big a deduction the first year as the tenth. On a property with a cost basis of $10,000, your first-year deduction would be $1,818.18 and the final year would be $181.82. The effect is a higher charge against revenue in the early years and a lower charge against revenue later. Since maintenance expenses tend to get bigger with the passing years, the combination of decreasing charges for depreciation and increasing charges for maintenance will approximately level off the total annual costs for these two big items.

The following table shows the comparative effect of each of the three basic methods of depreciation when applied to a $1,000 asset with a useful life of 10 years. We'll say salvage value is zero for the sake of simplicity.

You'll note that it pays to shift from the 200% declining-balance method to the straight-line method during the fifth year and from the sum-of-the-years'-digits method a year later. The break-even points would be at the same relative points in any asset's projected useful life. Unless you switch, the rate of recovery of the asset's value will continue to decline.

Moreover, if you use the declining-balance method, you'll be unable to write the asset's value off completely over its useful life. A switch from any accelerated method to the straight-line method can be made without approval of the tax authorities at any time. Switches from straight-line to accelerated methods or from one accelerated method to another can be made only with the written approval of the IRS, however.

Before the Tax Reform Act was passed in 1969, real estate inves-

| Year | Straight-Line | | 200% Declining-Balance | | Sum-of-Years'-Digits | |
	Annual Deduction	*Cumulative Cost Recovery*	*Annual Deduction*	*Cumulative Cost Recovery*	*Annual Deduction*	*Cumulative Cost Recovery*
1	$100	$100	$200	$200	$182	$182
2	$100	$200	$160	$360	$164	$346
3	$100	$300	$128	$488	$145	$491
4	$100	$400	$102	$590	$127	$618
5	$100	$500	$ 82	$672	$109	$727
6	$100	$600	$ 66	$738	$ 91	$818
7	$100	$700	$ 52	$790	$ 73	$891
8	$100	$800	$ 42	$832	$ 55	$946
9	$100	$900	$ 34	$866	$ 36	$982
10	$100	$1,000	$ 27	$893	$ 18	$1,000

tors could use accelerated depreciation methods virtually without restriction. Since then, however, they've been more cramped. The 200% declining-balance and sum-of-the-years'-digits methods may now be used only for new residential rental property and only if you are its original user. You are considered an original user if you bought the property directly from the builder and are the first party to rent it, but not if the builder had already rented it before you bought it. To be considered residential rental property, 80 percent or more of the gross rental income must come from non-transient dwelling units. Hotels and motels are not considered residential properties unless at least half of the units are rented to non-transients.

If you purchased used residential property after July 24, 1969, you may not use any depreciation rate that results in a more rapid write-off than 125 percent of the declining balance. And you can use this rate only if the property has a remaining useful life of at least twenty years. The straight-line method must be used where useful life is less than twenty years. These same rules apply to a personal residence that was not being rented out and therefore not being depreciated at the time it was first used, if it is converted to rental income property after July 24, 1969. The 80 percent gross rental test must be met for both used residential property and converted residences.

First-user non-residential real property bought after July 24, 1969, can be depreciated at a rate up to 150 percent of the declining balance. This rules out the sum-of-the-years'-digits method. Used non-residential realty bought after this date can be depreciated only by straight-line or certain other relatively slow IRS-approved methods.

Depreciable equipment, even though an integral part of your building, gets the benefit of somewhat more liberal depreciation rules. New equipment with a useful life of three years or more can be depreciated by either the 200 percent declining-balance or the sum-of-the-years'-digits method if you are the first user.

In the case of used equipment, you may use the 150 percent method if you elect to do so in the tax return you file for the year in which you make the purchase. Once you have made your election, you cannot switch to either a faster or slower rate of depreciation without permission from the IRS.

Component depreciation. You needn't use the same method of depreciation for all the individual assets associated with a realty investment. The declining-balance method may be used for some assets and the sum-of-the-years'-digits or straight-line method for others. And remember that parts of a building and its contents don't all depreciate in value at the same rate. The structure itself may have a forty-year useful life expectancy, but the plumbing may have to be replaced in fifteen years, the roof in twenty, the heating system in ten, and other items of fixtures and equipment in as little as five years.

By considering each of these items separately, instead of lumping them together, you will usually be able to claim much higher depreciation deductions during the early years of your ownership. You may be able to depreciate the basic structure at a 125 percent declining-balance rate over forty years, for example, but use a 200 percent declining-balance rate and a ten-year useful life for a new furnace. The difference will often amaze you. Sometimes you'll be able to take twice as much depreciation under the component method as you could if you didn't take the trouble to compute depreciation this way.

The IRS has discouraged the use of the component method on used buildings, arguing that taxpayers can't establish the value of the component accurately. But you can meet this argument. When you buy, take pains to list in your purchase agreement a specific supportable value for each component you wish to segregate. Having an expert give you his written opinion of value and remaining useful life of the various components will help you if the IRS later questions your depreciation schedules. You should be aware that this method may result in your tax return being audited.

Extra first-year depreciation can also be taken, in addition to the regular depreciation, when you buy tangible personal business property such as furniture, refrigerators, and individual air-conditioning units. (Central air-conditioning systems don't qualify since they're considered realty.) This extra deduction lets you write off as much as $2,000 (or $4,000 on a joint return with your spouse) in addition to other depreciation, in the year you acquire the property.

When you take this deduction, you don't subtract anything for the salvage value of the equipment. You must deduct a straight one-fifth of its cost (20 percent) up to the maximum of $2,000 or $4,000. In other words, you ignore investments over $10,000 or $20,000 in figuring the extra deduction.

After taking this deduction, you subtract it from your cost basis in computing the regular depreciation on the same equipment. So here's how your tax deductions would work out on some new furniture which we'll say cost you $3,000.

You estimate it will wear out in ten years. You're filing a joint return, so you claim the extra first-year depreciation allowance of $4,000 (20 percent of the $20,000 maximum). This reduces your $30,000 cost basis by the $4,000 deduction. On the remaining basis of $26,000 you figure your regular depreciation, using one of the methods previously explained. If you choose the straight-line method, and if you figure the salvage value will be $1,000, then your regular deduction will be $2,500. (You subtract the $1,000 salvage value from the $26,000 cost basis, and figure one-tenth of this since you've said its useful life will be ten years.)

If you're planning a sizable investment in furniture or equipment to increase the value of your property, you'll be smart to stagger your purchases over two or more years, so you can get the maximum benefit of the extra first-year depreciation allowance on each buy. For example, if you expect to put in $30,000 worth of new furniture and you're filing jointly, which enables you to take the deduction on a maximum of $20,000 worth, you might buy this much in December and the other $10,000 worth in January. If you're not filing a joint return, you'll be better off taxwise to spread your purchases over three different taxable years so you can take the maximum $2,000 first-year deduction in each of these years.

Any equipment or other asset on which you claim this first-year deduction must have a useful life of at least six years. But you can claim it for used as well as new items.

Combining the depreciation allowances can give you some impressive tax savings. Consider what happens if you put separate new air conditioners into a small apartment building. Say this equipment cost you $20,000 and has a useful life of ten years. If you take that special $4,000 first-year deduction, it reduces your cost basis to $16,000, but you can use the delightful 200 percent declining-balance method on this—which gives you another $3,200 in depreciation. The total of the two deductions is $7,200, which will save you $3,600 in taxes if you're in the 50 percent tax bracket. So in planning for new ventures or reviewing your investments as they stand, don't pass up the savings you can get by using these different depreciation methods.

Recapture of depreciation. One of the major tax benefits available to the investor in income-producing property has been the right to take depreciation deductions at ordinary income tax rates and report recovery of this depreciation on sale of the property as capital gain. Congress has not been unmindful of this special tax benefit, however, and in recent years it has passed several items of legislation narrowing the loophole.

Remember, when you sell a property for a gain, your profit isn't just the difference between what you paid and what you get. Your profit is the difference between the depreciated value on your books and the amount you receive from the buyer. So if you buy a property for $50,000, take $20,000 in depreciation on it, and then sell it for $60,000, you have a taxable gain of $30,000 to take into account.

Under the tax laws of some years ago, this entire gain would be taxable at capital gains rates. Under the current tax laws, much harsher treatment is given to the portion of the gain that results from depreciation. The new rules are pretty complex. I'll just mention them, and if any seem to apply to you, ask a tax accountant or expert.

Gain on the sale of business equipment attributable to depreciation claimed after December 31, 1961, is now all taxed as ordinary income. It doesn't matter how long you owned the equipment or what method of depreciation you used.

Likewise, when you sell real property held for one year or less, whatever part of any gain is attributable to depreciation is now taxed at ordinary income rates, regardless of the method of depreciation used.

Other rules make a distinction between depreciation taken at straight-line and accelerated rates. If you hold depreciable real estate for more than one year, the taxability of any gain on its sale attributable to depreciation taken at in excess of straight-line rates depends on the nature of the property, how long it has been held, and when the excess depreciation was taken.

Gain attributable to excess depreciation taken before 1964 is taxed 100 percent at capital gain rates. Gain on excess depreciation taken after that, however, has become increasingly subject to treatment as ordinary income. In the case of excess depreciation taken during the years 1964 through 1969, the extent to which the gain attributable to the excess is taxed as ordinary income depends strictly on how long the property was held—decreasing 1 percent per month for each full month beyond twenty months—with the amount escaping taxation as ordinary income being taxed as capital gain.

In the case of excess depreciation claimed from 1970 through 1975, there is no similar tempering of tax liability based on how long the property was held for any kind of real estate other than residential rental housing. With this sole exception, the gain resulting from excess depreciation taken after 1969 and before 1976 is taxed 100 percent as ordinary income, regardless of how long the property has been held. For residential rental housing, the excess depreciation is also recaptured 100 percent as ordinary income where the holding period is less than 101 months, but the recapture rate is reduced 1 percent per month for each full month by which the holding period exceeds 100 months. Only after 16⅔ years (200 months) is the entire profit taxed as capital gain, with no ordinary income recapture.

The Tax Reform Act of 1976 puts the final nail in the coffin. Under this legislation, any profits on a sale resulting from excess depreciation taken after December 31, 1975, are taxed 100 percent as ordinary income, regardless of the nature of the real estate or how long it has been held.

In youth we were taught never to put off until tomorrow what can be done today. But when it comes to paying taxes, the rule is usually against our best interests. Fortunately, the IRS regulations for recapturing depreciation won't hurt you a bit unless and until you dispose of your properties. And even then you won't necessarily become liable for any recapture tax (or capital gains tax either, for that matter). Suppose instead of selling it outright you trade it for another property in a tax-deferred exchange. In that case, any tax liability you might otherwise have will be postponed at least until you dispose of the new property. In effect, Uncle Sam has lent you a nice chunk of money entirely interest-free. And if that and other properties you may subsequently acquire are all disposed of in tax-deferred exchanges, you can postpone the tax bite indefinitely.

Remember, too, there is no commandment, regulation or tradition that says you must ever dispose of any property you own. You can keep it for life if you wish. What you do will depend on your personal goals and interests.

As you've surely realized already in reading this book, the fastest route to financial independence is to buy run-down properties, fix them up, and dispose of them for quick profits that you can put into more property. You've seen how tax-free exchanges will help you do this. But at some point you'll probably decide you have enough houses, apartments or other income properties. Instead of further trading, you'll prefer to sit back and relax. In that case, you'll never have to pay taxes on the gains you made, nor on the depreciation allowances that saved you taxes earlier. And when you die, your heirs won't be liable for any income taxes on the gains either, unless and until they dispose of the property. Then, at worst, they'll be taxed only on the amount by which the net sales price exceeds its fair market value on December 31, 1976.

Choosing a depreciation policy. In most cases you'll be money ahead by claiming depreciation deductions as rapidly as the law allows. But there could be exceptions. For example: maybe you've piled up such a comfortable reserve that you decide to spend the next few years traveling or beachcombing, and you expect to have little or no taxable income to report in the meantime. You plan to come back later on and sell a few properties, which will give you sizable capital gains. In that situation you'd be foolish to report fast depreciation on the properties. Doing this would merely give you bigger tax deductions in years when you have little or no income from which to deduct them. What you want is a depreciation policy that will let you postpone most of your deductions to later years when you hope to have substantial income.

Possibly you can even use an uncommon method of depreciation that will give you an ever-increasing deduction to offset increasing income. This method is "reverse accelerated depreciation." You use the same arithmetic you use on regular accelerated depreciation, but just reverse the order of the years. Since this method is rarely used, be sure to check it first with your tax adviser.

Even if you're not planning to take a year or two away from real estate investing, you very likely are looking ahead toward future years when your taxable income will be bigger. As you pay off your loans, you'll get smaller deductions for interest payments. At the same time, your rental income will probably be increasing, from the sheer pressure of inflation if nothing else. You'll be needing more and bigger deductions in those years in order to keep taxes within reason.

But you'd be foolish to sit and wait to get hit by the taxes, wouldn't you? If you remember what you've read earlier, you see an answer to this problem: just refinance some of your property—borrow money on it—so you'll get higher deductions for interest. If nothing else, you can always use the additional money to buy more property. Never forget that the central secret of success in realty investment is to stay as deeply in debt as is prudent. Use other people's money. They're glad to rent the money to you; it's a good deal for them too.

Refinancing property is easy when the rental income is increasing, because that means the value of the property is increasing. But of course the problem we've just been considering is purely academic for most readers of this book. Long before lower interest deductions or shrinking depreciation allowances cut sharply into your spendable income, you will have sold or exchanged the property, if you're following the Lowry method.

Therefore, you're thinking mostly about your income tax position for this year and the two or three years immediately ahead. Assuming that you want to offset as much as possible of your taxable income during this period, you'll choose the fastest depreciation method available to you. (Just be sure the deductions won't leave you with an overall loss. The loss would be wasted. If you wind up with minus income because of such deductions, the IRS won't let you carry this loss over to another year, although you may in later years be able to realize some tax benefit from it through income averaging.)

Improvements made by tenants are tax-free, whether you arrange with the tenants to compensate them for doing the work or whether they do it on their own initiative.

Quite often a tenant may offer to repaint his apartment if you will provide the paint. You can deduct the cost of the paint. And you're not required to report the value of his free labor as income or gain. (Just be sure he's covered by your workmen's compensation insurance, in case he has an accident while he's doing the work.)

Maybe a bathroom or kitchen needs modernizing. If you pay a contractor to do it, you'll probably have to capitalize the cost and get this back a little at a time in depreciation deductions spread over the expected life of the improvement. But if you make a deal with your tenant, whereby he pays for the modernizing and you deduct it from his rent, you get an immediate tax benefit—because you take in less rent on which you pay income tax.

Let's say a contractor tells you the work will cost $1,200. And you figure that the remaining useful life of the building is sixteen years. If you pay for the work, your depreciation deduction for it will average $75 a year over the sixteen-year period. But if the tenant pays for it, you get a tax saving equivalent to writing off the full $1,200 in one year.

Since you stand to gain so much, if the tenant is reluctant you might be smart to sweeten the deal for him. You could offer to deduct somewhat more from his rent than the improvement will cost. Another reason for making the concession is that the improvement will increase the apartment's rental value later on. You can't very well raise the current tenant's rent just because of the improvement, but you can certainly raise it when he moves out and someone else comes in. Anyhow, you'll more than recapture the full cost in additional value of the property at resale.

This has been a long chapter, yet it just gives you the basic information you need for taking advantage of the tax breaks available to real estate investors. The tax laws are full of fine points that can't be explored here.

The better you know the tax laws, the more opportunities you'll see for using them to unfreeze cash. Why not keep a good tax guide in your desk, and consult it whenever any question comes up? This way the answer will stick in your mind much better than if you try to read up ahead of time on many special situations in which you're not currently involved.

As your real estate activities blossom out, so will your need for sophisticated tax planning. You can get most of what you need from one or the other of the two best books I've seen in this line . . . J. K. Lasser's *Successful Tax Planning for Real Estate,* and *Managing Your Family Finances.* Both are available through Simon and Schuster, 1230 Avenue of the Americas, New York, New York 10020.

REMEMBER THESE HIGH POINTS:

You can acquire property with tax-free money by borrowing on property you already own, and investing the proceeds in more property.

No matter how small your down payment, you can take tax deductions for depreciation on the total value of the property (other than the land).

When you sell a mortgaged property, try to pay off the mortgage first and arrange a purchase-money mortgage with the buyer if necessary to qualify the transaction as an installment sale.

Make maximum use of depreciation allowances, and choose whichever of the basic methods of figuring them is best for you.

Encourage occupants to make improvements. There are tax advantages for you.

Many other tax breaks are available to realty investors who familiarize themselves with details of the tax laws.

XIV *How to Sell Your Property*

Since fairly quick turnover is the way to accumulate wealth in real estate, no doubt you'll be reselling what you've bought. As a seller, you can profit by careful planning and preparation.

Some investors simply put property on the market and sit back to let nature take its course. They're the ones who either net smaller profits than they should, or wait unnecessarily long for the right buyer to come along. Do the selling job right, and you'll be ahead in the long run.

The first step in your preparation is to make sure you have a good answer to the question that's sure to come up:

"Why do you want to sell?" Maybe you must move to another part of the country; maybe you've reached the point where you want to take your profits and go off to travel. Either of these answers should satisfy a prospect if he's convinced the property is a good buy. Another answer that can satisfy him is: "Because I need cash for a bigger investment." But this easy answer may fool you.

Do you really need capital urgently? Don't sell just for the sake of selling. One smart in-and-out trader said that a secret of his success was in liquidating investments only *after* he planned how to reinvest the proceeds. This was wise. With a sizable wad and no place to stash it except a savings account at comparatively low interest, an investor can get fidgety, and grab any investment that looks inviting. The dangers are obvious.

So figure out, for your own private satisfaction, why you really want to sell. Maybe your analysis will convince you that you *shouldn't* sell.

Have you made the obvious improvements that are worth many times their cost in added resale value? Will the sale bring you a short-term or long-term capital gain or loss? How much tax will you have to pay? If you've been taking accelerated depreciation, how will that affect your taxes on the sale? Would you do better by exchanging instead of selling? Should you qualify this sale as an installment sale, or insist on a big down payment?

If cashing out now will bring you back only 10 to 35 percent more than you put in, is it premature? Will rising realty values bring a 50 or 75 percent return a few years from now? Would refinancing or a junior mortgage bring you the capital you need?

At least yearly you should analyze your property's net yield on investment, its tax advantages or disadvantages, and the changing conditions in the neighborhood and the local realty market. That way, you can give a prompt answer if someone asks you unexpectedly, "Are you interested in selling?"

Obviously you'd answer, "For how much?" But when he offers a price, you should be in a position to judge whether it's a good offer. This brings us to the next part of the homework you should do when planning to sell. You need to know, coldly and realistically:

How much is the property worth? Maybe you should reread Chapter III's sections on estimating the value of a property you're thinking of buying, and go through the processes again to find the current value. You can even compare it again, point by point, with similar properties on the market—which may awaken you to changes in local conditions that make your property worth more—or less—than you anticipated.

What about the equipment and furnishings? Have you added some, removed some? They may change the annual costs for insurance, utilities, maintenance, replacements and other cash outlays.

Your estimate of what a fair price should be isn't necessarily the last word on the subject. We all make mistakes in arithmetic. We all fall in love with property and overestimate its worth sometimes. So we need to check our evaluation against outside thinking.

Even if you hope to sell without using a broker, it's a good idea to ask a few smart, sound brokers if they'll look at your property and tell you what they think it can sell for. Explain that you're going to try to sell it yourself but will call them later if you change your mind. They may be glad to help, especially if they know that you're an active investor who may buy or sell other properties through them.

Surveying the brokers and taking an average of prices they suggest can help you check your own judgment, but it has built-in drawbacks. Brokers are tempted to mention a higher price than they secretly think they can get, in order to sign up a would-be seller. They figure he'll use whichever broker claims to be able to get top dollar. Once they've landed the listing contract, they'll be in a position to suggest lowering the price if the property doesn't sell.

So take brokers' estimates with a grain of salt. You can still learn from them. Ask how they arrived at their price. They'll educate you about neighborhood conditions, current asking prices, and recent sales.

Ask what they see as the good and bad points of your property. Here again, remember that they may diplomatically withhold criticisms that they think you might resent. They know that pride makes the average owner see his building and its management as better than they really are.

Such flattery may inflate whatever naive ideas you've cherished about the worth of your property. As an antidote, you can hire a private appraiser for about $50 and up.

Another antidote—maybe too strong a remedy, sometimes—is to check the assessed value. Often a property is assessed at a certain fraction of its market value. The assessment may have been made years ago, when real estate was selling for less. Similarly, FHA and VA appraisals tend to be lower than sale prices in a rising market.

Anyhow, jotting government appraisals at the low end of your range, and optimistic brokers' figures at the high end, you may find that your own estimate, and a paid appraiser's figure, are about midway between. If so, you're not far wrong. Likewise, if estimates from several dissimilar sources cluster in a narrow range, this is excellent assurance that the market value is within the cluster.

Your asking price is what you need to consider next. The realty market—unlike the stock market and the supermarket—is an arena for haggling. Sophisticated buyers expect sellers to come down from their first demand. So add "bargaining room" to your fair market value in deciding how much to ask.

The spread between asking price and actual sale price varies from city to city. Ask realty people what the normal spread is in your market. Stay within it. Otherwise prospective buyers may turn away, figuring you're out of their range. Generally speaking, a markup of 5 or 10 percent will let you come down, and still keep you on target.

Your minimum price should be clear in your mind. To be effective in negotiating, you must know the limit below which you won't sell. Otherwise you won't be able to cut off negotiations, and prospective buyers will keep beating you down.

There's another important reason for knowing the least you'll accept. Suppose you decide to have a broker represent you. Normally you can't tell him your rock-bottom price, because if he's lazy he may not try hard for more—or may come in with even lower offers, hoping you'll compromise. Brokers are in a commission business where turnover is important; their time is money. But you can give your broker a true bottom figure if you ask him to sign an agreement that you'll receive this specified net amount from the sale, even if he must take less commission than usual. This puts him on notice that selling at an unfairly low price will mean a sacrifice for him, not you. A "con artist" broker won't sign such an agreement. Some brokers often take less than a full commission, at the closing stage of some negotiations, if the only visible alternative is to lose the sale.

So now you've figured how much the property is worth, how much you'll accept, and how much you'll begin by asking. (Never call it an "asking price," especially in ads or conversation with prospects; this implies that you expect to come down. Just say it's your price. Indicate that it is a "firm price," unless and until a prospect makes an offer within bargaining range of your true target.) But you'll need further preparations before you begin selling.

Selling tools must be prepared next. First you need a fact sheet, known to the public as a broker's income and expense statement, which can be handed out far and wide to everyone who might know of prospective buyers.

Above all, prospects want to know the cash flow, gross income, and expenses. You can begin your sheet as a broker would, with a top line that says something like: FOR SALE AT SEVEN TIMES GROSS INCOME.

But you might as well go on to give the true total of rent collected during the past year—not the "scheduled income" that brokers talk about. Any buyer with a spoonful of brains will want to know the actual income and the vacancy rate. You can save everyone's time by including this and other key facts in your original sheet.

The true operating net is important. How much were the taxes? The insurance premiums? The utility bills? The maintenance costs including trash collection? Just give the totals. A detailed breakdown should be ready in your file, because most prospects will want to see it.

There is no standard form for your sheet. Make it factual and crystal-clear, with all essential information (your name and phone number, for example) plus whatever additional facts might make a prospect want to buy—such as: "Completely refurbished. New heating and air conditioning. New kitchen and bathroom appliances," for example, or: "Within walking distance of shopping center," or: "In quiet high-class neighborhood."

Obviously you'll give the address of the property and tell how to find it. A facsimile of part of the city map, with the location marked, may help. You'll specify the lot size, total square feet in the building, number of units, approximate size of the units ("bachelor, 1-bedroom, 2-bedroom" may suffice unless they're unusually large), age of the building, and garage or parking space available.

Probably you'll want to mention draperies and carpeting, size of closets, amount of shelf space, if these are points that make the units easier to rent. In fact, just about everything that helps rent the apartments should be mentioned in conversation with serious buyers if not in the fact sheet.

On a bright sunny day, take some exterior photos of the property from the best angles. Maybe a few interior photos also, in case you decide to print both sides of your fact sheet. It's best to use the Kodak Pocket Instamatic or any 35 mm camera, because these give you 3½" × 5" glossy prints. You can use square 3" × 3" prints but they won't fill the space on the sheet as well as larger pictures. Shoot many and use the best-looking shots—or the shabbiest-looking if this happens to be a property that you haven't upgraded for some reason, and are selling as a prime opportunity for a renovation-conscious investor.

Get your fact sheet typed perfectly, and paste one or more photos in the space you've kept clear for them. Have about 200 copies of the sheet made at a nearby instant printing center (see listings in the Yellow Pages under "printing"). Ask the printer to prepare metal plates for half-tone reproductions of your photos. This may double your total cost, but without the plate your pictures won't reproduce well, and prospects will get a poor impression. Be prepared to spend $50 or more, because this is an important marketing tool.

The printer will take two or three days to get your sheets ready.

While you're waiting, you should begin your marketing campaign by word of mouth.

Spread the word to everyone you know that you're thinking about selling your property. (Don't mention price.) Virtually everyone likes to talk about local real estate. So make a point of passing the word to people who talk to many other people: barbers, beauty shop operators, dentists, service station operators, and of course your personal friends.

You might be lucky and get a few phone calls from people saying, "I've heard you're interested in selling your property. How much are you asking for it?" If you haven't yet released your fact sheet, you can quite logically reply, "Well, I'm only thinking about it. I haven't set a price. How much do you think you might pay?"

Obviously you're in a better position when buyers come to you unsolicited. Then you needn't seem eager to sell; it's up to them to persuade you. They might bid much higher than you'd hoped for, in which case you can try to close the sale promptly.

It's uncommon to get an offer high above the property's estimated value. You can't wait long for one. But at least give yourself a few days, while word is spreading. Ideally you should put the word out to all your good connections on the same day, so you can judge how long to wait before making your fact sheets available. Once your sheet, with its stated price for the property, is in circulation you can't hold a bidder to a higher offer than the price you've already set publicly.

But your sheet will be extremely helpful in negotiating with prospects who are thinking in the same price range you are. When they phone, you can offer to mail them the sheet. When they drop by, you can hand them one. Its facts should help convince them that the property is worth what you ask.

Moreover, it can help you locate prospects. Mail copies to everyone you can think of who might be interested: investors with whom you're acquainted; the Apartment Association; the Realtors. Your church may be a good place to leave some sheets, if you know that some church members are interested in realty investment. Ditto for clubs to which you may belong. And of course you'll follow up with all the "news broadcasters" to whom you spoke earlier—the barber and so on—by dropping off several copies of the sheet with each.

But be sure to keep plenty of copies in reserve. You'll need them if you find it necessary to take the logical next step in a marketing campaign: paid advertising in newspapers.

A newspaper ad may bring you dozens of prospects—or none, if you don't word your proposition clearly and attractively, or if you advertise in the wrong places.

Attractive wording can make the difference if you happen to be selling a duplex or fourplex. Investors in such properties have discovered that they can sell quickly with ads like these:

> **CAN YOU PAY $2,000 DOWN?**
> **CAN YOU PAY $34 PER MONTH?**
>
> This handsome three-family unit will cost you this much and not a cent more! You live in one unit and collect rent from the other two, add exactly $34 from your pocket, send it to the bank, and it pays INTEREST, PRINCIPAL AND TAXES. There are NO extra charges. Total price only $_____.
> Each unit has 4 rooms, large kitchen . . . (etc.)
>
> I will be there from 9 to 12 today. Come over and bring your deposit.
>
> YOUR APT. RENT-FREE PLUS $22 PER MONTH clear. Buy this well-built duplex, live on one floor, collect the rent from the other floor. Only $_____ down. Newly remodeled kitchens and baths . . . (etc.)

The amazing thing is that prospects flock to buy such offerings without even asking what the total cost is! And they don't care how long the mortgage runs. Their big concerns are how much down, and how much a month.

However, these prospects have probably never bought property before. They're afraid of being swindled, of unexpected gimmicks to get more money out of them. The secret of selling to them is to say unmistakably, "No extras will be sprung on you. Nobody will even try to raise the figures of down payment and monthly payments. If you can pay the advertised amounts, you can buy this property with an easy mind."

Sometimes they do have certain other fears—of repair bills, increased taxes, trouble with tenants. They fear they may dislike the apartment after they move in, and are stuck there for life. There's a simple but unorthodox way to overcome these fears.

A money-back trial is a tested, irresistible proposition. Most buyers of small income property, where they'll be resident manager as well as owner, are people accustomed to making their own small repairs. They have spare time, which they plan to use improving their property. But they dread the unknown hazards of ownership. So you tell them:

"You make the deposit and I give you the deed, on a free trial basis. You move in and try it out for a year. You own it. You collect rents, make your payments. If you decide you don't like it—and you alone will be the judge—simply come back and lay the deed on my desk, and tell me to give back your money. I won't argue with you. I'll take out $_____ per month for rent for the months you occupied, and refund the rest of your down payment.

"On the other hand, if you're completely satisfied, as I'm sure you will be, you just go along as before. About the time you're ready to retire, you'll own this building entirely, with no debts. You are sole owner. You have security and a steady income."

I've never heard of anyone asking for the refund. When a buyer knows the pride of ownership, with the status it gives him among friends, he never wants to rent again.

The moneyed people who buy larger properties can sometimes be attracted by "trial purchase" angles, such as a profit-sharing agreement or a performance guarantee (see Chapter XVII). But they're primarily interested in the percentage yield on cash invested—i.e., how much cash they'll get back each year for every dollar they put in. Play these figures up in your ads. Don't be coy. State what you have and what you want, and offer to provide a detailed financial analysis. Serious investors never reply to vague ads.

The bigger your property, the more important that you advertise it in the right place. A big-city paper isn't necessarily best, even if the property is in the heart of that city. Maybe a suburban newspaper nearby, read by a few hundred prosperous investors, will produce more inquiries.

If you use a metropolitan daily, be sure your ad appears in the separate column for Income Properties. Also think about using *The Wall Street Journal,* read by tens of thousands of money-minded people, if you're asking a half-million or more for your property. One day each week it has a "Real Estate Corner," and on other days it runs numerous one-column boxed ads for real estate. The only way to find out which advertising medium is your best bet is to take a close look at the real estate advertising in each one, check its "cost per thousand"—the cost of the ad divided by the circulation in thousands—and perhaps talk to some knowledgeable people in advertising.

Maybe you should put out a sign with your phone number in front of the property: "For Sale by Owner," if the property is attractive-looking and not too large. A sign outside a big apartment property has a tendency to frighten the occupants; they wonder if something is wrong with the property; if a tough new owner will soon be among them raising rents, and so on. In short, they begin to think of moving.

In smaller properties, however, you probably know everyone personally, or at least your manager does. Some of them might be interested in buying the property themselves, or might have friends who'd be interested; any occupant would like to have a personal friend as owner. So, after getting them used to the idea of a possible change in ownership, you can put out the sign. Maybe you can even hold an "Open House" to show the property on a given Sunday afternoon, if prospects haven't already come forward in satisfactory numbers. Include your fact sheet with the invitations, of course.

Meanwhile you're constantly spreading reminders that your property is up for sale. Mention it whenever you play tennis with friends, or go to a party, or attend a club meeting, or chat with churchgoers after services.

Sell on the telephone whenever people call up to ask about the property. Their first impression of your personality, as registered by your voice, will be enough to kill the sale if you sound unpleasant or unenthusiastic. So put a smile in your voice. Sound happy that the prospect called. Be friendly. Be quietly enthusiastic about the property.

Beforehand, you should have worked out exactly what you'll say to inquiries. Maybe your first response should be something like "Yes, I'm glad you called, would you like me to tell you a bit more about the property?" And if he is interested you should press for immediate action by asking "Which would be a better date for you to come and see the property, 10 A.M. on Tuesday or 3 P.M. on Wednesday?" You'll also make a point, as early in the conversation as possible, of getting the prospect's name—and jotting it down, so you can keep using it as you chat with him.

If he won't make an appointment to see the property, offer to mail him a fact sheet. Then ask for his phone number as well as his address, so you "can check back in a few days to see whether you want more information."

When a prospect comes to inspect the property, you're the salesman. You won't find it hard. You know a lot about your property, and you're highly motivated to sell. Just keep in mind a few rules that good salesmen follow:

Look successful. Your shoes should gleam. Your clothes should be neat and fresh, your grooming careful.

Be cheerful. Smile. Remark about anything that the buyer might be proud of, such as his car, his children, or his business judgment.

Be positive. Be ready to counter any negative remarks with an upbeat response such as, "Yes, usually that's very true, but in this case you may want to consider . . ."

A good salesman learns all he can about what he's selling. Try to find out about the shrubbery by taking sample leaves or trimmings to your local nursery and asking questions. Know the brand names of plumbing fixtures, and their qualities. Know the good points of the construction, the paint job, the roof. Be ready to pull out warranties if you have them.

Can you talk about the nearby schools? The shopping centers? Churches? These might be important to a prospect, if he's wondering whether vacancies in the building will be easy to fill.

Have you pulled together last year's repair bills, tax bills, insurance policies? An intelligent prospect may want to look at them. He'll almost surely want to see last year's records of rent payments, vacancies, number of prospects who looked at apartments, and similar data. You should have them at your fingertips.

Negotiating the terms should begin as soon as a prospect asks questions about terms. At that point you can stop selling the good points of the property and get down to money matters. Find out all you can about his financial position, because you may be able to sweeten the deal by adjusting the size of payments, term of mortgage, amount of down payment, or other variables.

Your best way to counter a suggestion that the purchase price is too high is to suggest that the prospect submit a purchase agreement, specifying the price and terms he'll offer, because you're not ready yet to make a decision and haven't given any thought to lowering the price. You can promise that you'll give him a prompt answer on his proposal, as soon as you've discussed it with your lawyer. Blame your lawyer for insisting that there must be a firm offer in writing, with earnest money.

Beyond this, you'll probably want to review the nuances of negotiating discussed in Chapter VIII. This will help even if you decide to have a broker handle the negotiations.

Many times it's better to use a broker than try to work out a transaction yourself. If you go the latter route, you expect to save the broker's commission—but any prospective buyer coming direct to you will also expect to save the commission. Obviously you can't both do this. It will be the buyer who saves, not you, if you're obviously eager to sell.

In deciding whether to use a broker, size up your own qualities. Can you deal with strangers intelligently and pleasantly, especially if they're wily and tough? Can you make useful suggestions about financing? Can you afford time for discussions with many prospects? A broker is expert at speeding up transactions, solving problems of financing, overcoming objections.

Maybe your best bet, if you're not in a hurry, is to try doing your own selling first. It's a worthwhile education anyhow. Then if it takes too long, or you find it too bothersome, you can turn to brokers.

REMEMBER THESE HIGH POINTS:

Don't sell impulsively, or just because you need quick cash. First analyze reasons for selling—and for not selling. Can you do better by refinancing the property, exchanging it, or holding for a rise in price?

Make sure you know your property's market value. Get estimates from brokers (which are likely to be too high) and from the tax assessors and FHA or VA appraisers (which tend to be too low in a rising market). If still in doubt, hire a professional appraiser.

Your offering price usually should be 5 or 10 percent above the fair market value, to allow room for concessions in negotiations.

Decide secretly on the minimum you'll accept. Stick to it.

Prepare a fact sheet to give to prospective buyers. Illustrate it with photos of your property.

Let all your acquaintances know that you're thinking of selling, but don't mention price before your fact sheet is distributed.

If no prospects are in sight, consider well-worded newspaper advertising.

You can sell small property quickly, at your price, on a money-back trial offer. Buyers almost never ask for their money back.

Plan carefully what you'll say when you get telephone inquiries, and how you'll show the property. Before talking terms, review Chapter VIII, on negotiating a good buy.

XV Want to Buy More Property?
Borrow More Money!

By the time you've owned and managed one or two pieces of real estate, and watched the spendable cash profits roll in, your appetite will probably be whetted for more. Let's consider how you can expand.

Basically, the way to do so is to go deeper into debt.

Do you flinch at the first thought of this? That's understandable. "Pay as you go" sounds more solid and sensible than "Go now, pay later." For generations our Puritan heritage has kept us feeling that we shouldn't borrow money except as a last resort, and should pay it back as quickly as possible. "Debtors" were much inferior to ordinary people, we were taught; in fact, debtors' prisons were part of the Anglo-American landscape for centuries.

But economics have changed, and so have our customs and beliefs. There's no longer anything discreditable or unwise in using carefully calculated amounts of "rented money"—which of course is what we do when we borrow.

Financial institutions are happy to lend us money if we pay enough rent (interest) for it, show that we'll be able to pay it back and secure the loan with something of sufficient value (the collateral or security) if the lender considers this necessary.

Using these other people's money is a sound and ethical way to build our own financial security. We're really helping the lending institutions as well as ourselves. They're in the business of lending money, for the profit of all concerned.

When we operate on credit—that is, on borrowed money—we use what financial people call "leverage." Leverage, as discussed in Chapter II, is the big basic principle behind all successful real estate buying. Therefore, we'd better examine it at sufficient length to make sure that it is clear.

Using leverage is part of many normal family transactions. It's what we do when we buy household appliances on the installment plan, or when we finance the purchase of a car.

Is this better than saving up until we can pay the whole price in cash? Paying cash means we pay no interest charges, so our total outlay is smaller. In that way we save. But maybe we lose in other ways. Let's consider a typical transaction. I buy a car. I pay the automobile dealer about one-fifth or more of his asking price, in cash. I agree to pay the rest—plus interest or a "financing charge"—to him or some financial institution in installments spread over a period of many months.

Why do I sign up for this kind of transaction, which obviously will cost me more than paying cash? Either because I don't have enough spare cash, or because I have the cash but prefer to use it for other purposes. I get immediate possession of the car for a fairly small down payment, and I figure that this offsets the disadvantages of the high cost over the long pull.

In buying a home, the same basic thinking applies. It's better to borrow heavily than to save up until the full purchase price is accumulated—which might mean forgoing ownership of a nice home for many years or maybe forever. Even the people who have an abundance of ready cash may find better uses for it than paying the full price for a house on the day they take possession. They prefer to eat their cake and have it too, in a sense—they become home owners and still keep most of their cash, by "leveraging" the transaction. For a small down payment they get a big immediate benefit, just as a small lever can move a big weight.

Smart investors use borrowed money in most realty investments even when they are rich enough to buy the property free and clear. They prefer a deal that keeps their own cash outlay at a minimum. They don't mind paying high interest on borrowed money if their overall return will be higher yet. The more leverage they can use (i.e., the smaller proportion of their own money, the greater proportion of other people's money), the bigger the potential for a high rate of return on their own money.

To see what a difference leverage makes, let's suppose you have $10,000 to invest, and have been offered two properties. Property A is for sale at $10,000, but the seller wants the full price in cash. Property B is priced at $50,000, but the seller says, "You can have it for a down payment of only $10,000 if you'll pay interest of 8 percent on the rest." This means you would take out a mortgage or trust deed for $40,000 on which you would pay $3,200 interest in the first year alone. Sounds like a lot to pay just for interest, doesn't it?

Which is the better deal? It depends on the approximate net income that each property would bring you. Property A's net income, you find, is $1,000 a year. Property B's net income is $5,000 a year. Both properties are thus yielding 10 percent on their selling prices. That's why the owner of B can price his property five times as high as the owner of A.

Now which is the better deal? Analyze them. If you put your money into Property A, you own it outright. Sounds great to "own it outright," doesn't it? Just thinking about it makes you feel solid and prosperous.

Furthermore, your thousand-dollar annual return on Property A will be a 10 percent yield on the ten thousand you invest. That also sounds good. It's hard to find a 10 percent yield in other types of investment.

But wait! Do you realize that Property B will bring you an 18 percent yield? Your net return, after paying interest, will be $1,800.

Here's the arithmetic on Property B. Its net operating income of

	Property A	Property B
Sales Price	$10,000	$50,000
Mortgage	-0-	40,000
Net Investment	$10,000	$10,000
Net Operating Income	$ 1,000	$ 5,000
Less Mortgage Interest	-0-	−3,200
Net Income	$ 1,000	$ 1,800
Net Return on Investment	10%	18%

$5,000 will be reduced by the $3,200 interest on the mortgage. But that still leaves $1,800 a year in your pocket for the $10,000 cash you put up.

In other words, Property B will earn an extra $800 for you every year, simply because the earning power of the borrowed money is $800 greater than what you pay to "rent" the money. Your investment in Property A would use no leverage; but Property B would give you considerable leverage—or, as some people phrase it, by investing in B you would "successfully trade on your equity."

You enhance the potential benefits of leverage whenever you find a way either to borrow at less cost or to increase the percentage of borrowed money you use in the transaction. For example, if you could acquire Property B with a mortgage loan at 6 percent instead of 8 percent, the interest on your $40,000 mortgage would then be only $2,400 a year. Subtract this $2,400 from your $5,000 income on the property, and you'd be netting $2,600, which is a 26 percent annual yield on the $10,000 you invested.

A second way to enhance the potential benefits of leverage is to borrow more—take out a bigger mortgage in proportion to your down payment. Let's imagine a Property C, also available to you for $10,000 down. Its operating income is $10,000 a year so the seller, logically enough, prices it at $100,000. But he's willing to carry back a $90,000 mortgage at 8 percent, the same rate charged by the owner of the $50,000 Property B.

Buying a $100,000 piece of property with only a $10,000 down payment sounds like a shoestring deal, doesn't it? But such deals are closed every day. They are perfectly sound for the buyer, the seller, and the lender. In the case of Property C, the leverage makes it even more attractive than Property B.

Sure, you'd be paying more interest each year than if you bought B. You'd pay $7,200 a year (8 percent of $90,000), which seems an awfully big chunk of the $10,000 operating income. Your net profit would be only $2,800 a year. But that's a 28 percent return on your $10,000 equity—more than half again as much as if you bought the $50,000 property with a $40,000 mortgage, and almost three times as much as if you bought the $10,000 property for cash.

Of course, you could further heighten the leverage you were using by making an even smaller down payment. If you bought Property A, B, or C at the same price, with the same mortgage terms, but made only a $5,000 down payment, say, or just a $1,000 down payment, then the potential return on cash you invested would be even greater. But there's a limit to how small a down payment most sellers will accept. Most expect 20 to 25 percent, although many will sell for as little as 10.

Moreover, an imaginative buyer can sometimes find ways for a seller to benefit by taking a smaller down payment. We'll look at some of these ways as we go along.

Before you go into debt with a mortgage, there are other considerations to evaluate. We won't try to go into all of these, but the

AN EXAMPLE OF LEVERAGE

$10,000 Cash Invested in Income-producing Property Supplemented by Varying Degrees of Assistance from Loans. Net Operating Income 10% of Total Purchase Price. Loans at 8% Interest Per Annum Amortizable Over 25 Years. (Amortization tables are available from most lending institutions and are usually given to customers at no charge.)

	(1)	(2) 50%	(3) 60%	(4) 70%	(5) 80%	(6) 90%
(1) Loans as % of Purchase Price	-0-	50%	60%	70%	80%	90%
(2) Cash Investment (Down Payment)	$10,000	$10,000	$10,000	$10,000	$10,000	$10,000
(3) Mortgage or Trust Deed Loans	-0-	$10,000	$15,000	$23,333	$40,000	$90,000
(4) Total Investment (Purchase Price)	$10,000	$20,000	$25,000	$33,333	$50,000	$100,000
Taxable Income from Investment:						
(5) Net Operating Income at 10%	$1,000	$2,000	$2,500	$3,333	$5,000	$10,000
(6) Less Interest on Loans at 8%	-0-	$800	$1,200	$1,867	$3,200	$7,200
(7) Less Allowable Depreciation*	$400	$800	$1,000	$1,333	$2,000	$4,000
(8) Net Taxable Income (LOSS)	$600	$400	$300	$133	$(200)	$(1,200)
Cash Flow from Investment:						
(9) Net Operating Income at 10%	$1,000	$2,000	$2,500	$3,333	$5,000	$10,000
(10) Less Loan Amortization Payments	-0-	$926	$1,389	$2,161	$3,705	$8,336
(11) Net Spendable Cash	$1,000	$1,074	$1,111	$1,172	$1,295	$1,664
(12) Cash Applied to Equity Build-up	-0-	$126	$189	$294	$505	$1,136
(13) Total Return on Investment	$1,000	$1,200	$1,300	$1,466	$1,800	$2,800
Return as Percentage of Down Payments:						
(14) Net Spendable Cash	10.0%	10.7%	11.1%	11.7%	13.0%	16.6%
(15) Equity Build-up	-0-	1.3	1.9	3.0	5.0	11.4
(16) Total Return on Cash Invested	10.0%	12.0%	13.0%	14.7%	18.0%	28.0%

* On building only. Assumes building represents 80% of total of value of property and is being depreciated over 25 years at 125% of the declining balance.

preceding chart will help you understand some of them. We are still talking about a cash investment (down payment) of $10,000 supplemented by loans of various amounts; we're still assuming that the mortgage calls for 8 percent interest, and that each property will produce an operating income equal to one-tenth of its selling price. The chart shows the effect on taxable income, and on cash flow before income taxes, of the degree of leverage used.

You'll notice that the first column represents Property A in the example we've just been considering; column 5 represents Property B, and column 6 is Property C. Columns 2, 3 and 4 work out the same arithmetic on other properties priced between ten and fifty thousand dollars.

The first four lines simply tabulate the calculations we've been talking about in the past few pages. They should be self-explanatory.

Lines 5, 6, 7 and 8 summarize the calculations you would make to find how much income you would have to report on your tax return. That is, line 5 shows each property's net operating income (scheduled rent minus property taxes, utilities, insurance, other operating expenses, maintenance and allowance for vacancies). We're continuing to assume that the net operating income is one-tenth of the asking price in each case—so that it is proportionately higher on the more expensive properties.

Line 6, the interest expense, naturally gets bigger with the size of the mortgage being assumed. Interest is tax deductible.

Line 7, depreciation, is the tax deduction Uncle Sam lets us take for the theoretical shrinkage in the value of a building we buy. He assumes that any building (and certain improvements to it) will gradually become less valuable because newer buildings will be competing with it—and that it also will deteriorate through aging, even if there is no competition. In practice this doesn't always happen, but Congress has laid down the rule and wants us to take the deduction. The word "depreciation," of course, simply means "decrease in value," just as "appreciation," which we'll be using later, means an increase in value.

Depreciation doesn't involve any cash outlay by the investor. In fact, the long-term upward trend of real estate values usually means that an owner of property doesn't really suffer any loss from depreciation if he buys a good sound building, maintains it properly, and modernizes or improves it as circumstances make advisable.

Line 8 is where the chart gets slightly harder to understand. It is the amount that must be reported to the tax collector as net income from the investment made in the property. This line is affected by the delightful fact that we can take depreciation not only on the value of the investment represented by our own money, but also on the value represented by the money we have borrowed. This means that the higher the leverage we use, the lower our taxable income will usually be.

This is why on line 8 the taxable income actually turns into a loss—which can be deducted from our other income—in the case of the 80 percent and 90 percent loans (columns 5 and 6). Anyone in the 50 percent tax bracket will get back half the theoretical loss in the form of lower income taxes.

However, our net profit for income tax purposes is only one consideration. We're not putting money into real estate just to avoid paying it to the tax man. Most of us are interested not only in cutting our tax bill but more importantly in getting a spendable cash return from our investment. We arrive at this on line 14 by making certain calculations on the intervening lines (i.e., net spendable cash divided by the original down payment).

Line 9 just duplicates line 5, for convenience in making the calculations; it shows again the net cash we can expect to have after paying all normal operating expenses, but before making any payments on the mortgage or trust deed. Line 10 shows how much we'll be paying to "service" the mortgage—in other words, to pay the 8 percent interest plus a specified fraction of the principal. Most lenders want to get back the full amount of their loan, plus interest, in installments over a stated period of time. The chart assumes that this time is twenty-five years, since twenty-five-year mortgages are fairly common. And line 10 assumes that the investor is to amortize (pay off, or liquidate) the entire debt in equal installments during each of the twenty-five years. Not all mortgages read this way; remember the tricky "balloon payments" mentioned in Chapter IX.

Line 11, pre-tax net spendable cash, shows how much the investor will have left after he makes the mortgage payments but before he pays his tax. Line 12 shows how many dollars of the mortgage payments will be applied to reducing the mortgage principal—which is the same thing as increasing our investment (equity) in the property and is therefore often called "equity build-up." Only the dollars applied to interest, and not those for equity build-up, can be deducted from taxable income. So the difference is important. But equity build-up is also important for another reason, reflected in line 13: the bigger our equity in the property, the wealthier we are on paper, because we own a bigger fraction of it and the mortgage lender owns a smaller fraction.

Therefore, equity build-up represents a financial benefit to us. In later chapters we'll see how our equity can put hard dollars in our pocket when we sell or exchange the property in various types of deals.

Another way of thinking about line 13 is that it shows the total pre-tax benefit we can expect to realize from the investment: equity build-up (just a paper profit, for the moment) plus actual cash left in our pockets after meeting the mortgage payments and all other normal expenses.

Now an interesting and pleasant fact begins to emerge as you look at the chart. In the chart—as in most actual situations—both the net spendable cash and the equity build-up are higher in the more highly leveraged investments. Why is this so pleasant? Because the total return represented by the sum of these two items isn't fully taxable. Some of it is tax-free! We pay taxes only to the extent of the income shown on line 8. In the case of the 80 and 90 percent loans, the non-taxable income will actually be supplemented by a reduction in taxes on income from other sources.

Lines 14, 15 and 16 show this net spendable cash and equity build-up in percentage terms: the rate of return on the cash we would put up as a down payment. Notice how this bottom line, the real payoff, gets larger as the mortgage gets larger—or as our down payment is proportionately smaller, in other words. In the case of Property C, for which the down payment was only 10 percent of the total price, return on our $10,000 down payment is a juicy 28 percent.

Negative leverage would come into play when the interest rate on a mortgage is higher than the overall rate of return from the cash invested. If you'll look again at the chart and do some arithmetic of your own, you'll find that an 11 percent mortgage on Property B (column 5) would cost you $4,400. This deducted from the $5,000 operating income would leave you only $600. In this case the net return on your cash investment of $10,000 would actually be smaller than if you hadn't borrowed at all.

Likewise if you have to pay interest at 12 percent, this would be $4,800 for the $40,000 mortgage. This would eat up all but $200 of the $5,000 operating income, and leave a mere 2 percent return on your $10,000 equity. From an income standpoint, at least, leverage would be working against any investor who put money into such a deal.

The figures get worse if you use your $10,000 to buy Property C at $100,000 but have to pay 12 percent on the mortgage. You'd be left with a negative cash flow of $800 a year. That is, you'd be paying interest of $10,800 (12 percent of $90,000) while receiving income of $10,000 from the property. Even if your interest rate is only 8 percent, as assumed on the chart, you'd feel the painful effect of negative leverage if the property's operating income shrank for any reason.

Negative leverage can put money in your pocket, however, if you make a big enough profit when you sell, exchange, or otherwise dispose of the property. The whole thrust of this book so far has been to show you how to buy real estate at markedly lower prices than you'll eventually sell it for.

To understand the paradox of negative leverage becoming profitable, let's go back to the three hypothetical properties we considered earlier in this chapter. Whichever property you bought, we'll assume, you've upgraded it and managed it so well that its rental income and market value have gone up by 35 percent. Anyone following this method should be able to do this almost automatically. But of course repairs and upgrading cost money; let's say it cost 17 percent of your original purchase price, so your net gain is 18 percent.

When you sell the property, you'll pay a commission to the broker —perhaps 6 percent—and there'll be other costs involved in selling. Let's say the commission and other costs reduce your net profit on the sale to only 10 percent.

These figures would mean that when you sold Property A, which you theoretically bought for $10,000 in an all-cash deal, your 10 percent would equal $1,000 (plus whatever profits you pocketed from rents during the period you owned it).

If you made the same 10 percent profit in selling Property B, you'd end up $5,000 better off than at the start (again, plus—or minus— whatever income or deficit the property generated in the meantime). And the profit on the $100,000 Property C would be $10,000—a full 100 percent return on your investment.

Now what effect would negative income leverage have on these figures? Even a little negative income leverage (operating at a loss on borrowed money, in other words) could ultimately bring you more profit than if you had paid all cash for a lower-priced property. In fact, the negative income leverage could have put you $800 into the red each year for as many as five years on the $100,000 property, yet would bring you an overall pre-tax profit as big as you could have made on the all-cash Property A deal. This tabulation shows why:

	$100,000 Property C Gain or (Loss)	$10,000 Property A Gain
1st year income	($ 800.00)	$1,000.00
2nd year income	($ 800.00)	$1,000.00
3rd year income	($ 800.00)	$1,000.00
4th year income	($ 800.00)	$1,000.00
5th year income	($ 800.00)	$1,000.00
PROFIT ON SALE	($10,000.00)	$1,000.00
NET PRE-TAX PROFIT	$ 6,000.00	$6,000.00

This points up the principle that you're usually better off with a small equity in a high-priced property, even if it operates at a little loss, than with full ownership of a lower-priced property operating at a profit—when you finally sell, that is. And profit on sales, not income from rents, is where real estate investors make real money.

Naturally we're oversimplifying a bit. In practice there would be other factors to take into account, such as the timing of the cash flow, payments on the mortgage principal, and the impact of taxes.

One of the times when leverage can really hurt you most, rather than help you, would be when you sold a property for less than its purchase price. A 10 percent loss on a $10,000 all-cash investment would be $1,000. But a 10 percent loss on a $100,000 property bought with a $10,000 down payment would be $10,000. In the first case you'd lose one-tenth of your investment; in the second case you'd lose all of it. However, there is negligible risk of any loss at all on resale if an investor sticks to the principles we have been discussing. Just make reasonable allowances for unforeseen problems and contingencies.

REMEMBER THESE HIGH POINTS:

You can afford to pay high interest when borrowing, if your overall return will be higher yet.

The smaller the proportion of your own money used in a transaction, the higher your potential rate of return.

You can get more "leverage" by either:

1. borrowing at a lower interest rate; or
2. taking out a bigger mortgage in proportion to your down payment; or
3. making a smaller down payment.

XVI *You Can Buy with No Down Payment*

When I give seminars on real estate investment, I often ask, "How many of you have ever bought a property with no down payment? Let's see your hands."

There are always a few people who raise their hands. Sometimes, with a hundred or more students in the room, as many as forty hands go up. The rest of the group looks dumbfounded.

Buy property with only a few dollars for closing costs—or perhaps no money at all? It sounds utterly impossible. Yet it is done every day.

Not by most people, of course. And seldom by one person over and over. Yet almost anyone can do it once in a while. When the right situation comes along, the would-be buyer just needs a little know-how plus patience and persistence.

"No down payment" terms aren't often advertised. Nor are sellers or brokers likely to hint that a down payment might be waived. The average seller needs and expects to get a reasonable hunk of cash. Not only must the seller figure on paying a commission and other sales costs, but he or she probably wants money for some other purpose—maybe another real estate purchase.

Even a seller who doesn't especially need cash at the moment may be unenthusiastic about turning over a valuable asset to someone who offers nothing more than a promise to pay over a period of years. Could this would-be buyer be a phony? What happens if the promised payments aren't forthcoming? What certainty is there that the payments *will* be forthcoming? Can't this buyer just walk away from the property, perhaps leaving it in bad condition?

Let's say you're this would-be buyer who hopes to acquire the property for no down payment. Even if you show an owner you've been investing successfully in real estate for many years, have plenty of assets and a good credit rating, the owner is likely to prefer selling to someone who'll make a reasonable down payment. In fact, his only reason for selling may be to get his hands on some cash.

Still there are exceptions. Watch for them.

Some sellers don't need cash, and realize they may come out ahead in the long run by selling for nothing down. Other sellers have let property run down so badly that a no-cash buyer usually is the only kind who'd be interested. Both types may yearn to free themselves from the work of managing their property. They'd prefer the steady income and high interest yield from a long-term trust deed or mortgage.

Then too, certain kinds of real estate—country acreage, desert land, and resort properties, for example—are often hard to sell at a good price unless the seller will waive most or all of the down payment.

Distress situations offer similar opportunities. If an owner is awash in red ink, he's mainly concerned about cutting his losses. He'll sometimes grudgingly pass up the down payment in order to get the problem off his hands. Likewise, lenders who've had to foreclose on a property they don't want will often be happy to rid themselves of it for nothing down and on generous terms.

Divorces, remarriages, illnesses, deaths, and job changes can often make people eager to sell as quickly as possible, with immediate cash a secondary consideration. In such circumstances, the steady income from payment of principal and interest on notes can often be more attractive than cash that would be immediately and heavily taxable.

Still other chances for no-cash-down purchases may crop up in FHA programs that enable responsible buyers to arrange 100 percent financing for the purchase and rehabilitation of housing for low-income families. Then too, if you're a veteran with a reasonably steady income, you're probably eligible for a loan guarantee that may enable you to buy at least one residential or farm property without a down payment.

However, such situations are seldom visible to the casual shopper. Only when you draw the owner or broker into lengthy conversation will you become aware of them. From then on, your chance to buy without cash will depend heavily on your willingness to ask for such terms and negotiate for them. "Ask, and it shall be given you; seek, and ye shall find," Saint Matthew tells us in the New Testament—and this is just as true in real estate as in other fields.

When you suggest a no-down-payment purchase, brokers almost always look horrified and say, "My client wouldn't consider it." Remember that any broker wants to know where the cash is coming from to pay his or her commission. But this is no reason to let a broker talk you out of submitting such an offer.

A broker must pass all offers along to the seller, no matter how outrageous or ridiculous they may seem. And the broker isn't always in the seller's confidence. Sellers sometimes are willing to sell on far more liberal terms than their brokers imagine. This is especially true when their property has been on the market for quite some time with no sale in prospect.

In persuading a seller not to insist on a substantial down payment, you can use various talking points. I'll just mention them here, and describe them in detail in later chapters.

1. You might suggest that he refinance the property before selling it to you. This would give him the cash he wants, with no immediate liability for taxes on any cash he receives. Then he might be able to sell the property to you on a contract of sale for the full agreed price without accelerating the due date on the loan. That way he could report his gain in installments and spread its taxability.
2. You might offer him a higher total price on condition that he accept your personal note in lieu of the cash down payment. This would enable him to get cash by pledging the note as security for a loan. If he needs a specific amount of cash, you might write your note for enough more than that amount to cover the discount that would be charged by a lender. And you'd cover the balance of the purchase price by a contract of sale. This transaction too would qualify for tax treatment as an installment sale.
3. You might offer to pay a higher interest rate on the personal note or the installment contract or both.
4. You might offer a speedier payoff of either or both. Remember, the best way to get a concession is to offer one. You can afford to concede quite a bit to get a quality property with no down payment.

Is it good business to buy this way? Not necessarily, if you commit yourself to unrealistically heavy installment payments. But it usually can be an advantageous transaction for both parties. Let's consider an actual case, to see how it works out.

A client of mine—we'll call him Mr. Morganfellow—sold an apartment house for $61,350. A normal down payment would have been about one-fifth of the total, or $12,270. But the buyer, Mrs. Keen, didn't have this much. Morganfellow accepted an IOU—a note—from her for this amount. I won't go into all the details, but the fact that Morganfellow didn't insist on a down payment was certainly what enabled him to get as much for his property as he did. He probably couldn't have sold for more than $55,000 to anyone who would have paid one-fifth in cash.

The $12,270 "down payment" note Mrs. Keen signed was payable in installments of 1 percent ($123) per month including interest at the rate of 9 percent a year for fifteen and a half years. The other four-fifths of the purchase price was covered by a contract of sale. The contract committed her to pay $412 per month for twenty-five years. These installments included interest at the same rate, 9 percent.

Thus Mrs. Keen would be paying a total of only $535 a month. She wouldn't have to dig into her savings for any down payment, nor for any balloon payment later.

The gross scheduled income from Morganfellow's apartments was $7,319, out of which Mrs. Keen would have to pay operating expenses of $1,742, leaving her a net operating income of $5,577 per year—only about $465 a month. Looks as if she'll have a negative cash flow, won't she?

But remember that those installments are partly interest and partly principal. It's important to know the proportion of each, because every dollar she pays in interest is tax-deductible. The tax savings are what make this a good deal for her.

During the first year she'll be paying $5,484 interest on the declining balance of her two debts. Thus only $93 of the property's net operating income for that year will be taxable.

Nevertheless she's actually paying out more cash than she takes in. She'll run a cash deficit of $843 the first year, and each of the many years to follow—as you see on the seventh line of the chart at the end of this chapter. Is this any way to grow rich?

Sure it is. That cash deficit won't hurt Mrs. Keen a bit. In the meantime her bank account will be getting bigger because of the sums she won't have to pay in income taxes. And the property will also be appreciating—that is, gradually rising in market value because of the long-term uptrend in the worth of real estate.

Appreciation won't put anything in her bank account until she resells the apartments. But the tax advantages actually give her more spendable dollars every year. Let's look at those advantages.

You'll notice from the chart that the tax men will allow her to deduct $3,067 in depreciation from her otherwise taxable first-year income of $93. So, presto! On paper she has a loss (overflow depreciation, it's called) of $2,974 to show the IRS. How much will this reduce her tax? It depends on what income bracket she's in.

In the chart we're assuming that she is in the 40 percent bracket, which means that every dollar of deductions will reduce her tax by 40 cents. Therefore she can keep $1,189 (40 percent of $2,974) that she would otherwise pay in income tax. So this more than covers her pre-tax cash deficit in owning the property. She'll find herself with $346 extra cash in pocket the first year, as you can see on the chart by subtracting the negative cash flow on the seventh line from the tax benefit on the twelfth line. Each of the first three years she winds up with a little less cash after taxes. Starting with the fourth year she'll have a negative cash flow even after taxes. It will be small but gradually increasing, as shown on the chart.

Again Mrs. Keen seems to come out a loser, doesn't she? But we have to look deeper. Let's go on to the final five lines of the chart, which show her return on investment. This is the real good news.

At the end of ten years Mrs. Keen will have put only $532 of her own money into the property (the difference between her pre-tax cash flow and her tax benefits). Meanwhile, as we noted a few paragraphs ago, she will have been gradually paying off the principal due on her loans, thereby increasing her equity position in the property she's buying. The more of the equity she owns, the more she'll get when she resells.

Meanwhile, as we noted earlier, the resale price tag on the property will be going up year by year. We're not even figuring in the long-term uptrend in realty prices through growing population, higher incomes, and other factors. Inflation alone will push it up. On the chart I reckon this inflation factor at only 3 percent per year—which you'll probably agree is quite conservative. Anyhow, the property's rise in value is shown on the next-to-bottom line.

That's why the bottom line shows, very conservatively, that in ten years Mrs. Keen's equity in the property will have a resale value of at least $35,062. She'll be that much better off than if she had stayed out of the transaction with Morganfellow. Is there any investor who wouldn't want to pay out $532 cash, spread over ten years, on the virtual certainty that it will enrich him or her by some $35,000?

10 Year Projection of Cash Flow, Tax Benefits, and Return on Investment From Purchase
of a $61,350 Property With No Cash Down Payment

Year #:	1	2	3	4	5	6	7	8	9	10
ANNUAL CASH FLOW:										
Gross Scheduled Income	$ 7,319									
Less: Operating Expenses	– 1,742									
=Net Operating Income	= 5,577	$ 5,577	$ 5,577	$ 5,577	$ 5,577	$ 5,577	$ 5,577	$ 5,577	$ 5,577	$ 5,577
Less: Interest	5,484	5,395	5,299	5,194	5,079	4,953	4,816	4,665	4,501	4,320
=Taxable Income Before Deprec$	93	182	278	383	498	624	761	912	1,076	1,257
Less: Principal	– 936	1,025	1,121	1,226	1,341	1,467	1,604	1,755	1,919	2,100
=CASH FLOW	($843)	($843)	($843)	($843)	($843)	($843)	($843)	($843)	($843)	($843)
ANNUAL TAX BENEFIT										
Taxable Income Before Deprec$	93	182	278	383	498	624	761	912	1,076	1,257
Less: Depreciation	(3,067)	(2,876)	(2,696)	(2,529)	(2,454)	(2,454)	(2,454)	(2,454)	(2,454)	(2,454)
=Overflow Depreciation	(2,974)	(2,694)	(2,418)	(2,071)	(1,956)	(1,830)	(1,693)	(1,542)	(1,378)	(1,197)
Times: 40% Tax Bracket	x 40%	x 40%	x 40%	x 40%	x 40%	x 40%	x 40%	x 40%	x 40%	x 40%
=Tax Benefit	$ 1,189	$ 1,078	$ 967	$ 828	$ 782	$ 732	$ 677	$ 616	$ 551	$ 478
CUMULATIVE RETURN ON INVESTMT.										
Principal Paydown	$ 936	$ 1,961	$ 3,082	$ 4,308	$ 5,649	$ 7,116	$ 8,720	$10,475	$12,394	$14,494
Cash Flow	(843)	(1,686)	(2,529)	(3,372)	(4,215)	(5,058)	(5,901)	(6,744)	(7,587)	(8,430)
Tax Benefit	1,189	2,269	3,234	4,062	4,844	5,576	6,253	6,869	7,420	7,898
Appreciation	1,840	3,736	5,689	7,699	9,771	11,905	14,102	16,366	18,699	21,100
TOTAL RETURN ON INVESTMENT..	$ 3,122	$ 6,280	$ 9,476	$12,697	$16,049	$19,539	$23,174	$26,966	$30,926	$33,062

NOTE:

1) "Down payment" consists of a $12,270 note payable at $123 per month including interest at 9% per annum over a period of 15½ years. Balance of purchase price is represented by a $49,080 contract of sale payable over 25 years at $412 per month, also including 9% per annum interest.

2) Gross scheduled income is assumed to remain unchanged throughout the 10 years. Although it might very well be increased, the expenses could probably be expected to go up more or less proportionately so that the net operating income would remain about the same.

3) Operating expenses do not include an allowance for vacancies or maintenance, which should be nominal since the building is well located and has recently been completely renovated.

4) Depreciation is computed on the basis of what can reasonably be expected to be allowed by the I.R.S. on the building and other land improvements. The 125% of declining balance method is used until the 4th year and straight-line thereafter.

5) Principal paydown and appreciation are benefits that will not be realized until there is a sale or other disposition of the property. Appreciation is assumed to take place at a rate of 3% per year.

6) The return-on-investment figures do not reflect any sales costs or tax consequences that may be incurred if the property is disposed of at that time. Note, however, that the down payment note would have a $6,275 balance due at the end of the 10th year.

So again we see what leverage can do. We see why it usually makes good sense to borrow as much as possible when investing in real estate.

Donald A. Yule, executive vice president of the Arizona Association of Realtors and a partner of mine in many real estate ventures, has summed up the principle in these words:

"Leverage is to real estate investment what scientific agriculture is to an investment in good seed. The more of it you use, the greater the harvest you can expect to reap."

REMEMBER THESE HIGH POINTS:

Sellers seldom hint that they might waive a down payment. But they can be persuaded if they don't need cash, or if they must sell quickly. Feel them out if you think there's any possibility.

You can suggest that the seller refinance the property before selling it to you.

You can offer your personal note in lieu of down payment, and suggest that he get cash by pledging it as security for a loan.

You can offer to pay higher interest rates.

You can offer a shorter repayment term.

XVII Eight Ways to Reduce the Down Payment

The most common obstacle to buying or selling property is that the buyer can't afford to put up enough cash for the down payment the seller feels he must have.

However, there are plenty of ways to solve this problem. As we've already seen, a seller often changes his mind when offered more attractive long-term inducements such as collecting a higher interest rate, receiving bigger monthly payments and/or a bigger total price.

In this chapter we'll look at eight other solutions. There are times when a seller (who may be you, or may be the fellow you're trying to make a deal with) seems adamant about the need for a big chunk of cash on the barrelhead. Let's see what can be done at such times.

Using your broker's credit is a magically simple solution, if you have a smart broker with good credit or good connections. He can often call up the savings and loan, or some other lending institution, and get a loan that you couldn't otherwise get. (We're assuming now that you're the would-be buyer who can't come up with enough cash for the down payment.) Sometimes he just knows the right person to talk to, and can persuade that person to grant you the loan. At other times he may be willing to put his own credit on the line by cosigning your note, so that if you default for any reason the lender can still collect from the broker. Also, brokers have been known to advance their own cash as payments for improvements to a property, if this is needed before the deal will make sense.

We saw in Chapter X how you can sometimes use a mortgage or trust deed to sweeten a bargain. Now we'll see how a broker may help you do this. Let's assume you've recently sold a house, getting $6,000 in cash from the sale, and agreeing to carry back a $5,000 purchase-money second trust deed. Now you want to use both the cash and the trust deed to buy another house, for which the seller is asking an $11,000 down payment.

You make this offer to the seller, but he shakes his head. He doubts the value of the property securing your second trust deed. He's afraid the borrower might default and leave him holding the bag.

Here is where your broker will come in handy, if he knows the true value of the house you've just sold and is sure that any foreclosure sale would bring in enough to pay off both the first and second trust deeds. Since he has a commission at stake, he has an incentive to take a hand.

The broker's unsecured personal note may be perfectly acceptable to the seller, if the broker's credit rating is good. It could be written to provide for payments to the seller on the same basic terms that payments were scheduled to be made to you on the trust deed note. Then you would simply assign your trust deed to the broker. He would collect on it for his own account and make payments to the seller at the same rate on the unsecured personal note. If your broker doesn't think of this, suggest it to him.

You can add that he has a chance of plucking out a juicy plum. Second trust deeds are often paid off before they are due. If this happens, the broker will have the use of the extra money while he continues to make payments as scheduled on his personal note.

Your broker may advance cash out of his own pocket rather than see a sale fall through and lose his commission. For example, let's say you want to buy a $40,000 house and take over an existing $25,000 FHA loan in the process. It would be common for you to offer a $7,500 cash down payment, and ask the seller to carry back a $7,500 purchase-money mortgage or deed of trust to make up the gap. But what if the seller says, "Sorry, $7,500 cash isn't enough," when it's all you can scrape up?

He knows he'll have to pay a $2,400 commission to the broker out of cash you're offering. He'll also have to pay several hundred dollars in closing costs. So there won't be enough cash left from your $7,500 to enable him to make a down payment on another house he has in mind.

Maybe you can nudge the broker into suggesting, "Instead of taking my $2,400 commission in cash, I'll take it in the form of a note secured by a third mortgage on this house." This would mean cutting down the second mortgage by $2,400—the amount of the broker's commission—and, more important, it would mean the seller would retain $2,400 more of the cash you're offering. It would also mean you'd be making monthly payments on three mortgages instead of two, but your total payments would probably be the same as if you had only two.

A still better solution for all concerned: You might execute just one $7,500 subsidiary mortgage, payable to the broker, under an agreement whereby he'll apply 32 percent of each payment toward his commission and pass along the remainder to the seller. This way you'll have only two mortgages on which to make payments. The broker will probably feel safer than if he had accepted a separate third mortgage. And the seller will probably feel safer too, because he assumes the broker will do a professional job of collecting the payments on the second mortgage. Again, the seller is $2,400 better off cashwise because the broker isn't taking his commission in cash.

This same basic financing structure could be used if the seller in the above situation was asking a minimum of $7,500 down but you only had $5,100 to put into the investment. Here again the solution would be to get the broker to agree to defer his $2,400 commission so the seller wouldn't have to pay it out of the cash he receives. That way if the seller accepted a $5,100 down payment he would come out with as much cash as he would if he continued to demand $7,500 and had to pay a $2,400 commission out of it. In this case, the $2,400 commission would be added to the second mortgage note, making the total $9,900 instead of $7,500. The only difference would be the amount of the monthly payments and the proportion of each payment that the broker would forward to the seller.

Like most people, brokers prefer to be paid in cash for their services. But they're usually brainy enough to realize that lending money to a buyer or seller makes good sense when this is the way to make a profitable transaction possible.

A seller may pay a buyer's closing costs in order to swing a sale, if he's anxious to sell. Let's suppose that you're the seller now, dickering with a prospective buyer who has only enough cash for a down payment but can depend on plenty of income to meet the monthly payment requirements. If you want to enable him to buy your house, one way of doing so is to pay his share of the closing costs as well as your own.

Normally a buyer and seller each pay part of these costs. Customs vary from one area to another, but in most situations an escrow can be set up so that a seller pays most if not all the closing costs and even the taxes, insurance, and impounds. If you as seller are willing, it still depends on the lender and the nature of the primary financing. New VA loans fit well into this situation. In VA financing, the seller must pay both the discount points and the buyer's escrow fee; all other costs and fees may be paid by either party. Thus your prospect, if he is eligible for a VA loan, conceivably could buy your house for absolutely no out-of-pocket costs, if you're willing.

Naturally you won't want to pay these extra costs, in most cases. But if this will ensure a quick sale, you may find it worthwhile.

If the buyer is getting FHA financing, this plan won't work. FHA doesn't mind if the seller pays all the loan costs, but the seller gains nothing because under FHA financing the amount of the loan to the buyer is reduced by one dollar for every dollar paid by the seller in the name of the buyer.

The plan may or may not work in conventional loans, depending on the lender. Many banks and savings and loan firms won't allow a seller to pay part of a buyer's closing costs. Even so, you can get substantially the same results by adjusting the terms of purchase money or secondary financing or by other techniques.

Two VA loans to the same veteran are perfectly possible. Few people know this. Many veterans who bought homes under VA guarantees some years ago are now buying other homes on stiffer financing terms because they think they've used up their GI eligibility, when they really haven't. They may be eligible for still more VA-backed money.

During World War II, VA loans guaranteed the lenders against loss up to $4,000. In 1951 this guarantee was upped to $7,500. In 1968 it was upped again to $12,500. And in January 1975 the guarantee was increased still further to $17,500. As the law stands at this writing, any veteran of the armed forces who has paid off a home loan guaranteed by the VA is eligible for another VA-backed loan with a guarantee up to a maximum equal to the difference between $17,500 and whatever guarantee he used previously.

So if you're a veteran—or if you want to sell your property to a veteran—be sure to look into this. All veterans who took out a GI loan before January 1975 have a remaining guarantee entitlement of at least $5,000 and maybe much more.

Remember, neither the Veterans Administration nor the law sets any maximum on the size of the loan the veteran can take out with any given amount of guarantee. This is up to the lender. However, if a vet meets the basic credit qualifications, he can generally buy a home with no down payment if it is appraised and priced at no more than four times the amount of his remaining guarantee entitlement. This means that someone with the full $17,500 entitlement can probably purchase a $70,000 home with no down payment except closing costs if he qualifies for the loan.

The delayed close is an arrangement that can help a buyer when the money market is so tight that he can't get a mortgage loan. Many deals fell through in 1974 and certain other years for no reason except that lenders had no funds available. If anyone involved had known about delayed-closing arrangements, many of these transactions could have gone through.

Imagine a situation where you and the other party have agreed on a sale price and down payment. All that is needed is a new modest-sized first mortgage loan. Often, in such situations, a bank or savings and loan knows it will have money available to lend again a few weeks or months later. If so, you needn't wait to sign the papers. Set up an escrow with a delayed close.

The lender is usually willing to give tentative approval, and to say approximately what the terms of the loan will be. If so, the escrow can be arranged to run for six months or longer, but with a "pre-release" clause. Under this clause the whole down payment is released to the seller within a few days, and the seller deposits a grant deed. The deed will be recorded in the buyer's name when the loan has been obtained and/or other specified conditions met.

Under delayed-close escrows, the buyer can usually take possession of the property under an "interim occupancy agreement" at about the same time the seller receives the down payment. The buyer pays monthly occupancy fees to the seller. The seller keeps on making the payments on any existing loans. Then when the escrow finally closes, the buyer stops paying occupancy fees to the seller, and switches over to making whatever monthly payments the new lender is to receive under the terms of the mortgage loan.

Temporary inability to get a loan is only one of many reasons why you may want a delayed close. Here are some other reasons: Maybe you expect interest rates to come down in a few months. Maybe you expect an uptrend in economic conditions so that lenders will be flush and will be competing to make loans, thereby liberalizing their terms. Or maybe you are waiting for cash from the sale of another property, and need to use it in your purchase. (In this case, you and the seller might agree to a smaller down payment, to be supplemented with additional money later.)

Still another reason for delaying the close of an escrow might arise when there is (or will be) a second mortgage on a property for which you're negotiating a new first mortgage. A note you give a lender can't say "second mortgage" or "first mortgage." The same is true of trust deeds. Whether your note is a first or second normally depends on the date it is recorded. The first one recorded has the first claim against the property, and the second one recorded has the second claim. So in cases where you pay off an old first mortgage and want to take out a new one, if there's a second mortgage in the picture you usually must get the holder to agree in writing that his mortgage (or trust deed) will be subordinate to the new first one. However, if you're taking out a new second mortgage while the first one is still being negotiated, you can instruct the escrow agent to delay the close until you've obtained the new first mortgage, and then to record the second mortgage immediately behind the first. This is a simpler way of keeping the priorities straight without getting the second lender to agree in writing that his claim will be subordinate.

The delayed close can also simplify a two-stage deal—a sequence of selling one property in order to get cash for the down payment on another. To illustrate, let's suppose you want to buy Mr. White's house and you've reached an agreement with him on the terms. These terms call for a down payment of $6,000, say—which you don't have at the moment. But you expect to have it in a few weeks, because Mr. Green is buying a house from you, and his down payment is to be somewhat more than $6,000. So you explain this to Mr. White and propose, "Let's set up a delayed-close escrow on my purchase from you. We can work out all the arrangements and get them in writing, on the understanding that they're conditional on my collecting this other down payment from Mr. Green."

White may ask, "What if your deal with Green falls through for any reason? Then my deal with you also collapses, doesn't it?"

You admit, "It would mean that I wouldn't have the six grand I need for your down payment, so our delayed escrow would never close. But you and I wouldn't necessarily have to call off my purchase of your house. We'd just have to renegotiate the terms. I'd have to figure out some inducements to make it worth your while to accept a smaller down payment."

With this understanding, almost any seller is willing to go along with a delayed close.

Using a second mortgage as a guarantee can be another way of getting around the down-payment obstacle, in cases where a seller doesn't necessarily need a lot of cash but feels uneasy about a second mortgage that the prospective buyer offers in lieu of a down payment.

For example, imagine that you own a $125,000 apartment house, are ready to sell it, and are negotiating with a prospective buyer, Mr. Nemo. He offers you a $25,000 second trust deed he owns. "This will be my down payment," he proposes. "It will bring you $250 a month in payments from the borrower."

But you say, "What if that borrower defaults? Whoever holds the first mortgage on the property will get his money first. And I don't think the property will bring enough at a foreclosure sale to leave any money left over for me. If that should happen, then in effect I would have sold you my building for $25,000 less than I'm asking."

Nemo says, "Well, will you sell it to me for nothing down? I'm willing to pay more per month if you will, and maybe shorten the term for paying off the whole amount."

You think this over. You don't know much about Nemo. If he gets in a bind, he'd have little to lose by making a payment or two and then walking away from your building. So you finally tell him, "No, I'm sorry, Mr. Nemo, but I just wouldn't feel safe with a nothing-down sale, and I wouldn't feel safe with your second mortgage either."

So is the deal off? Not at all, if you or Nemo or the broker do a little creative financial thinking. Here's what negotiators might work out—and actually did, in a recent transaction I happen to know about:

Nemo finally said, "Okay, I'll give you security against my defaulting on my contract to pay you $125,000 over the agreed-on term of years. I'll put up this $25,000 second trust deed as collateral. If I default, I'll lose the trust deed and it will be yours. Then will you feel safe with a no-cash-down sale?"

This arrangement is good for Nemo. He continues to collect $250 a month in payments on the second mortgage. The rents he collects as new owner of the $125,000 apartments are enough to meet the monthly payments on it. And the seller has enough extra security so that the deal is worthwhile for him too. Of course there's still some possibility that both Nemo and the man who's paying on the second mortgage might default, but such a double disaster is unlikely. Even if it occurred, the $125,000 apartment house would revert to the earlier owner. So if you were the seller in such a situation, the deal with Nemo would be not only profitable but reasonably safe.

A performance second or third mortgage is one way that a buyer can safeguard himself when a seller demands more money than the property seems to be worth.

The phrase "performance mortgage" means a mortgage agreement that hinges on the rental income brought in by the property. Let's say you want to buy the Golconda Apartments, but you and the owner can't agree on the purchase price. He swears up and down that the Golconda will produce at least $800 a month in rental income for you, and he's priced the building accordingly. But you've analyzed the property, and you're afraid the vacancy rate will be higher than he says. So you don't feel sure of collecting more than about $700 monthly in rents, which means that you want to pay less for the building.

It looks like a stalemate, because neither you nor the Golconda owner will compromise on your estimates of the rental income. But a "performance mortgage" agreement can bring you together, if he's willing to take the risk that Golconda rents won't fall.

The agreement can be set up in a number of different ways. You and he might agree that your payments of principal and/or interest on this second or third mortgage will be only as large as can be covered by the cash income produced by the Golconda. Or you might set the loan up so you'll be entitled to a minimum cash return on your investment (say 10 percent) before you'll be obligated to make any payments on this mortgage. Or you and he might agree to share cash flow from the building up to a point where you were collecting a specified amount, and apply all cash flow above that toward payments on the performance document. Often you may want to include a clause providing that you'll owe nothing further on this mortgage after a stipulated number of years (perhaps ten) if the property hasn't generated enough income to pay off the loan by that time.

When you propose a "performance mortgage" to an owner who seems to be asking too much, you make him put up or shut up. He says the property will generate enough income to justify the price he asks. If it really is worth this much, he has nothing to lose by signing a performance agreement. If he won't sign, he tacitly admits that he isn't so sure after all that his property will bring in as much income as he predicts. All you're doing is asking him to share some of the risk you'd take in accepting his estimate.

Performance-money mortgages are often used when a buyer takes over an apartment house with many vacancies. The seller says, "I'm sure you'll have no trouble getting enough tenants to fill up the building." Then the buyer may say, "All right, let's agree that you'll give me one dollar's worth of credit toward payments on the performance mortgage for every two dollars' worth of scheduled rent I don't receive because of vacancies. Then you won't be taking all the risk, and neither will I. On a one-for-two scale, I'll still have a strong incentive to try to fill up the building. But I won't lose my shirt if this is impossible, because you'll forgive part of my mortgage debt to you." A seller who is sincere can scarcely refuse such a proposition.

A profit-sharing agreement is possibility number eight, of those we've explored in this chapter, for persuading a seller to accept a smaller down payment than he is asking.

Incidentally, please don't jump to the conclusion that this exhausts the list of possibilities. There are many, many other possible ways of structuring a purchase through creative financing. In fact, I've counted more than a hundred such ways.*

Suppose Mr. Morganfellow owns an apartment building that produces enough rents to be worth $200,000. This is the price he asks, and you know that it's fair. But he wants $30,000 down. And you have only $20,000 cash in sight for a down payment. You try the usual negotiating tactics, such as offering to pay a higher total price, bigger monthly payments, or a higher interest rate. But for one reason or another these terms don't suit him, even though you can see that he genuinely wants to sell his property to you.

So you try something more creative. You offer to share with him the profits that you expect to make as owner of the building in return for his agreeing to accept the $20,000 down and carrying back a $180,000 instead of $170,000 mortgage.

There are several ways to do this. One way might be simply to say, "Let's sign an agreement whereby our accountants figure how much profit I make from this building every year, and I'll pay you a specified percentage of it in addition to the regular payments I'll be making to you on the $180,000 loan."

He might reply, "Sounds good, but I wonder if your accountant and mine could agree. There are various ways to figure profits. For example, how should depreciation be figured?"

---

* For a free brochure on creative financing and other courses held in your area, contact Dr. Albert J. Lowry, 50 Washington Street, Reno, Nevada 89503.

If there seems to be too much likelihood of a dispute, another possibility would be to offer Mr. Morganfellow a fixed percentage of all cash flow you produce above the amount needed to cover the mortgage payments. But here again there might be arguments about the bookkeeping. What if you were putting cash into capital improvements? Paying money to a hired manager? What if you wanted to refinance your debt? Should your general office overhead be included as a deductible cost? There could also be questions about whether the cash flow was to be figured on a periodic or cumulative basis. Should you make monthly payments to Morganfellow based on the amount of cash you receive that month? Or should you pay him quarterly or yearly, based on the cumulative cash flow? Then too, you and he must look ahead to the possibility that you may want to resell this property to someone else in a few years. What becomes of his share of the profits then?

Maybe a simpler agreement would be best. You could simply offer Morganfellow a fixed share of the gross rents (in addition, of course, to your mortgage payments). Or you could offer to share these rents with him on a sliding scale, so that he'd get a larger share if the monthly gross rose above a stipulated amount.

Best of all might be a straight bonus deal. You'd pay him only when the gross rents reached an agreed level. Then if your efforts to improve the property are successful, he should share handsomely in the fattening of the gross. But if the property doesn't earn enough, you won't be obligated to divvy up a meager profit.

Suppose Mr. Morganfellow rejects all these ideas, saying, "I'm sorry, my friend, but I absolutely must receive a $30,000 down payment." You're still not licked.

Either you or your broker may know some private investor who'd be glad to put up the additional $10,000 cash for 10 percent yearly interest plus a "kicker" that would pay a bonus if your profits reach a certain point. This gives him a realistic chance at a substantially higher return on his money.

However, if this private investor is a suspicious soul, he might say, "Maybe you're following the Lowry formula. Maybe you plan to upgrade this property in a hurry, raise the rents so you can resell for a higher price, and then pay off my loan. The higher rents wouldn't bring me much of a bonus, would they?"

It's a valid objection. But you can meet it by saying, "We'll put a special clause in the loan agreement. If you wish, the clause will entitle you to share in whatever profit I make from a resale. Or the clause can prohibit the loan from being paid off before a certain date, no matter whether I resell the property or not. If we write the clause this way, it would require any new buyer to assume my obligation to pay you whatever bonus the property earns."

This tactic can often enable you to buy income property with absolutely nothing down. The private investor puts up the full down payment in return for a stipulated interest rate plus a share in the profits, or the cash flow, or the gross rental income. Do you see what tremendous leverage you get when you buy a property this way? You're acquiring a money-maker without putting any cash on the line. Therefore, you can well afford to offer a lender a much bigger share of the prospective benefits of ownership than he is likely to expect or demand. It's a great deal for both of you.

In effect he is becoming at least a minor partner in your enterprise.

REMEMBER THESE HIGH POINTS:

To get around a seller's demand for a big down payment, you may—

1. Use your broker's credit. His note may be acceptable.
2. Suggest that the broker advance cash.
3. Suggest that the broker defer his commission.
4. Propose that the seller accept a "performance mortgage."
5. Offer the seller a profit-sharing agreement.

To get around a buyer's inability to make as big a down payment as you need, you may—

1. Pay his share of the closing costs.
2. If he is a veteran, see if he can get a VA loan.
3. Set up an escrow with a delayed close.
4. Use a second mortgage as a guarantee.

XVIII Magic with Mortgages

Most people think that a home loan agreement is a standard printed form with a few blanks to be filled for amounts, interest rate, and number of payments. This needn't be true.

Sure, the basic transaction is simple. When you borrow money, you sign a note, which is proof of your debt. Then as security, to be forfeited if you don't pay, you sign an agreement giving the lender the right to force the sale of the property to recover the amount owed him. A mortgage or a trust deed is the agreement showing that your property is the collateral for your note.

In reading this book you've become aware that the terms of a real estate loan may vary from one lending institution to another—or may vary in the same institution from month to month depending on the state of the money market. But maybe you think this is the extent of the possible variations.

Even some people who've done a lot of business in real estate think this way. "A mortgage is a mortgage," they say. "A trust deed is a trust deed. These documents are always the same fundamentally."

Now you're going to find out how mistaken such beliefs are.

In this chapter we'll see how the orthodox real estate loan agreement can be sculpted, shaped, tacked, trimmed, and transformed to bring you additional spectacular profits. We'll look into wraparound mortgages, overlapping mortgages, contracts of sale, lease options, and other sophisticated strategies you can use when you put up real estate as collateral.

The average lending officer at a bank or an S & L isn't likely to suggest any such agreements to you—mainly because they're a bit hard to explain. But he'll usually go along if you ask for one of them and if he sees that you and your real estate broker understand them too. They're well worth understanding.

All-inclusive trust deed or mortgage, also sometimes referred to as a wraparound or overriding trust deed or mortgage. This is a trust deed or mortgage that is subordinate to, yet includes all the encumbrances to which it is subordinated. It is a junior deed of trust or mortgage that includes the unpaid balance of all existing trust deeds senior to it, in addition to a possible further encumbrance on the property. It is generally used in connection with a sale, but sometimes in connection with a refinancing.

It is easier to illustrate than to explain. Recently I knew an owner who wanted to sell a property on which he was paying off a twenty-five-year loan. The unpaid balance was $30,000. He was paying 6 percent interest. He found a would-be buyer, and the two of them agreed on a price of $60,000, with the buyer to put up $10,000 in cash, leaving $50,000 to be financed somehow.

One possibility was for the buyer to try to refinance the $30,000 first mortgage with a new, larger loan. However, the money market was tight at the time. Any new loan he might get probably would not be for more than $42,000 and would cost him 10 percent interest plus at least two points. In addition, there would be a repayment fee on the existing loan equal to six months' unearned interest, or another $900.

A second possibility: The buyer might assume the $30,000 existing loan and have the seller carry back a purchase-money second trust deed or mortgage for the remaining $20,000 of the sales price. The interest rate could be whatever the buyer and seller agreed on up to the maximum legal rate, which in their state was 10 percent.

A third possibility (and the one they finally decided on) was to use an all-inclusive deed of trust. The buyer gave the seller a promissory note in the amount of $50,000 with interest at 8½ percent. The note contained a clause to the effect that its face amount included the unpaid balance of the first mortgage, and that the seller would still be responsible for making payments on that underlying obligation as it stood.

So the seller was in the comfortable position of receiving interest at an annual rate of $4,250 (8½% of $50,000) while paying out interest at an annual rate of $1,800 (6% of $30,000), thereby netting $2,450, or 12.25%, on the $20,000 difference between the two notes. This is 2.25 percentage points higher than he could legally have charged if he had carried back a $20,000 purchase-money second. The arrangement put an extra $450 per year into his pocket.

The buyer made more money too. He avoided completely the $900 prepayment penalty and some $1,000 in loan-origination costs he would have incurred if he had taken out the new 10% $42,000 first mortgage. Furthermore, he ended up paying 1½ percentage points ($750) less annual interest than he would have paid on a new first and second totaling $50,000.

Unfortunately, the option to use an all-inclusive note is limited to cases where there is no acceleration or other alienation clause in any of the notes or mortgages against the property, or, if there is such a clause, the lender agrees to waive it. He will seldom waive it unless he has little to lose by doing so. In that case the borrower may also have little to gain from the lender's willingness to allow the loan to stand intact.

When to use an all-inclusive mortgage. Where there is no clause in the existing loans that blocks them, all-inclusive loans can be good to use when:

1. There is a locked-in loan that cannot be paid off—at least without severe penalties.
2. The buyer is a poor risk and is making a small down payment.
3. A property is overpriced and the seller sticks to the price but not to the terms of sale.
4. The existing loans are at lower interest rates than you could get on new financing.
5. There is little time to shop for new loans and little chance of the buyer's qualifying for them.
6. The down payment offered is so low that the only practical alternative would be for the seller to carry back a large purchase-money mortgage.

The advantages to a seller from using an all-inclusive loan can include:

1. Retaining favorable terms of existing financing in case it becomes necessary to repossess the property.
2. Disposing of property that has a locked-in loan against it.
3. Obtaining legally a much higher effective interest rate (as in the foregoing example).
4. Because of this higher effective interest rate, being able to sell or borrow against the all-inclusive note at a lower discount than against a similar purchase-money note.

5. Getting a higher price because you can afford to offer more liberal terms on the sale (more apparent than real).

The advantages to you as a buyer can also be weighty:

1. Being able to acquire a much bigger property for the same down payment.
2. Being able to buy property for which you could not qualify if you had to apply for new financing.
3. Being able to set up greater tax benefits by adjusting price and terms.
4. Saving the cost of new loan appraisal fees, points, escrow charges, etc.
5. Saving the time it would take to shop for new loans and fill out loan applications.
6. Tailoring payment terms more directly to your needs for cash.
7. Getting title to property with an owner's policy of title insurance, which might be difficult under certain other arrangements.
8. Being able to bargain for better terms by offering a higher price.
9. Being responsible for only one loan payment, rather than two or more.

I strongly urge that you get a real estate attorney's help when preparing all-inclusive deeds of trust and contracts providing for their use.

Contracts of sale (also referred to as land contracts, real property sales contracts, conditional sales contracts, agreements of sale, contracts for deeds, and conditional contracts of sale) are agreements to convey title to property when certain specific conditions are fulfilled, with title staying where it is until these conditions are met.

Contracts of sale are often used as alternatives to all-inclusive trust deeds. The two types of agreement have many features in common. In both types the buyer pays the seller, who is still responsible for payments due on existing mortgages against the property. Most of my pointers about one type apply to the other too.

However, some tricky differences arise from the fact that title doesn't pass to the buyer, under a contract of sale, until stipulated conditions are met. A buyer entering into a contract of sale must wait until the conditions of the contract are fulfilled in order to acquire title, but in the meantime he does become an equitable owner of the property with rights of possession.

To protect himself, he should insist that the contract be recorded and that title insurance be issued in his favor. The seller will usually prefer to leave the contract unrecorded. Why? Because if the buyer defaults, having the contract recorded would cloud the title. Court action would be needed to clear the title if the buyer refused to grant a release.

Many lenders flinch at the thought of accepting an equitable interest instead of an equity interest as security for their loan. Another problem: After having made all payments in accordance with the contract, the buyer may find that the title is defective or that he can't obtain title at all. And what happens if the seller should die, become incompetent, or be adjudged bankrupt? The buyer would have to go to court to acquire title.

The seller is uneasy because he might have to institute court action to regain possession if the buyer stops paying and refuses to move out. Or he might make the painful discovery that there are liens against his title because the buyer was negligent or dishonest.

Even so, a contract of sale can be a useful instrument. It just needs to be drawn up by competent legal counsel with a view to protecting both parties. It would be still more useful in the future, if a recent decision of the California Supreme Court gets a favorable nod from courts in other states.

Until this decision (Tucker *v.* Lassen Savings & Loan Association, Supreme Court 42006, October 1974), courts hadn't done much to prevent a lender from enforcing a ferocious "due-on-sale" alienation clause in his loan if property securing it was sold under a contract of sale. It didn't make any difference that the seller hadn't actually transferred title to the property; he got socked because he had agreed to do so at some future date if certain stipulated conditions were met.

In the Tucker–Lassen case, the court turned thumbs down on this time-honored trick clause. It said in effect: "Even if an installment land contract may not appear feasible because of a typical due-on-sale clause, the lender doesn't have an *automatic* right to accelerate. If the buyer's credit qualifications are reasonably satisfactory and the seller is keeping a substantial equity interest, the lender must prove the transaction has impaired his security before he can enforce such a drastic clause against the seller."

So now one state has given a seller the right to retain existing favorable loans despite "due-on-sale" clauses. This could be far-reaching, but don't let it go to your head. The only thing reasonably sure so far is that acceleration clauses can't be enforced in a contract of sale in California if these three tests are met: (1) the buyer is credit-worthy, (2) the seller is keeping legal title and substantial equity interest, (3) the lender's security is unimpaired.

The decision may lead to similar rulings by courts in other states. Some day—maybe soon—lenders may be prevented from putting the screws on a borrower who enters into any agreement to dispose of his property. But not yet. So far, the new mercy would appear to apply only to contracts of sale subject to California law, and only to those that have the characteristics I've mentioned. Let's hope that the same reasoning will lead courts in other states to reach the same judicial conclusion. Then court protection may extend to any sale where the seller keeps a substantial interest in the property.

Take a long hard look at any situation where existing loans you want to retain are booby-trapped with a due-on-sale clause. If you hope to kick out such clauses, get good legal advice first, and have your lawyer prepare or approve the contract documents.

An all-inclusive loan is probably a better choice where there are no due-on-sale clauses in the existing loans. It is generally much cleaner and more forthright from a legal point of view. It leaves less room for acts by either party that could lead to litigation. Here too, an attorney should approve the documents.

You can buy under a partnership name as another way of protecting yourself when due-on-sale clauses hang over you.

If a husband and wife take title to an investment property, they usually do so as "joint tenants with right of survivorship" or as "tenants in common." They seldom think of forming a partnership and taking title in the partnership name. Yet this is usually just as easy, and the legal and tax angles are about the same. As partners, when they get ready to dispose of the property, they sell their interest in the partnership. The due-on-sale clause can't be used against them because there's no alienation of title; title remains in the same name. Neat, eh?

To illustrate, suppose Mr. and Mrs. Jones are buying an apartment house at 10 North Cumberland Road. They form a partnership, which they might call "10 North Cumberland Road," or "Montlake Plaza" or any equally jazzy name. They'd better not use their own names, however, as this would cause complications if they later sell their interests in the partnership to someone else. Using the address of the property as the name of the partnership is probably best. They register ownership in the name of the partnership, and take out a loan that gives the lender the option to demand that it be paid off in full if title to the property changes hands.

But title never changes hands. If a Mr. and Mrs. Smith come along and strike a bargain with the Joneses to acquire the property, they don't buy it from them and they don't buy it from the partnership. They buy the partnership instead.

If you are considering ownership in the name of a partnership with this sort of switch in mind, of course you'll want to get good legal advice in drawing up the documents.

The lease-option is another method of private financing that may protect you from due-on-sale clauses and similar speed-up demands by a lending institution. Instead of selling your property outright, you enter into a master lease and option-to-purchase agreement with the prospective buyer.

Typical loan agreements say nothing about a right to call the loan if the owner gives some third party a lease with an option to buy. Even if a loan agreement does contain such a clause, a court might well nullify it by reasoning similar to that in the Tucker–Lassen decision.

Furthermore, granting someone an option to buy isn't the same as signing an agreement to sell. Giving an option is simply promising to hold an offer open for a period of time, usually in return for money or some other consideration.

Suppose you want to sell your apartment house for $120,000, and a Mr. Emptor has agreed in principle to buy it at that price with $30,000 down. However, the proposed sale is snagged by the fact that the nice $90,000, 6 percent, seventeen-year loan you have on the property has a clause in it that makes the whole amount due-on-sale. Mr. Emptor figures he can't afford to buy the property at the price you're asking if he must refinance it at the prevailing 9 percent interest rates. Seemingly you'll have to lower your price, or else the proposed sale will fall through.

You and Emptor consider various alternatives but discard them for one reason or another. Then you solve the problem by working out a lease-option proposal. Here's how it might go:

Of Emptor's $30,000 cash that he has available for a down payment, he'll put up $25,500 as a security deposit for a twenty-year lease on your apartments. Under this lease, he'll make monthly rental payments to you equal to or slightly larger than the payments you're committed to make on your $90,000 loan. (One reason for making them slightly larger would be to compensate you for your trouble in the matter. The transaction would still be sound if Emptor's payments to you were just the same as the payments you were making on your loan. In fact, you might conceivably arrange to have him pay your bank, and have the bank pass along the payments to the lender on your loan.)

At the same time you give Emptor an option to buy your property at any time during the twenty-year term of his lease. By the terms of this option, he can buy it for $4,500 cash plus whatever amount is then required to pay off the loan on the understanding that he'll also forfeit the $25,500 he paid you as a "security deposit." These two amounts, of course, add up to $30,000—the same amount he's already agreed would be his down payment.

The agreement also commits Emptor to pay all property taxes and other expenses. The entire agreement is filed with the county recorder. You're free of all expenses connected with the property. You're in essentially the same position as if you'd sold it—and you're better off in at least one way. You can still take tax deductions for depreciation because you still legally own the apartments.

After Emptor's payments reduce the balance on the seventeen-year loan to zero, the due-on-sale clause is no longer an obstacle to selling the property. Thereupon Emptor pays you the $4,500 option price, forfeits his $25,500 security deposit, and takes title to the property.

This same strategy is one more solution to the problem of a down payment that the prospective buyer feels is too big for him. By some quirk of human nature, the same seller who demands a $20,000 down payment will often settle for $5,000 as a "lease security deposit" and let the prospective buyer lease the property for ten years, say, with an option to purchase it at the seller's original price by putting up the rest of the $20,000 any time during those years. Although a seller may not think of it this way, what he's doing is roughly the same as selling his property for $5,000 down on an interest-only basis with $15,000 balloon payment due in ten years.

So you see a lease-option arrangement can be useful to a buyer or seller or both. Just in case you may want to use it as the solution to some difficult investment problem, I'm inserting here a copy of an agreement, worded so that it gives good legal protection to both sides.

AGREEMENT TO LEASE WITH OPTION TO PURCHASE

Received from BONANZA INVESTMENTS hereinafter called Lessee:
Address: 18 Gold Coast Road, Yuma, Arizona,
The sum of ONE THOUSAND AND No/100 DOLLARS ($1,000.00).
In the form of: Note (to be converted to cash within five [5] business days from the date Lessee accepts the property) as deposit for Lease with Option to Purchase on the property of LUCIUS B. VON ANZA AND ANN ANZA, his wife; hereinafter called Lessor: Said property situated in the City of MIDWAY, County of EUPHORIA, described as follows:

TO WIT: ALL THAT REAL AND CERTAIN PROPERTY BEING:

1.0 A THIRTY-TWO (32) unit apartment building commonly known as 100 Palm Street, Yuma, Arizona, including all equipment, appliances, furnishings, and draperies used in the normal operation of the property.

SAID PROPERTY SUBJECT TO:

1.1 A Note and First Deed of Trust in the approximate amount of ONE HUNDRED THIRTY EIGHT THOUSAND AND No/100 DOLLARS ($138,000.00) payable at ONE THOUSAND TWO HUNDRED FORTY-TWO AND 72/100 DOLLARS ($1,242.72) per month including principal and interest at SIX AND THREE QUARTERS PERCENT (6¾%) per annum.

1.2 General and special taxes for the 1974–75 fiscal year.

Which property said Lessee agrees to lease subject to the restrictions, conditions, covenants, easements and rights of way that are now of record.

TERMS AND CONDITIONS

2.0 Lessee and Lessor mutually agree that said Lease shall be for a period of TWENTY (20) years and shall contain an option to purchase for an option price of THREE HUNDRED TWENTY THOUSAND AND No/100 DOLLARS ($320,000.00).

2.1 As consideration for the option to be given Lessee, Lessee agrees to pay Lessor TWENTY THOUSAND AND No/100 DOLLARS ($20,-000.00) including the above deposit, the balance of NINETEEN THOUSAND AND No/100 DOLLARS ($19,000.00) to be deposited into escrow within thirty (30) days.

2.2 Lessee agrees to pay Lessor rental payments in the amount of TWO THOUSAND ONE HUNDRED AND No/100 DOLLARS ($2,100.00) or more per month for a period of TWENTY-FOUR MONTHS, then TWO THOUSAND TWO HUNDRED AND No/100 DOLLARS ($2,-200.00) for the next TWENTY-FOUR MONTHS, then TWO THOU-

SAND THREE HUNDRED AND No/100 DOLLARS ($2,300.00) for the next TWENTY-FOUR MONTHS, and then TWO THOUSAND FOUR HUNDRED AND No/100 DOLLARS ($2,400.00) per month for the remainder of the lease period. In the event Lessee shall exercise his option such rent shall be applied first to interest and then to principal of the sum of THREE HUNDRED THOUSAND AND No/100 DOLLARS ($300,000.00) at the rate of EIGHT AND ONE-HALF PERCENT (8½%) per annum; and all principal when applied shall be credited against the option price.

2.3 Lessor agrees to have property fully rented upon close of escrow. Tenants accepted by Lessor after final approval of this agreement by both parties shall have Lessee's prior approval.

2.4 Said Lease and Option shall contain a subordination agreement whereby if Lessee should exercise his option and therefore wish to refinance Lessor will subordinate to a new first loan. Any proceeds remaining from the refinance after retirement of the existing first loan and payment of reasonable refinance costs shall be paid to Lessor and credited to the principal due under the Lease. Should this refinance occur Lessee agrees to execute a Note and Second Deed of Trust in favor of Lessor for the remaining amount due Lessor, said Note to be at 8½% interest per annum and payable in monthly installments of interest only and due on January 1, 1995.

2.5 If Lessee shall exercise his option to purchase without refinance or assumption of the existing First Note and Deed of Trust, then said loan shall remain in Lessor's name until such assumption or refinance shall occur. Lessee is aware that loan contains an Acceleration Clause and that the Beneficiary (Mercy Savings and Loan) has the right to call said loan or require a formal assumption. Lessee is further aware that it may be necessary for him to pay loan points, assumption fees, title insurance fees and other costs involved in obtaining an assumption or replacing the existing loan with alternative financing.

2.6 Concurrently with the execution of said Lease, Lessor shall execute in favor of Lessee a Note and All-Inclusive Deed of Trust in the amount of approximately THREE HUNDRED THOUSAND AND No/100 DOLLARS ($300,000.00), said note to bear interest at EIGHT AND ONE-HALF PERCENT (8½%) per annum and to contain a due date of TWENTY (20) years. The payments on said Note shall correspond to the payments on the Lease for the period of the Lease still remaining when the option is exercised, and thereafter shall be in monthly installments of TWO THOUSAND FOUR HUNDRED AND No/100 DOLLARS until paid. Said Note and Deed of Trust shall contain a subordination clause as described in paragraph 2.4, but shall not contain an Acceleration Clause.

2.7 Concurrently with the execution of said Lease, Lessor shall execute in favor of Lessee a Grant Deed to the property, said Deed to be held by Lessor until such time as Lessee has delivered the Note and Second Deed of Trust described in paragraph 2.6 or until Lessee shall pay in full the THREE HUNDRED THOUSAND AND No/100 DOLLARS ($300,000.00) amount described in paragraph 2.6. Upon the earliest occurrence of either event Lessor shall deliver to a Title Company of Lessee's choice the Grant Deed for recording.

2.8 Lessor agrees to furnish Lessee with a signed statement of rents and deposits for his property. Advance rents, cleaning fees and security deposits shall be transferred to Lessee in escrow.

2.10 Lessor to provide the other with an inventory of all personal property within FIVE (5) days of final acceptance hereof by Lessee.

2.11 This agreement is subject to:

(a) Lessee and/or his agents inspecting and accepting the property including all units and contents thereof within TEN (10) working days of acceptance hereof. Each party to provide access as required.

(b) Lessee's inspection and acceptance of all rental or lease agreements and operating records showing rental history for one year, current tenant's rental amount, amounts past due, records of payment and security or cleaning deposits received, prior to close of escrow. Lessor agrees to provide said records or statements as required.

Lessee to indicate acceptance of the above by writing the date and his initials next to each paragraph.

And it is hereby agreed: That in the event said Lessee shall fail to pay the balance of said option amount or complete the transaction as herein provided, time being of the essence of this contract, the amount of said deposit shall at the option of the Lessor be retained by Lessor as consideration for the execution of this agreement.

That the evidence of title shall be a policy of Title Insurance issued by the LAWYERS TITLE, premium to be paid by Lessor. Title is to be free of liens and encumbrances except as above mentioned.

That should the title to said property prove defective or unmerchantable and the Lessor be unable to perfect same within 90 days from date hereof all amounts paid hereon shall be returned to the Lessee upon demand.

That should the improvements on said premises be destroyed or materially damaged prior to the close of escrow, all amounts paid hereon shall be returned to the Lessee unless the Lessee elects to complete the transaction regardless of the then condition of the improvements.

That the taxes for the fiscal year ending June 30th following the date hereof, the rents and insurance, shall be prorated as of the date of closing.

Any existing assessments and/or improvement bonds are to be PAID BY LESSOR.

That the real estate Agent is allowed FIVE (5) days to secure the acceptance of the Lessor.

Time is the essence of this contract, but the time for any act required hereunder may for sufficient cause be extended not longer than thirty days (30) by the undersigned real estate agent.

Possession of premises to be given upon recordation of a memorandum of said Lease.

All terms and conditions of this Agreement shall be binding to the heirs, executors, administrators, successors and assigns of the undersigned parties.

The above deposit is received and this agreement is executed by the agent on behalf of the Lessee subject to the Lessor's approval.

By _____

I agree to lease the above described property on the terms and conditions herein stated, and acknowledge receipt of a copy hereof.

Dated _____, 1975 _____

Lessee

_____

Lessee

ACCEPTANCE

I agree to lease the above property on the terms and conditions herein stated, and agree to pay the below signed agent as commission SIX PERCENT (6%) of the above option price, or one-half the deposit in case same is forfeited by Lessee, provided same shall not exceed the full amount of the commission, and I hereby authorize the Title Company to pay said commission from escrow upon closing.

Dated _____, 1975 _____

(Lessor)

_____

(Lessor)

Variable-rate mortgages are a comparatively new idea that you're likely to run into. In some states you may find that a variable-rate mortgage (VRM) is the only kind you can get from some lenders for certain types of residential property.

You can probably guess what a VRM is from its name. Instead of carrying a fixed interest rate, it has a rate that moves up or down in gear with a formula based on some specific index such as the lender's cost of money.

The VRM has been around for years, but until lately it has been used only on a limited basis. But now, with repeated sieges of tight money pushing interest rates up, S & L and other mortgage lenders have gotten tired watching hundreds of millions of dollars in savings lured out the door by higher yields elsewhere. For the most part they couldn't prevent these withdrawals by offering higher interest on savings accounts, because their loan portfolios were laden with mortgages written at lower interest rates. As you know if you followed the news, this caused a severe squeeze on availability of funds for mortgage financing—especially for residential buildings—and brought hard times to the real estate and construction industries. Lending officers began to see the VRM as a cure for all this trouble.

If you're offered a VRM, the lender might say to you in effect, "I'll give you a loan at the going rate of interest, on condition that you agree to let me adjust your rate later to put it in line with whatever changes hit our index. We won't change rates oftener than six months. And we'll put a ceiling on how far and fast your interest rate can go up, but no floor under the extent to which it can sink." Many lenders are further brightening this picture by making the VRM assumable by the new owner if you sell the property, and by letting you pay off the loan at any time without prepayment penalty.

This could be good for you if you're taking a mortgage when prevailing rates are high. Contrariwise, if money is cheap and plentiful when you borrow, you'd better calculate carefully. What will happen to you when the pendulum swings the other way, as it undoubtedly will sooner or later? Exactly how much more will you be committed to pay? Will you be able to afford the higher payment rates? Or does your loan give you an option to extend its term and continue to make payments at more or less the same monthly rate over a longer period of time? This latter feature is advocated by many VRM proponents as a solution to the burden-of-higher-payments problem.

If you have a choice between a VRM and a standard fixed-rate mortgage, your best bet will depend on the terms of the loan contracts, and the circumstances involved. Study every clause of the proposed contracts, and figure what each will mean to you as rates rise or fall.

REMEMBER THESE HIGH POINTS:

Don't settle for a "standard" mortgage or trust deed. Consider possible variations.

Consider an all-inclusive loan (wraparound) when there is a locked-in loan that can't be paid off without severe penalties, or when you want to buy property for which you couldn't qualify if you had to seek new financing.

Consider buying under a partnership maybe, to avoid due-on-sale acceleration clauses.

Consider lease-options as another way of avoiding refinancing.

A variable-rate mortgage can be good for a borrower when existing rates are unusually high.

XIX *Creative Financing for Bigger Profits*

A quick turnover with a big profit becomes easier during tight money periods if you use an all-inclusive or wraparound mortgage. You buy property on which there is an existing assumable mortgage at a favorable interest rate (using the lowest down payment you can negotiate plus a second) and resell it with a wraparound.

For example, you find an apartment house on sale for $100,000. The owner tells you he's borrowed $70,000 on it at 6 percent from an insurance company, which is willing to let a new owner assume the loan.

Borrowing money at 6 percent is usually a bargain. So you're eager to acquire the apartment house and take over the payments on it. You manage to negotiate a $10,000 down payment, and the seller agrees to carry back a $20,000 second mortgage on which you'll pay him 9 percent.

So you hustle up the $10,000 and close the deal. You then turn around and resell the apartment house to someone else for the same $10,000 down payment and the same total price of $100,000. Sounds crazy? It isn't.

From the new buyer you carry back an all-inclusive mortgage or trust deed for $90,000 at 9 percent. Look what's happened. The $10,000 cash you put up is back in your hands. You're out-of-pocket only the transaction costs, which would be nominal if you didn't use a broker. And for many years to come you'll be drawing a nice profit.

Here's how it works out. The first year you'll collect almost $8,100 interest on the wraparound trust deed (9% of $90,000). From this you'll pay out something less than $6,000 interest on your underlying loans (6 percent of $70,000 plus 9 percent of $20,000). The difference between the interest you pay and the interest you collect leaves you with a clear profit of about $2,100 the first year and for some years to come—for which you do nothing except put money in the bank and write checks. I know someone who made exactly this deal. Since his total transaction costs were only $1,600—mainly legal, title insurance, and escrow fees—he earned well over 100 percent a year on the net amount he had invested after completing the two transactions.

This same technique can bring you even more generous profits if you use it on run-down property that you put back in shape and resell for more than your purchase price. In this case, you might well be able to resell for a down payment big enough to recover your entire cash outlay and generate a double profit—on the increase in value as well as the leverage in the financing.

An overlapping mortgage (or trust deed), sometimes called a blanket mortgage, is one that covers two or more separate parcels of property. It's a way to get more financing than you could by mortgaging each separately, because the lender is spreading his risk and therefore feels safer.

Here's how it might solve some problems as you expand your investments. Imagine you've bought an apartment house for $125,000, paying $35,000 down and carrying $90,000 in mortgages. You plan to fix it up for resale at $165,000 or so.

But you've barely begun the renovation when you come across another run-down building that you decide is a real steal at the $200,000 price the owner asks. You find that this second property is mortgaged for $110,000, leaving the owner with $90,000 in equity.

Your problem is that you can't offer him any cash. Completing the improvements on your first property will use up most of the money you can count on, and you're too smart to risk getting caught in a cash squeeze. You find that lenders don't want to advance you any more money on either of the properties because they look so seedy.

Nevertheless the owner of the second property, Mr. Scrimp, wants you to plunk down a substantial down payment. He doesn't need the cash particularly. He simply wants you to have an equity interest in the property big enough so he can be fairly sure you won't be tempted to walk away from it, leaving him holding the bag.

The average investor in this position would give up, assuming that there's no way he can buy Scrimp's property. But you know better. You say, "I can understand why you're worried about selling to me, Mr. Scrimp. You're not sure I mean business. So here's what I'll do for you. I'll give you a $90,000 note secured by an overlapping mortgage on both properties. Look at the security you'll have: not only the $90,000 equity in the property you own but also the $35,000 equity I have in my own property—a total of $125,000. It would be virtually impossible for you to lose any money under the circumstances."

You reassure him further by explaining your plans to put both buildings into better condition while whittling down the mortgages on them. "All I ask," you continue, "is that you agree to release my first property from the overlapping mortgage when I've renovated both of them, maybe two or three years from now. By then I'll have paid off quite a bit on the existing mortgage on your property as well as the overlapping one, and your refurbished apartment house will be even better security than the two shabby ones are now."

If Mr. Scrimp is still reluctant, you can sweeten the deal by promising that you'll make some additional lump sum payment against his note in return for his releasing your first property from the mortgage. You should be able to afford this with no trouble, because when you've improved the property you can generate cash either by selling it or by refinancing it.

This technique is a way of acquiring a second property with a first, while still retaining the appreciation potential of the first, and without giving up the cash you'll need to make the potential a reality. And, as soon as you've improved the two properties to the point where the release clause goes into effect, you'll be free to sell or exchange either property at a profit.

The key to the success of any such arrangement is getting the seller to agree in writing that he'll release each of the various properties covered by an overlapping mortgage as you complete the improvements you have stipulated you will be making and/or you reduce the overlapping loan by a specified amount. If you don't do this, the seller might refuse to release a property from the mortgage, or might hold you up for an exorbitant payment before he'll do so. And you could find yourself blocked from doing anything with any of the properties.

An overlapping mortgage can be a first on some properties and a junior on others, or may include all firsts or all juniors. Keep it in mind whenever you own property and want to add to your holdings but are short of cash.

You can sell a mortgage with option to repurchase. Whoever buys your mortgage may grant you an option to buy it back before a certain date, for the price he paid plus a bonus. How much bonus? It might be on a sliding scale, related to the length of time elapsed before you exercise your option. This is something to negotiate when you're working out the written terms of the sale.

This sort of deal is usually good for both parties. If you don't exercise the option, you're no worse off than if you'd sold the mortgage outright. If you do exercise it, the other party gets his money back plus the bonus and whatever mortgage payments he's received in the meantime. Your option gives you the chance to recover the bulk of your $10,000 loss (assuming that you sell a $40,000 mortgage for $30,000) if your financial pinch eases and you don't need the cash.

You can borrow against a mortgage at reasonable terms if you seek out an individual who is looking for profitable ways to invest excess cash. There are many such people. They'll often be glad to lend up to 60 percent of the face value of the mortgage, at 10 percent interest, without charging you a loan fee. All you need do is convince them that the loan would be safe. On the other hand, if you went to a mortgage broker or some other professional moneylender, he almost surely would charge you a loan fee of 10 or 15 points in addition to the 10 percent interest.

A good way to locate potential private lenders is to ask the real estate broker who is representing you in your other dealings. If he's any good, he keeps an up-to-date file of people who have recently taken in sizable wads of cash from the sale of property. Such people often don't see any quick and safe way to reinvest their gain, so they just put it in a savings account. If the broker can show them how to get higher interest on this money through a good, safe private loan, they'll often jump at the chance. Some of them will consider it a highly attractive proposition to lend you $25,000 at 10 percent a year against the security of a $40,000 mortgage.

This should be quite attractive to you too, since you'll continue to earn interest on the full $40,000. Even if that interest is being paid at a lower rate, it should amount to more than enough to offset the 10 percent rate on the $25,000 you're borrowing.

Assigning mortgage payments is another technique you can use, if you hold a mortgage and want to expand your investments. Suppose you've sold some land and taken back a $40,000 mortgage payable at $400 per month. You can say to a private investor, "How would you like to lend me $8,000 and get back $9,600 in the next two years? I can sign over to you the right to receive the next twenty-four monthly payments of $400 each on this mortgage I hold."

It's a good way to get your hands on $8,000 cash, if that's what you need to make a down payment on an apartment building or upgrade property you already have. The $1,600 you'd lose during the two years should be repaid many times over from your increased cash flow generated by the tenants who pay rent to live in your property. By assigning the mortgage payments you're giving up only $400 a month in income, and your rental income is bound to increase much more than that if you're following sound principles.

You could also use the right to receive these payments as a down payment itself, if you're buying property. You simply offer the seller an assignment of the payments in lieu of cash down. If he is reluctant, maybe you sweeten the deal by offering to throw in some nominal amount of interest, or make some other concession (see Chapter XVI). If he still says, "No, I've gotta have a cash down payment," either you can get the cash by assigning the payments elsewhere, as described in the preceding two paragraphs, or you can point out to the seller that he can in turn sell the right to receive these payments. Some third party will probably be glad to give him cash for the assignment.

You can sell a part interest in your mortgage, as still another key to profitable expansion of your holdings. If you hold a mortgage for $40,000 you can probably sell a half interest in it for $17,500, on condition that you give the buyer (in writing) the first claim on whatever money might be brought in by a foreclosure sale. In other words, if you and your new partner have to foreclose on the property because the mortgagor doesn't keep up his payments, you won't get anything until your partner gets his $20,000. In effect you give him a mortgage that's senior to yours. So it's a pretty safe deal for him, assuming that the property is a sound value, and he'll probably be willing to put up $17,500. He might go only $15,000 if you won't grant him this prior claim.

You can sell part of your equity in a property, much as you would sell a piece of your mortgage in the example just described. Let's suppose you've made a $20,000 down payment on an apartment house, against a purchase price of $100,000. Property values have been climbing, and the apartment house is now recognized to be worth $150,000. This means your equity is worth an extra $50,000—or

$70,000 in all. (To simplify the example we'll ignore whatever additional installments you've paid on the principal.)

And now, perhaps, there's another property you also want to buy. You're looking for a way to do so. How can you make use of that $50,000 paper profit on the first property? One way would be to sell a half-share of your $70,000 equity in the property. A big money man may be glad to pay you $35,000 or more for it, especially if you agree to keep full responsibility for the management of the property, so he won't be saddled with a bunch of detail work. (One point to watch: if you're still going to manage the property or pay for its management, your co-investor shouldn't have any right to an equal voice in decisions. A two-headed management team is likely to disagree on operational matters. The tug-of-war could be irritating and expensive.)

If you sell half your equity for $35,000 or more, you get back all the cash you put into the down payment plus an extra $15,000. This can put you in a position to acquire other property immediately.

You'll notice I said "$35,000 or more." Your new partner may be willing to put up more than $35,000 for a half-share of a $70,000 equity if you offer him some other special consideration such as first claim on the net cash flow up to a certain point. Sometimes the mere fact that you'll relieve him of management worries will make him willing to pay more. If he bought other property with his money, he'd have to pay additional for a manager, or else manage it himself. So by going in with you he's acquiring not only part-ownership of a valuable property but a manager as well.

Subordination is a word that comes up often in real estate. If you own a property and are making payments on one or more mortgages against it, normally the only way you can refinance it with a new first mortgage is to pay off the existing loan as part of the transaction. Otherwise your new borrowing won't be a first mortgage; it will be a second, third, or fourth, depending on how many other loans are already outstanding against your property.

As a borrower, you naturally prefer the lower interest and longer term of a first mortgage. But the only way you can get a new first mortgage without paying off all existing loans against the property is to persuade the holders of the existing loans to subordinate them. That is, they must agree in writing that the new lender will get paid off before they do, if you default on your debts.

Suppose you buy a run-down property for $120,000—putting up

$20,000 in cash, taking over the previous owner's $60,000 debt on his first mortgage, and giving him a $40,000 second mortgage for the rest of the purchase price. You figure that you can increase the property's value to $160,000 by spending $10,000 on improvements. But you don't have the $10,000. Unless you get it, the property may not be a good investment for you. What do you do?

You discuss your plans with a lender, who says he is willing to give you a new $80,000 first loan on the property (two-thirds of its existing value) but that's all. And you can't get this $80,000 first mortgage from him unless you pay off the two existing loans, which total $100,000.

Impossible? Not necessarily. You must go and talk to whoever holds the $40,000 second mortgage. You must show him that he'll be better off to subordinate his loan to the proposed new first mortgage.

So you say to him, "The appraisers will tell you that this property is worth $120,000 as it stands. Your $40,000 second sits behind a $60,000 first on a $120,000 piece of real estate. This means there is a margin of $20,000 in equity value as additional security for your loan. If you'll subordinate your $40,000 loan to a new $80,000 first so I can get the money for some needed improvements, you'll find yourself with the same $40,000 second behind an $80,000 first but on an apartment house worth $160,000. This will mean you'll have a $40,000 instead of $20,000 margin of equity in back of your loan."

If this logic isn't enough to satisfy him, you have other cards to play. You can offer to pay him a higher interest rate on his second; to make bigger monthly payments on it; or to put some of the extra $20,000 cash you'll get from the new lender, after subtracting the cost of the new improvements, into a lump sum payment on the second, reducing its amount accordingly. This last offer would be especially attractive to him if his second mortgage calls for fairly nominal payments and has some years to run.

Ideally it's much better to postpone trying to get a new first mortgage until after you've completed the improvements, thereby clearly establishing the higher value of the property. Since your new first lender will be basing his loan maximum on something like 66⅔ percent of value, he can lend you $120,000 on the property after you've upped its value to $160,000.

The three points to keep in mind about subordination are (1) whenever you take on a second mortgage obligation, try to get the lender to agree that he'll subordinate it if you refinance with a new first mortgage; (2) unless you have no alternative, postpone refinancing a run-down property, because you can get a better loan after you increase its value through improvements; (3) know where your cash is coming from to pay for needed improvements. This third point was mentioned earlier, but it's worth reemphasizing. Never put so much money into an investment that you'll be unable to take care of it properly. Pass it up and go on to something more modest.

Trading on the down payment. As I've already mentioned, there is usually much more leeway for give-and-take concerning prices, down payments, and other terms and conditions of real estate sales than you'd imagine from the initial demands of sellers. Prices and terms can often be traded one against the other.

Rex Johnson, a Realtor friend of mine in Honolulu, recently had a case in which a seller was asking $50,000 down on an apartment building he had listed at a price of $100,000. There was an assumable $50,000 first loan on the property at 7 percent interest. The seller demanded cash to this first loan. He wouldn't consider anything less, he said. The property was bringing in a net operating income of $9,000, or 9 percent on the asking price. The price was thus about $10,000 too high in terms of the 10 percent return we normally shoot for in buying residential income property.

However, this 10 percent target is simply a target. We needn't necessarily hit the bull's-eye every time. A price that yielded a 9 percent return could be considered quite reasonable for a building of good quality in a better area, whereas a price that produced an 11 percent or 12 percent return might be too high for a lower-quality building in a deteriorating neighborhood. The particular building being offered scored exceptionally high in both these respects. So it was well worth the $100,000 price tag.

The problem was the down payment. A buyer who put up the $50,000 would have to pay out $3,500 a year for interest on the $50,000 mortgage, thus leaving him with a net return of only $5,500, or 11 percent on his $50,000 investment. This might not be too bad if he had no alternatives. But he would certainly be remiss if he did not consider the other opportunities available at the time. A similar investment in commercial property leased to a good, solid commercial tenant could bring him essentially the same return virtually risk-free and management-free.

Rex tried to convince the seller that he would have a hard time finding anyone who would pay all cash to the loan at that $100,000 price. He suggested as an alternative that the seller slash his down payment requirements to $10,000, take back a second of $50,000 at 8 percent, and boost the price he was asking to $110,000. The logic he used went somewhat like this:

1. It was extremely unlikely that any buyer with $50,000 to invest would be willing to pay the $100,000 asking price. He would probably insist on a substantial discount in return for paying all cash to the loan.
2. The seller would be broadening his potential market several-fold. There are many more buyers with $10,000 than with $50,000.
3. The attractiveness to any potential buyer would be greatly increased. The return on his $10,000 cash investment would be $1,500, or 15 percent (the $9,000 net operating income less the $7,500 in interest he would have to pay on the two $50,000 mortgages) instead of the 11 percent he would generate if he bought the property for $100,000 with $50,000 cash.
   a. The tax benefits that would accrue to the buyer from depreciation would also be greater. (The higher the price the greater the amount of depreciation that could be taken.)
4. If the seller sold for $100,000 with $50,000 down, he would in the same year have to pay out a substantial portion of the proceeds in capital gains taxes since his cost basis in the property was only $40,000. If he sold for $110,000 with $10,000 down, however, he would qualify for installment treatment and spread the taxability of his gain over an extended period of years.
5. The extra money he would eventually get from a sale at $110,000 plus the deferral of tax liability should more than compensate the seller for agreeing to sell on the more liberal terms.

The seller remained unconvinced. He was obsessed by the idea of getting his hands on that $50,000 (regardless of the other considerations and even though he had no specific plans for using it). After listing it with Rex for six months the best offer he received was $40,000 down against a total price of $90,000. The $20,000 discount he would suffer by holding out for all cash, as compared with offering the property for sale under the terms Rex had suggested, was just too painful to contemplate, so he finally went along with Rex's suggestion. Three weeks later, Rex found someone who bought the property for $10,000 down at the new $110,000 asking price. The seller is now enjoying a comfortable income from the principal and income payments on the $50,000 carry-back mortgage and will continue to do so for many years to come.

From the buyer's point of view, the opportunity to generate a higher rate of return on the cash he was putting up was only one of the reasons he was willing to pay a total price of $110,000 with the low down payment terms that were finally offered. If the property increased in value, as it surely would, whatever increase was realized would, because of the greater leverage, represent a higher percentage gain on the cash invested.

Another reason: Since the value of the building and other depreciable improvements was about 85 percent of the total value of the property, his $10,000 down would bring him $93,500 worth of depreciation ($9.35 worth for every dollar of cash he had invested). Spread over the remaining thirty-year life of the building, this would average at $3,117 per year, thus completely tax-sheltering his anticipated $1,500 per year net return and contributing $1,617 of deductible expense as an offset to other income. On the other hand, if he had bought the property for $90,000 with $40,000 down, he would be getting only $76,500 worth of depreciation (85% of $90,000) for the $40,000, or about $1.91 worth for every dollar of cash he had invested. And this spread over the thirty years would come to only $2,550 per year, leaving him with a taxable income of $2,950 on his anticipated pre-tax return of $5,500.

In other words, by purchasing for $10,000 down against a total price of $110,000, he would be reducing the taxability of his income from other sources. It would have been foolish to put up five times as much cash while getting a considerably lower pre-tax return per dollar invested, and also increasing his tax liability.

The point I'm making is that price and terms cannot be considered independently. Each is meaningless without the other. What might be considered a very reasonable price on soft terms could be outrageously high if the seller was demanding all cash. Conversely, what might be considered a reasonable price on all-cash terms could expand noticeably and still be considered reasonable if the terms were made softer.

Therefore, when you are quoted a reasonable price on hard terms, get a pencil and do some figuring. Take the tax consequences to the seller into account. Take the prospective pre-tax rate of return on your cash investment into account. Take depreciation and its tax consequences into account. You may be able to convince the seller that both of you will be much better off if he relaxes his down payment requirements in return for a higher price than would otherwise be warranted.

You might start by asking the seller why he wants cash. Often he will not be able to come up with a good answer. You then ask if he understands the tax consequences of selling for cash vs. those of selling on terms. Quite often he does not. You next point out the competition—literally hundreds of equally good properties being offered for very little down. Finally, if all else fails, you might casually suggest that you might even be willing to pay a bit more if he will sell on more liberal terms.

There is, of course, a limit to how high you can afford to go to get softer terms. But if you have done your homework, the additional price you can reasonably afford to pay will look enticing to the seller.

Should you refinance your existing mortgage? No doubt the house you now own is mortgaged. Let's make up some numbers and play with them, to help you understand the principles involved.

Say the house cost you $30,000 but is now worth $50,000. Say you're making mortgage payments at 6 percent and now owe only $14,000 of an original debt of $24,000. This means you have an equity of $36,000 in the property.

So maybe you shop around among lenders, and find that you can borrow $35,000 on the house by paying off your existing $14,000 mortgage debt and taking out a new and bigger mortgage. This is called refinancing.

However, sometimes interest rates go up, as you may have noticed. Your friendly savings and loan officer may say he must charge you 9 percent on the new mortgage, plus a loan fee of "two points"—in other words, a one-time charge of 2 percent of the face value of the mortgage, which would come to $700.

Of course, there'll also be other loan costs, as always. And there may be a penalty for prepayment of the old loan. This will bring the total cost of the refinancing to $1,500, we'll say. So you'll come out with net proceeds of $19,500 (the $35,000 face value of the mortgage, minus the $14,000 of it you would use to pay off the old mortgage, minus the $1,500 refinancing cost). You wouldn't owe any income tax on the $19,500 that would go into your bank account, because it would be borrowed money. And you could take a bigger tax deduction for the bigger interest payments you'd be making.

Would it be a good deal for you? It might be good in the sense that the $19,500 could be seed money that could produce an abundant growth of income for you. But it might not be as good as other possible financing strategies. Let's examine the costs more carefully, and then see whether other strategies might put you further ahead.

Your interest payments alone on this mortgage would start out at a rate of $3,150 per year (9 percent of $35,000). Quite a difference from the $840 a year interest you're paying on your old mortgage (6 percent of $14,000).

Look at it this way. If you take on the new mortgage, you'll be paying $2,310 more in interest for the $19,500 capital you'll acquire. This works out to be an effective interest rate of 11.8 percent annually. Then too, in addition to the interest payments, you'll have to pay off part of the principal each year (including the $1,500 difference between the $19,500 cash you receive and the $21,000 face value of the new loan). Naturally this will cut deeper into your cash flow if you take on the big new mortgage.

A junior mortgage (second mortgage) is another alternative. Experts say that about three of every four real estate transactions involve some form of junior mortgage. Most money for junior mortgages comes from private individuals—often the sellers of the real estate involved in the transactions.

As you recall from earlier chapters, the holder of a second or third mortgage or some other subordinate claim is taking a much bigger risk than the holder of the first mortgage. The holder of any junior mortgage can't get any money from a foreclosure sale until the first mortgage and costs have been paid. So if the debtor stops payments, the secondary lender may face a total loss. In most states he does have the right to assume payments on the first mortgage himself, and then to foreclose on the property, but this may be throwing good money after bad.

Even so, lots of people lend money on second mortgages because they can charge higher interest rates than on first mortgages, and this makes the risk worthwhile. So you'll probably be able to get a second mortgage on your property. This would mean you could leave your 6 percent first mortgage undisturbed.

How big a second? This would depend on a number of things, including your income and general credit standing. But with a home worth $50,000 and a first mortgage of only $14,000 against it, you probably wouldn't have much difficulty finding someone who would lend you at least $21,000 on a second mortgage. After all, this would bring the total encumbrances against your $50,000 home to only $35,000—the same they would be under the new first you were considering, and a modest percentage of total value by almost any lending standards. With such a margin, both lenders can feel safe. They'll almost certainly get their money back if you default. (In reality, you might be able to raise considerably more money by taking out a second than by taking out a new first. This is because lenders on seconds generally charge higher interest rates and will often take higher risks in return.)

So let's assume someone is willing to lend you $21,000 on a second mortgage and you are considering his offer.

Still he wants a big yield on what he lends. Usually he'll charge you about 10 percent a year interest, plus a loan fee of 7½ points, say. After you've paid this fee and all other loan costs, you'll probably come out with about $19,000 in cash although you'll be borrowing $21,000.

So how much interest are you really paying for the $19,000 capital you'd get? You're paying at a rate that initially amounts to $2,100 a year. This makes the effective annual rate a little more than 11 percent. In addition you'll presumably have to make some arrangement for repayment of the $21,000 principal over the loan term. And this can hurt you. Junior mortgages tend to be shorter-term loans than first mortgages. A four-year second mortgage, for example, would mean you'd owe another $500 per year, on the average, just on the difference between the $21,000 you "borrowed" and the $19,000 you actually received. Altogether you'd have to dig up an average of $5,250 a year for principal repayment, whether you paid it back in equal installments or arranged to pay smaller portions plus a big balloon payment at the end of the four years. We've already seen how balloon payments can be booby traps. If you can't come up with a big chunk of cash when the balloon is due, you might have to refinance, and pay the same or higher loan costs all over again.

So we see that the total annual costs of the $19,000 from a second mortgage might be even bigger than the average total annual cost of the $19,500 you'd get from a new first mortgage. At this point you might shudder and decide to give up the whole idea of finding cash for the down payment on an apartment house investment.

But don't despair. Other alternatives may be open to you. And they may cost considerably less with ideas from the next chapter.

REMEMBER THESE HIGH POINTS:

When you plan to buy and resell a property quickly, an all-inclusive (wraparound) mortgage may increase your profits.

When buying two or more properties, an overlapping (blanket) mortgage may enable you to get more financing than by mortgaging each separately.

When you're pinched financially, you can generate cash by selling a mortgage with option to repurchase,

   —or by borrowing against a mortgage

   —or by assigning mortgage payments

   —or by selling part interest in your equity.

When there are two mortgages on a property you may be able to persuade the holder of the second mortgage to subordinate his loan to a new first mortgage.

XX   *Huge Profits Can Be Tax-Free*

Almost two hundred years ago, George Washington wrote a letter to his stepson, J. P. Custis, advising him not to convert his lands into cash unless he could immediately put that cash back into other lands more valuable to him. In effect, he was telling his stepson to exchange real estate only for other real estate.

Reflection must convince you of two things; first, that lands are of permanent value; that there is scarcely a possibility of their falling in price, but almost a certainty of their rising exceedingly in value; and secondly, that our paper currency has depreciated considerably, and that no human foresight can tell how low it may get.

By parting from your lands, you give a certainty for an uncertainty. The advice I give you is not to convert the lands you now hold into cash faster than a certain prospect of vesting it in other lands more convenient requires of you.

This will, in effect, exchange land for land, it being of no concern to you how much the money depreciates if you can get land of equal value to that you sell.

It may be said that our money may receive a proper tone again. I shall only observe that this is a lottery. If it should happen, you have lost nothing. If it should not, you have saved your estate.

Neither Washington nor Custis had to contend with the taxes we have nowadays. So they didn't lose by converting real estate momentarily into cash—provided they reinvested that cash immediately in other real estate more suitable to their needs. Today the same basic considerations still prevail. But today, because of our tax laws, a substantial portion of our invested capital can be lost if we sell one property and purchase another instead of trading for the new one directly. We will get back to this awesome fact in a moment.

Nobody loses, everybody wins in any well-planned exchange of property. Each trader acquires something more valuable to him than he gives up. Otherwise, of course, there'd be no point in his trading.

How can all parties to a swap come out ahead? Fortunately for all of us, value, like beauty, is in the eyes of the beholder. Something of small value to you may be immensely desirable to someone else, and vice versa. Only when this is true is any exchange feasible. But you'll be amazed at how many times it *is* true!

The tax laws can help you when you trade instead of sell. We saw this in Chapter XII. Section 1031 of the Internal Revenue Code makes it possible for you to use exchanges to unload one property and acquire another, time after time, without loss of investment capital through taxes on the gains. This is one of the most important single tools for building wealth fast through realty transactions.

In fact, if you ignore the profit potential in exchanges, you'll be slowed down considerably in reaching worry-free financial independence, because an important part of your profits in realty sales will go to Uncle Sam in taxes.

Are all exchanges of property tax-free? No. Some are wholly or partially subject to tax. It depends on whether the exchange includes any other goodies besides real property of like kind held for productive use in a trade or business, or for investment.

Even if a deal isn't taxed at the time, remember that the tax is only postponed. When a string of exchanges finally ends in a sale, the tax becomes due on the accumulated profits made in all the exchanges (subject only to the special provisions that apply where the property being sold was acquired by inheritance). Death of the property owner would not, in itself, trigger taxes on the accumulated profits, although there would be taxes on the estate if it was large enough.

As I mentioned above, an exchange isn't taxed at the time if the properties are held for productive use in a trade or business, or for investment purposes—and if they are entirely "of like kind."

"Like kind" includes just about any other kind of real property to be held for the same purpose, whether improved or unimproved, plus fixtures to the property, and leaseholds with a remaining life of at least thirty years.

However, "like kind" does not include any real property used as the taxpayer's personal residence, or any real property held primarily for resale (dealer property). It likewise doesn't include any non-real property or other inducements or benefits received in the exchange—such as cash, notes, furniture, automobiles, or other personal property, mortgage relief (i.e., reduction of mortgage debt), or the assumption by another party of any of a taxpayer's other liabilities.

As we saw in Chapter XII, when an exchange includes something besides real estate of like kind (qualifying property), the something else is called boot. If boot is included, the exchange will be considered partially taxable and any gain realized will be taxed to the extent of the fair market value of such boot.

Sometimes various kinds of boot are given and received. Generally their total values can be netted out in figuring the portion of any realized gain to be taxed. But there's one big exception: mortgage relief given cannot be used as an offset to other boot received. The taxpayer will still be taxed on any gain realized to the full extent of this other boot even though he may have shouldered a much bigger mortgage debt than was lifted from him by other parties to the exchange.

Let's go on to look at near-miraculous profit possibilities in typical exchanges. As we consider special examples, you'll get a better understanding of the tax angles.

Trading even is the simplest and most straightforward way, of course. How can both parties be gainers? We'll see.

Say you paid $15,000 cash for a house twenty years ago, and have been collecting rent on it ever since. You've spent $3,000 improving it, and have taken tax deductions of $8,000 for depreciation. So your cost basis, as the tax collectors figure it, is now $10,000 ($15,000 plus $3,000 minus $8,000).

But in twenty years the property values in the neighborhood have soared. You can probably sell the house for $40,000 if you choose. You're tempted to do so, because the neighborhood now seems to be going to seed, which means that property values will stop rising. The only thing that stops you is the whopping capital gains tax. Your gain would be $30,000—on which your tax could be $7,500 or more, leaving you only about $32,500 (minus costs) to reinvest.

Sure, you can get off easier if you arrange an installment sale, accepting less than 30 percent down and carrying back a high mortgage. In later years you may be in a lower tax bracket, so the installment payments may not be taxed so heavily.

However, this too would leave you with much less to reinvest—even though you could probably raise a substantial amount of additional cash tax-free by borrowing against the mortgage you had carried back. Why sell and pay taxes at all, when you may easily accomplish the same thing without triggering any liability for taxes? Why not try for a tax-free exchange of your free and clear property solely for other free and clear property with the same fair market value in an area you feel offers more current potential?

This way you could duck the capital gains taxes that would fall due if you were to sell your property outright and buy the new one in a separate transaction. Moreover, you would keep your $40,000 equity fully at work (with the exception of the usual transaction costs) instead of finding it severely diluted by taxes and/or steps you had taken to defer their payment.

An exchange of this type would be fully tax-free to both parties. Neither party would be getting anything out of the exchange other than property of like kind.

The situation would be somewhat different, however, if the $40,000 property you were acquiring was encumbered by a $10,000 mortgage. In this case, you would be trading a $40,000 equity for a $30,000 equity and would naturally expect to receive an additional $10,000 from the other party in some form to make up the difference. The situation could be summarized in table form this way:

	You would be giving up	You would be receiving
Fair Market Value	$40,000.00	$40,000.00
Existing Mortgage	-0-	− 10,000.00
Equity Value	$40,000.00	$30,000.00
Other Consideration Needed to Equalize	-0-	10,000.00
TOTAL	$40,000.00	$40,000.00

In the above situation, the $10,000 worth of something or other you would rake in would be considered as boot and taxed at capital gains rates to the extent it did not exceed the actual gain you were realizing. The fact you were taking over responsibility for a $10,000 mortgage from your counterpart would be irrelevant because mortgage relief given cannot be used to offset other boot received.

For your counterpart, however, the exchange would be entirely tax-free. True, he would be receiving $10,000 in boot in the form of being relieved of a mortgage obligation, but this would be fully offset by the $10,000 in boot he would be paying to you as an equalizing consideration.

But with a little better planning you won't have to pay any tax at all. In the situation I have just described there would be no need for the other party to pay you $10,000 in boot to equalize the equities if the equities could be equalized before the exchange took place. Your co-exchanger could simply use $10,000 in cash to pay off his $10,000 loan before the exchange. As an alternative, you could take out a $10,000 loan on your own property, also before the exchange. Either way you would then be able to exchange entirely boot-free and tax-free. The first way your counterpart would increase his equity interest in his own property to $40,000 (the same as your equity interest in yours). The second way you would reduce your equity interest in your own property to $30,000 (the same as his equity interest in his). The only other major difference in the two methods would be the cash flow involved. The first would require a cash outlay of $10,000 by your co-exchanger, but produce no cash flow to you, while the second would leave you with $10,000 in cash without any cash outlay on your co-exchanger's part.

Trading up. Normally, with an equity of $40,000 and a desire to build financial independence, anyone following the principles in this book won't be satisfied just to trade even. An equity of $40,000 can easily and safely be used to acquire a property worth $160,000 to $200,000 and even one worth twice that.

"But why," you may well ask at this point, "would anyone with a property worth $160,000 or $200,000 be willing to trade it for one with only one-quarter or one-fifth as much?" The answer is that people who own larger properties sometimes get tired of the problems involved in managing them, and are happy to convert their equity into a relatively management-free income if they can do so on a favorable basis. Since there are more people who would like to trade up than there are cash buyers who can make a reasonable down payment, it's usually possible to get much more for a larger property by trading down than by selling outright. Furthermore, it's generally much easier for the owner of a large property to cash out on a smaller property he is trading into than on the more expensive property he has been holding. Far more buyers can put up a respectable down payment on small properties than on big ones. Also, as we shall see later, if the party who is to receive the smaller property does not want it, an advance commitment can often be obtained from some third party to buy the property from its new owner.

So let's assume that you want to trade up and that the owner of a $160,000 apartment house is willing to take your $40,000 free and clear property in an exchange. Let's assume also that the $160,000 property has a $40,000 mortgage on it, leaving the owner with a $120,000 equity. This makes his equity $80,000 greater than yours. You agree with the owner of the larger property to equalize the difference by giving him an $80,000 purchase-money second mortgage.

What have you accomplished? For one thing, you've made a swap that is completely tax-free to you, since you received no boot of any kind in the transaction. Furthermore, through the magic of the leverage you employed, you now have $160,000 working for you instead of the $40,000 you had previously. You have presumably multiplied your net operating income some four-fold, and are in a position to reap four times as much benefit from future increases in property values.

There's theoretically no reason you couldn't keep trading up time and time again as long as you live, indefinitely postponing taxes on your capital gains. In practice, you might run into some situations where you couldn't avoid accepting taxable boot, but you should be able to keep these taxable gains nominal as compared with the increase in equity values you would be achieving.

Trading down. What about the other party to this exchange? You'd be trading up, but he'd be trading down. What are the tax consequences, if any, for him? Let's prepare a table so we can visualize his position better.

	You would give up and he would receive	He would give up and you would receive
Fair Market Value	$40,000.00	$160,000.00
Existing Mortgages	-0-	− 40,000.00
	$40,000.00	$120,000.00
Purchase-money Mortgage Needed to Equalize	$80,000.00	-0-
TOTAL	$120,000.00	$120,000.00

The owner of the bigger property would be unhooking himself from a $40,000 mortgage and would have received boot to this extent. He would also be receiving an $80,000 purchase-money mortgage note. This too would be boot since it would not be property of "like kind." If his gain on the sale were $50,000, he'd have to pay capital gains taxes on this entire amount (the lesser of the gain or the

$120,000 boot). What could be done to minimize his liability for taxes or otherwise improve his tax position?

One thing he could do, you will remember, is pay off the $40,000 mortgage and thereby eliminate the mortgage relief he would otherwise realize. As a corollary to this, he'd have you substitute a new $120,000 purchase-money first mortgage for the $80,000 purchase-money second you had previously planned to give him. Then he would treat his side of the exchange as an installment sale, because only $40,000 of the $160,000 sales price is being received at that point. This means that only 25 percent of whatever gain he had realized would be taxable that year. If this mortgage ran for twenty or twenty-five years, reporting of the balance of the gain, of course, would also be spread over twenty or twenty-five years.

Only one problem. Where is our co-exchanger going to get $40,000 to pay off the existing mortgage? Most of us don't have that kind of money sitting idly in a checking account. You'll recall from earlier chapters, however, that first mortgages can often be pledged as security for loans. In this case the new $120,000 mortgage carried back by our counterpart to the exchange would simply be pledged as security for a new loan at least big enough to pay off the existing $40,000 first mortgage, and thus make the new mortgage a first instead of a second. Under normal circumstances, our co-exchanger could probably get a loan for as much as 60 percent or more of the $120,000 mortgage he would be pledging, and thereby end up with some $32,000 or more in non-taxable cash as a by-product of the transaction, after paying off the $40,000 mortgage. If the interest rate on his loan were less than on the $120,000 mortgage, he would gain some additional leverage.

Three-way exchanges can solve many problems. Many prospective two-way swaps are stymied because one of the parties has no desire to own the other party's property.

There could be all sorts of reasons for this. Maybe someone wants to trade a farm for an apartment house. It's easy to see why most apartment house owners wouldn't want the complexities of running a farm. Or maybe somebody is being transferred from Chicago to Los Angeles, and wants to exchange his Chicago property for something in the other city. Very few people in Los Angeles want to acquire Chicago real estate unless they happen to be moving there. Or it could be that the owner of an apartment house won't trade for another apartment house just because he's fed up with tenant problems and wants to get out of the business.

Such obstacles to an exchange are quite common. In fact, it's a bit uncommon to find two investors who each want the other's property. But by bringing in a third party to buy one of the two properties, a tax-free or partly tax-free exchange can often be worked out.

Let's look at some examples, and see how all three investors can benefit.

Suppose you've found an apartment house that could be a profitable investment for you. The owner, Mr. Olde, wants to get rid of it. But he doesn't want any real estate in exchange. He wants to sell outright and go off on a trip around the world. This doesn't mean you can't work out an exchange with Mr. Olde, however. You just need to find some third party who would like to acquire your property.

Let's say you find a Mr. Terzio who is interested. Now you have two possible three-way deals. You can trade properties with Mr. Olde, who can then sell the property he acquired from you to Mr. Terzio. Or you can have Terzio buy Olde's property and then exchange it for yours.

As you read this, perhaps you're thinking, "It's sometimes hard enough to get two people to agree. How could I ever work out a three-way deal, with all the variables of value and timing that would make their interests different?"

Brokers specializing in exchanges will tell you it's done every day. They'll probably find a prospective purchaser for one of the properties as a first step. They'll get him to sign an agreement that he'll buy this property from some third party if and when such a person acquires the property in an exchange. Then they can show this agreement to some other property owner who wants to sell and wouldn't otherwise consider an exchange.

The agreement is a powerful selling tool. The fact that someone has committed himself to buy a property at a stipulated price removes all doubt about its value. And if you happen to own this property, the purchase agreement puts you in position to bargain for a bigger equity interest than you might be able to get in a straight two-way exchange where no third party purchaser was involved.

But suppose the prospective buyer of your property doesn't want to sign this kind of purchase agreement? He might object, "This deal could be stalled for months while your brokers shop around for someone who is willing to exchange. If you don't want to sell direct to me, forget it."

In this case your broker can advise you, "Go ahead. Sign a binding agreement to sell your property to this man. But we'll set up the agreement so the close is delayed long enough to give us time to find other property you'd like to get in a trade. And the agreement will be clearly worded to say that your basic intent is to make a tax-free exchange and that the agreement is only to be the first step toward this end." This will help you in case the tax authorities raise a question later.

Or your broker can go another way. He can begin by finding a property you'd like to acquire. Then he'll see how the owner of the property feels about an exchange. If the owner doesn't want your property, your broker can probably still get him to sign an agreement to switch with you conditioned on finding someone to purchase the property you would be giving up in the exchange.

For you, such an agreement has one advantage and one disadvantage. The good news is that you're not blocked from making an exchange, if someone turns up who does want your property. You haven't committed yourself to sell it to someone else. The bad news is that you lack the bargaining power you'd have in the unquestioned value of your property, as shown by an existing commitment to buy it at a set price.

I personally prefer to try to set up the exchange agreement first. There are at least two good reasons for doing this. One, it gives the owner of another property an option to take over and keep your property if he chooses. Two, the tax collectors are less likely to look at the records and say, "For tax purposes, we consider this a separate sale and purchase."

Regardless of how you exchange, you intend it to be partially or wholly tax-free so you should always be sure to get good tax and legal advice before committing yourself. It doesn't come cheap. But it's much cheaper than the sometimes monumental losses and other costs you can incur through not employing it.

Talk purchase, not exchange when you negotiate with someone whose property you'd like to acquire. Unless he has hinted that he's interested in a trade, you may turn him off completely by proposing one, and may lose all chance to explore possibilities with him.

You'll be surprised how few owners understand exchanges and the tax and other advantages they may provide. It's human nature to shy away from anything you don't understand. So don't throw yourself against their mental block. Talk first about your interest in acquiring a property like theirs. Go on to size up its value, and negotiate for it, applying the principles you've learned earlier in this book. Get on a firm friendly footing with the owners. Find out what their problems and goals are. Only when they're close to agreement with you on price and terms should you mention the possibility of an exchange.

You can ease into it by saying something like this: "Gee, Mr. Robinson, I'm glad we see eye to eye. I can hardly wait to sign the papers and take possession of such a fine building. I do have one problem, however. I'd like to get your thoughts on the best way to resolve it. I own a small apartment house over on 86th Street. My equity in it comes to quite a bit more than the down payment we've agreed on. I plan to sell the apartment house to get cash for the down payment. My broker says it should sell quickly at the price I'm asking, but he doesn't have a purchaser at the moment.

"I don't know what your tax situation is, but it would be a big help to me if we could set this up as an exchange of our two properties, to take effect whenever either of us can find a qualified buyer for my apartment house with enough cash for whatever down payment you consider necessary. His down payment would go into the same escrow as part of the deal between you and me. You'd be the owner of my property just momentarily, as part of a three-way exchange. We can set things up so you'll come out exactly the same as if I bought your building from you instead of exchanging my building for it. And of course if you should decide that you'd like to keep my property in a tax-free exchange, there would be nothing to prevent this. We could make a trade immediately without bringing in any third party."

At this point he'll hesitate to turn you down cold, because he's happy at the near-completion of the deal. He's already begun to enjoy the thought of not having his property to worry about. He'll hate the thought of starting to negotiate all over again with someone else.

If he does refuse to consider delaying, you still have trump cards to play. No doubt you've used the tactics you learned in this book to drive a good bargain. So you probably have some leeway to offer him various inducements. You can afford to make concessions in order to put those extra thousands in your pocket through a tax-free or partly tax-free exchange.

Multiple-party exchanges are always a possibility, even though it takes time to set them up. There's no limit to the number of properties and owners that can be included. The only basic difference between a two-way exchange and a trade between four, five or six different owners is the longer time it takes to get everybody in agreement about what they are to give up and receive. Naturally the details are more complex—trying to comb out unnecessary boot, figuring the best tax advantages, and making sure every detail is properly spelled out in the written exchange agreement.

An owner who doesn't want to trade his property for yours may have nothing against exchanges as such. He may be as eager as you are for a tax-free exchange. But perhaps he just doesn't like your property. He'd be foolish to take title he didn't want, solely to save on taxes.

If could be that the owner of an apartment house who refused to trade for your farm has his heart set on owning a small commercial building leased out to a solid long-term business tenant, so he can get rid of the details of managing a residential building. There's no way he'll exchange his apartments for a farm. But it also could be that some owner of a small commercial building is tired of the city hubbub and is dreaming of owning a farm like yours. Put the three properties together in an essentially tax-free exchange and you may make three people happy.

Exchange counselors are magicians. No doubt you've realized, in reading this chapter, that even the simplest exchange takes extra work and imagination to negotiate, set up, and close. The average broker who is reasonably competent at handling buy–sell transactions will get flustered if you want to swap instead of sell. He may be willing to tackle exchanging one apartment house for another in the same city—but along the line he may unwittingly botch the operation. He may create unnecessary boot, overlook details that should be spelled out, or even make a slip that causes the transaction to be legally classed as two sales and two purchases rather than an exchange. As for trying to exchange land you own in Wyoming for an industrial property in New York, he wouldn't have the vaguest idea how to go about it.

Therefore you'll be smart to seek a professional real estate exchanger when you're interested in making an exchange. These people are brokers who have gone on to specialize in exchanges, and who spend virtually all their time working on them. The more competent ones usually belong to such professional organizations as the Society of Exchange Counselors and the National Association of Realtors, Commercial Investment division. Not all good exchangers belong to these, but membership is a good indication that the broker is well qualified. If the other party's broker is a professional exchanger and yours is not, you'll probably be at a disadvantage.

The true professional exchanger is in a good position to fulfill his clients' needs and desires through information he has available about countless properties that are prospects for exchange. There are local, state, regional, and national exchange organizations. Their members meet periodically to pass around information. Between meetings they work with one another to find solutions to their clients' problems. They depend heavily on one another to match up various clients. Through membership in national exchange organizations, the professional exchanger will almost certainly sooner or later be able to work out a multi-party agreement whereby you'll end up getting that industrial property you want in New York for your Wyoming land. On a local level, it should be much easier for him to match up owners for a multi-party exchange.

Most professional exchangers can save you considerable money in drawing up the exchange agreement and other necessary documents. You'll want to have these reviewed by an accountant, and by a lawyer who knows the real estate business. But the accountant and lawyer will charge you less if you present them with well-prepared papers.

REMEMBER THESE HIGH POINTS:

Before trading, look for ways to equalize equities.

Often you can trade up by giving a purchase-money second mortgage.

Sometimes you can pocket non-taxable cash by trading down. This is possible by pledging first mortgages as security for loans.

If a prospective buyer of your property doesn't want to trade, look into possibilities for a multiple exchange. It may be attractive to him as well as owners of other properties.

Talk purchase, not exchange, when beginning to negotiate.

Get help from competent exchange counselors when you want to arrange an exchange.

XXI *Don't Let Them Call You a Dealer*

Investor or dealer? Which are you? Presumably you're an investor, since that's the kind of person for whom I'm writing this book. But you may find yourself having so much fun buying properties and fixing them up and reselling them that pretty soon you own quite a string of duplexes and small apartment buildings in various stages of renovation. If you continue to buy and sell, sooner or later somebody in the Internal Revenue Service is going to look at your tax return and say, "This person is a dealer in real estate. These properties are dealer properties." If the IRS classifies you as a dealer, your transactions will be taxed as ordinary income instead of capital gains—which means, of course, they'll be taxed twice as heavily.

You can do two things to lessen the chance of looking like a dealer. One is to state very clearly, in the papers you submit when you buy a property, that you're buying it for investment purposes or for your personal investment portfolio. The second is to act like an investor, not like a dealer. Actions speak louder than any words you write. If you buy and sell too often in too short a time, you'll be running a high risk of being classified as a professional real estate dealer.

This is another reason why you're better off to keep your sales transactions to a minimum and trade wherever possible. But try not to trade each property individually. Put together a package of four, five, six or seven of them and trade these for one big building. Maybe the big building's owner doesn't want your smaller properties, but you've already seen how to overcome this obstacle. You tell your broker to find other parties to take over the properties from their new owner as soon as the exchange has been completed. You thus pack several transactions into one. You also strengthen your image as an investor.

Upping the depreciation is one of the most important techniques that make real estate investors wealthy. As we saw in Chapter XIII, you get a substantial tax shelter through the depreciation allowances you can take on buildings, equipment and furnishings.

Take a look at the depreciable improvements, too, when you're sizing up a property you might want to trade for. Are they larger, or smaller, in relation to the value of the land under the property you now own? You remember, of course, that land can't be depreciated. So if you trade for a property where the value of the depreciable improvements is relatively greater as compared with the land, you can cut your tax bill further.

In general, the best way to boost your depreciation allowances is to trade up. Stated as simply as possible, your new property's tax basis will be its fair market value minus any gain on the old property that hasn't been recognized for tax purposes. Or, stated in a much more roundabout way, it will be:

1. The adjusted basis of the old property
2. PLUS boot given
3. MINUS boot received
4. PLUS mortgages you assume on new property
5. MINUS mortgages on your old property
6. PLUS any taxed gain on old property.

Here's an example. Suppose the property you now own has a tax basis of $20,000, a market value of $50,000, and a mortgage debt of $10,000 outstanding against it. You exchange this property for one worth $140,000 encumbered by a $95,000 mortgage, which you assume. To make up the difference in equities you toss in cash boot of $5,000. The exchange will be totally tax-free to you, because you get no net mortgage relief or other boot.

By such a trade, you rake in a bonanza. You now own a property three times as valuable as the old one, and presumably with a net operating income some three times as great. In addition you've upped your tax basis from $20,000 to $110,000—entitling you to take several times as much annual depreciation on your future tax returns.

You can determine your new tax basis by either of the two methods mentioned above. If you use the first, simply subtract your unrecognized gain of $30,000 (the $50,000 fair market value of the property you traded away, minus its $20,000 tax basis) from the $140,000 fair market value of the property you acquire.

If you use the second, you add to the $20,000 basis of your old property the $95,000 mortgage you're taking on, and the $5,000 in cash you're coughing up as boot; from this total you subtract the $10,000 debt you're getting rid of. The basis of the property isn't affected by your profit on the old, because you won't be paying any tax on this gain.

Is it always better to exchange? Some real estate people will contend that in a situation like the one above it might be better to sell the old property, pay the capital gains tax on the profit, and buy the new in a separate transaction. Their reasoning might run something like this: (1) you would fatten the tax basis of the property you were acquiring from $110,000 to $140,000, thereby swelling the depreciation you could ultimately take on the new property proportionately, and (2) you would be paying a tax on your gain at capital gains rates (that is, generally paying tax on only half your gain at whatever ordinary tax rates would apply) while being able to deduct every dollar of whatever additional depreciation you could take from future income.

They could be right from a strictly tax angle—depending mostly on how the gain would affect your tax bracket in the year or years you'd be liable for taxes on it, and what your income might otherwise be in the years in which you'd be taking the extra depreciation. But you should look at other angles besides taxes. Whether you sell your old property on terms that render the gain immediately taxable or qualify the sale for installment treatment, you'll have much less available to reinvest than if you exchange. In fact, there might be a serious question as to whether you'd be able to buy the new property at all. You might find the owner was still expecting a down payment of $40,000, while all you could scrape up after considering your liability for taxes and/or the borrowing power or discount value of your paper was $32,500. Whatever the circumstances, you wouldn't be able to control as valuable a property on reinvesting, nor could you step up to the same high tax basis you were seeking.

I have mentioned this point before but it's worth repeating. A dollar now is worth much more to you than a dollar one year or ten years from now, if only because of what you can earn with it in the meantime. It might take you ten, fifteen or twenty years to save as much in taxes from an additional depreciation deduction as you'd pay out in taxes if you were to sell instead of exchange. And this isn't even considering the value of the additional property you could probably acquire with the tax money in the meantime!

All this, of course, is one more reason for having a competent tax consultant (and preferably one who works extensively in real estate matters) review and advise you on any contemplated sale, exchange, or purchase of real estate. I can state only general principles here. There could be situations where, despite the advantages I have mentioned, a sale instead of an exchange would be better for you.

One such situation might be where you're disposing of property at a loss. Losses realized in qualified exchanges aren't counted for income tax purposes, and any boot received in the exchange merely results in an adjustment to the tax basis of the property being exchanged. If your other income is such that you can take advantage of the loss, you'll probably be better off selling the old property and buying the new in separate transactions.

No mortgages wanted? There are people in this world who want nothing to do with mortgages, either as borrowers or as lenders. Maybe they once got burned as a mortgagor or mortgagee. Or maybe they cling to the old Puritan belief in staying out of debt, as well as to the Shakespearean advice: "Neither a borrower nor a lender be."

A broker friend of mine once met one of these people. The broker's client owned land worth $80,000, which he wanted to trade for a small apartment house. A $60,000 purchase-money mortgage was owed against the land, so the client had a $20,000 equity to work with.

Another broker in the same town knew a lady who owned an apartment house free and clear. She was looking for a chance to trade it for land. And she happened to want exactly the kind of land my broker friend's client owned. Moreover, the value of the apartment house was virtually identical with the value of the land—making a trade seem all the more feasible. All that was needed to equalize the equities was for the landowner to give the lady a $60,000 purchase-money first mortgage for the difference.

But the lady wouldn't accept a mortgage as part of the trade. Nor would she assume responsibility for the existing mortgage on the land. Unless she could have the land free and clear, she didn't want it.

The landowner couldn't come close to raising $60,000 to pay off the land mortgage before the trade. But a little imagination and resourcefulness paid off. My broker friend and I went to see the man who held the mortgage on the land. We found as I suspected that he was delighted to exchange his mortgage for what he regarded as a much more secure similar mortgage on the apartment house. So the lady got her land free and clear—with no payments or collections to be made on mortgages of any kind—and my friend's client got the apartment house on which he continued to make payments to the same creditor as before.

Boot can be a troublesome question when you're trying to arrange a tax-free exchange. Since boot is taxable to the extent of any gain being realized, the party receiving it may want to back out. Often there is no way to eliminate boot or reduce it to an acceptable level. But sometimes what appears to be impossible can be done.

Suppose, for instance, you've been investing in residential property for some years, and now include among your holdings a free and clear apartment building worth $275,000. But the properties are getting burdensome because they make you spend too much time on managerial details. So you'd like to trade the apartment house for some other income-producing property that will be simpler to manage. You tell your broker this, and he starts searching.

He finds a Mr. Steel, owner of a small industrial building, who would like to trade for an apartment house of the type you're offering. Everything seems to fit perfectly. Mr. Steel's building is leased to a strong national company for the next twenty years. You can just sit back and watch the cash roll in without any bothersome detail work. Its fair market value, based on the income it produces, is $425,000. Mr. Steel owes $150,000 on the mortgage against it, so his equity is $275,000—exactly the same as your equity in the apartment house. What could be sweeter?

You and Steel inspect each other's property. You both like what you see. You agree in principle to the proposed exchange.

But then Mr. Steel's accountant points out that he'll make a profit on the exchange, and that $150,000 (the value of the mortgage you'll be taking over) will be taxable as long-term gain. Mr. Steel is shocked. He's already in such a high tax bracket that the exchange would cost him $42,000 in taxes to Uncle Sam, and several thousand more to the state.

He tells you it's all off. He just can't afford to pay out that much money in taxes. It would more than offset any advantage he expected to get from the exchange.

So you and your broker grope for some way to eliminate or drastically reduce the mortgage-relief boot.

Should you take out a $150,000 mortgage loan on the apartment house, to equalize mortgage debt and eliminate boot? No, because this would reduce your equity in the apartment house to $125,000 as compared with his equity of $275,000, and you'd have to make up the $150,000 difference in some other form of boot. Thus Mr. Steel would owe just as much tax as he would with the mortgage relief.

Should you try to find some way for him to pay off his $150,000 mortgage before the exchange? No, because even if you could arrange it, this would simply increase his equity to $425,000 as compared with your equity of $275,000—leaving you both with essentially the same problem but less money to work with.

But at last a brilliant idea dawns on you. Why not try to borrow that $150,000 on your apartment house to eliminate the mortgage boot (as you'd previously considered) but with a startling difference? Instead of paying this $150,000 to Mr. Steel, why not use it to buy free and clear another apartment house Mr. Steel might want? This would enable you to limit the entire exchange to properties of like kind—with no net mortgage relief or other boot to be received by either party and therefore no taxes! He'd be getting $425,000 worth of qualifying property with a $150,000 mortgage on it and you'd be getting the same!

Then other creative ideas come to your mind. What if you find you can borrow only $100,000 against your apartment house? No problem! You'll still buy another $150,000 apartment house, but with a $50,000 mortgage against it instead of 100 percent cash. This would still offset $150,000 in mortgage debt on the one property with $150,000 in mortgage debt on the other two properties—so, again, there'll be no mortgage relief and no tax bill for either you or Mr. Steel.

Even this isn't necessarily the best possible solution. Suddenly you realize that you may not have to borrow directly at all. Instead, you can simply create a mortgage against your original apartment property. You can use this mortgage as part or full payment for the new $150,000 property, taking out a purchase-money mortgage to finance whatever balance may be needed.

Doing this is surprisingly easy. You just pick up some mortgage forms from a stationery store, put them in a typewriter, and type up a mortgage on your own property in favor of the owner of the property you want to buy. If you're not sure how to fill in the blanks, or how to word the terms, your banker or an escrow company will be glad to prepare the papers for you, charging a fee of only ten dollars or so. Normally you won't have to pay any points, and you'll escape most of the other charges that would be tacked on if you borrowed in the usual way. Better still, you'll probably have much more room to negotiate provisions favorable to you than you would with an outside lender.

If the owner of the property is willing to go along, this creation could be the best solution for both of you.

Two dollars can do the work of four when they're in the form of mortgage notes instead of cash. What I mean by this paradox is that you can often use existing mortgage notes at face value in exchanges, even though the same notes would be sharply discounted if you sold them for cash. This can sometimes give you a chance to turn a profit of as much as 50 percent virtually overnight.

Let's assume you've got $12,000 in cash, and want to invest it in income-producing real estate. You figure that this much money can probably make you the owner of a property worth at least $60,000.

But you can really do much better than that, if you know how.

Instead of beginning with a direct purchase of property, you can scan the "Mortgages and Trust Deeds for Sale" ads in the papers. Or you can make a few inquiries among builders and Realtors. You'll almost certainly find that you can buy one or more high-quality mortgages or trust deeds having a total face value of as much as $24,000 with the same $12,000 cash.

Then you go looking for property. Instead of cash, you offer your newly bought mortgages or trust deeds in exchange for a $24,000 equity in real estate worth perhaps as much as $120,000. This has been done many times.

Even though most sellers want cash down payments, there are always some who don't need cash and would much prefer to watch the dollars roll in every month from a properly secured mortgage or trust deed. If they took cash on the sale, they'd simply put it into a savings account at much lower interest than they can collect from your realty notes.

Taking a repurchase option when you exchange is a money-making technique you can use when you're temporarily strapped for cash but are sure you'll have ample income a few years from now.

Let's assume you own some free and clear land worth $100,000 in a rapidly developing area. You find yourself operating on a very tight cash budget and badly in need of a tax shelter. You consider trading your land for income property that will provide you with both cash flow and tax shelter. But you're reluctant to do so because you feel pretty sure the land will be worth three or four times as much in another five years.

While pondering the problem, you become acquainted with a wealthy widow, Mrs. Lodge. She is willing to accept a $50,000 created mortgage against your land as down payment on a $200,000 income property she'd like to sell. This would permit you to acquire a tax shelter through ownership of her property, without giving up the appreciation potential of the land.

You do see one big problem, however. Although the after-tax cash flow from the property will more than cover the payments you'll have to make on the $150,000 balance of the purchase price, there won't be enough left over to take care of the payments on the $50,000 created mortgage as well. And you simply can't afford to take on additional cash obligations now. It will be a different story three years from now when your four kids finish college and your new business reaches its full potential.

What should you do about Mrs. Lodge's offer? Accept it and hope you can scrape up the payments somehow? Or play safe and pass up the opportunity?

Neither. Instead you offer to exchange your entire $100,000 equity interest in the land for a $50,000 equity interest in her $200,000 income property. You do this on the condition she'll grant you an option to buy the land back at any time within the next five years at the same $50,000 price plus an additional amount of, say, 8 percent compounded annually (plus taxes and other costs) for each year your option remains unexercised.

Do you see what you're doing? In effect, you're asking her to lend you $50,000 for up to five years without committing yourself to make any payments on it.

But it's not a one-way street. It will enrich Mrs. Lodge, too, if she's in no immediate need of cash. The worst that can happen to her (if you exercise your option) is that she'll get an 8 percent per annum return on the $50,000 *and it will all be capital gain!* If you don't exercise your option, she'll get free and clear title to land currently worth twice the $50,000 she was giving up for it. It probably will be worth much more later.

Thus, to sum things up, you'll have feathered your nest five ways at once:

1. stepped into the tax shelter you were seeking;
2. held on to the chance to profit from further fattening in the value of the land;
3. dodged any further immediate drain on your cash resources;
4. picked up some added cash flow from the income property;
5. set up a chance at another profit from improvement and resale of the income property.

Trade and leaseback is another technique that has helped build financial independence for numerous investors. Here's how it works.

You own an apartment house. It's bringing in plenty of rent money. But you need a tax shelter. Your apartment house doesn't give you the deductions you need, because it is located on valuable land that can't be depreciated; the value of your building and improvements is too small in relation to the value of the land. (This is a common problem vexing investors who own a small building in a particularly desirable location.)

How can you hold on to as many as possible of the thousands of dollars you will otherwise be paying out in taxes? One way would be to sell your property, and buy something else for which the value of the improvements is greater in relation to the value of the land. Another way would be to try to work the same switch through an exchange. But there is something else you might do to get even greater tax and other benefits.

If you don't need cash flow, you might consider exchanging your property for a highly leveraged position (that is, heavily mortgaged) in land that seems likely to go up in value. This would both reduce your current income and give you an additional tax saving from the interest you'd be paying. What you'd really be doing, however, is speculating on an increase in land values.

But there's a still better way, especially if you want to keep the cash flowing in. Remember that your building and the land under it can be owned, sold, or traded separately. Maybe somebody would like to own this land and lease it back to you. In exchange for your land, maybe he'll give up another investment property where the depreciable assets are comparatively high in relation to the land value. The ideal candidate for such a trade would be someone who is tired of managing his investment property, isn't in danger of uncomfortably heavy tax bills, and would prefer the steady management-free income that a long-term land lease would provide.

Would this be a good deal for you too? Yes indeed. First of all, the payments you make on the land lease can be charged off against income from other sources. You'll thus get back a good share of these rental payments in the form of lower income taxes.

Second, you'll boost your depreciation deduction delightfully. You can still take whatever deduction is available from your original property, and also charge off depreciation on the newly acquired property.

Third (assuming that you've planned your trade wisely), the cash flow from the new property should more than cover your payments on the land lease and be mostly or wholly tax-free.

Fourth, you can stand to gain in two ways if real estate values keep rising: you can gain from any increase in the rental income or resale value of the new income property you're acquiring, and you can gain the same way on the building you still own, even though you've sold and leased back the land under it.

Not too bad for a little exercise of creative financial thinking, and perhaps a few days' work!

Trading with someone who is short of cash can often be worked out to the benefit of both parties, if you use some of the special techniques that have been developed by imaginative investors.

Here's an example. We'll imagine you own a piece of land worth $60,000. You owe $15,000 on an assumable mortgage against it, which you're paying off at $150 per month. So your equity is $45,000.

But you confront two problems. Making those mortgage payments is keeping you uncomfortably short of cash. And you'll owe a big tax bill in April unless you find some tax shelter.

A logical solution is to trade your land for income-producing property that will at least carry itself and give you a deduction for depreciation. So you advertise in the paper. You get a call from a Mr. Short, who owns an apartment house and is interested in your land.

You look at his property. He looks at yours. Both of you are pleased. A trade will benefit both of you, if you can just work out an agreement on values and terms.

Finally you do so. Mr. Short agrees to accept your land at its fair market value of $60,000. You agree that his apartments are worth $160,000. You both decide that you'll get together in a few days to figure out the final details.

Mr. Short owes $120,000 on his apartments. The mortgage can be assumed. So your final problem is to balance Mr. Short's equity of

$40,000 in the apartments against your $45,000 equity in the land (its $60,000 value minus the $15,000 mortgage).

Mr. Short's apartments are bringing in net spendable cash of $300 every month—over and above the amount needed to make the mortgage payments and cover all other expenses including maintenance, repairs, and a comfortable reserve for vacancies. This is better than you'd expected. All you were trying to do was to find a legal solution to your tax problem and escape the pinch caused by your land's property taxes and mortgage payments. So you happily await the meeting with Mr. Short to close the trade.

But suddenly he phones you: "I'm afraid our deal is off. I still want your land and would like to trade for it on the terms we figured out. But I just can't find any way to raise the $5,000 I'd have to pay you to make up for the difference in equities."

You think fast. "No problem," you say. "I'll be glad to carry back a $5,000 purchase-money second mortgage on the land. I'll only charge 7 percent interest, and I'll let you pay in installments as small as fifty dollars a month."

Mr. Short sighs. "That's mighty nice of you. But I'd still have to pay $150 a month on the existing land mortgage, plus the property taxes and $50 to you—and I don't think I'll have that much cash available every month. I should have figured this out sooner, but the cash flow from my apartments has kept me feeling prosperous, and I didn't realize what a difference it would make not to be getting that income any more."

In other words, his problem is similar to yours. Both of you own valuable assets but you both need more cash than you can count on.

Fighting down the impulse to hang up in disgust, you say, "Let me mull it over. Would you still be interested if I think of some way for you to acquire my land with no more cash outlay than the land taxes?"

He sure would. He knows, as you do, that your land is likely to be extremely valuable someday. So you think and you think.

You realize that you'll have enough cash to get by if you just don't have to make those mortgage payments on the land. That $300 monthly cash flow from Mr. Short's apartments won't be terribly important to you. Is there some way you can equitably divert part of it to him?

At last you find an astounding answer. Write two new mortgages instead of one!

By cleverly adjusting the terms of payment on the two mortgages, you can overcome Mr. Short's cash flow problem. Remember that you must get $5,000 from Mr. Short to compensate for the difference in equities, and that he can neither scrape up $5,000 nor undertake to pay $150 per month on the existing land mortgage. Let's take the solution step by step.

1. You'll write a second mortgage for, say, $10,000 in Mr. Short's favor, with the apartment house you'll be acquiring as collateral, on condition that—
2. He'll give you a similar second mortgage on the land he'll acquire from you. But this mortgage will be $5,000 bigger than yours, to balance the difference in equities.
3. You'll make payments of $300 per month to Mr. Short on the $10,000 mortgage he'll carry back, on condition that—
4. He'll make monthly payments of $150 to you on the $15,000 mortgage you'll carry back.

Of course, the net effect is that every month for the next few years Mr. Short will receive $150 more from you than he'll be paying you. This will give him the money he needs for the $150 monthly payment on the land mortgage.

You'll be paying off your debt to him much faster than he'll be paying what he owes you. So the time will come when he'll have to rely on his own resources to cover the two $150 monthly mortgage payments. You point this out to him. "That's all right," he answers. "A few years from now I'll have ample cash flow from other sources."

So you've solved his problem and your own problem as well. You'll have improved your net cash flow by several hundred dollars a month, and you'll have acquired a tax shelter in the depreciation allowance you can take on the apartments, thus increasing your net cash spendable even more.

Making money by giving it away is another strategy that millionaires use—and that you may be able to use too, even though you're not quite in that category. It's a good idea to keep in mind for the time when you're tired of the fun of buying and selling and managing properties, and would like to stop work without stopping your income.

When you reach such a point, you'll quite possibly find yourself in a high tax bracket, despite your know-how in minimizing taxes.

Moreover, if you start selling off your investments, you'll be forced to pay the heavy capital gains taxes that you've kept deferring through tax-free exchanges.

You can postpone a good part of this tax bite by qualifying your sales for installment treatment. And you can very likely make additional savings by trading down. But this would probably intensify your management problems before it would ease them.

There's a better way. Instead of selling and paying the taxes, you can just give away some or all of your properties. Foolish? Impractical? Not at all. You can still keep the cash rolling in to you from these investments. You can even bequeath the income to your heirs for twenty years, without anyone being taxed on the capital gains you've piled up. It's like giving away your cake and having it too.

You can do this by giving away the property to a charity—a youth movement, a church, a college, a fraternal order, a service club such as Kiwanis or Rotary, or virtually any other organization that the Internal Revenue code recognizes as a tax-deductible charity.

Congress wrote certain provisions of our tax laws for the avowed purpose of encouraging charitable gifts. The provisions that concern us here apply to something called a unitrust. This may be a new word to you, so let's define it before we go further.

A unitrust, or "charitable remainder unitrust," to give it its full name, is a special kind of trust. You set up a trust fund, into which you put property and from which a fixed percentage (at least 5 percent) of the net market value of the trust's assets as valued each year is:

1. distributed at least annually;
2. to one or more beneficiaries named by you;
3. at least one of which is not a charity;
4. for the beneficiary's lifetime or for twenty years, whichever is shorter;
5. with an irrevocable remainder interest to be paid to, or held for, a qualified charity.

In other words, you set aside property or other assets that will eventually go to a designated charity, meanwhile continuing to provide yourself and/or other beneficiaries with a steady income from these assets. You're really exchanging your property for income, even though you're also making a charitable contribution that is income-tax deductible.

You work out the details with the charitable organization that you want to benefit, including the percentage of the trust's assets that will be paid yearly to you or other beneficiaries. You can write the terms of your gift in such a way that the beneficiaries will be paid a fixed percentage of the value of the trust's assets, whether the trust actually earns any income or not. Or you can stipulate that the beneficiaries will be paid the actual income, up to the percentage you set. In this latter case, you can specify whether any shortages in early distributions will or won't be made up if the income from the trust's assets gets bigger than the stated percentage in later years.

In the eyes of the tax collectors, the income paid to the beneficiaries by the trust will remain the same kind it was in the trust, and will be taxed as such. Ordinary income (including short-term capital gains) is considered distributed first; long-term capital gains second; tax-exempt income third; and any return of principal (also non-taxable) last—until the stated percentage return has been reached, computed on that year's fair market value of the trust's assets.

The percentage itself is a matter of negotiation with the charitable organization. Normally this percentage should be somewhat smaller than the trust's prospective yearly income. Otherwise the principal might dwindle, and the charity might eventually get little or nothing.

The unitrust gives you both tangible and intangible benefits. The tangible benefit is the tax savings, which could be huge. Remember that you can deduct from your other taxable income the full market value of the property you're contributing, regardless of how little you originally paid for it. In addition, you avoid any liability for taxes on the capital gains. So if you're in the 50 percent bracket, you'll get half the value of your contribution back in reduced income taxes. And, of course, you can take that half and reinvest it to produce an income that could easily total half what you were previously getting on the donated property.

Moreover, for many years to come the unitrust will presumably be paying you and/or other beneficiaries something approaching the income you were receiving from the property before you "exchanged" it for a beneficial interest in the trust. Thus the near-miraculous result of your generosity is that this property could conceivably bring you and your loved ones substantially (perhaps as much as 20 or 30 percent) more income than it brought you before you deeded it over to charity!

There are other tangible benefits too. A unitrust is a hedge against inflation, because the income you're entitled to receive from it is based on a percentage of the fair market value of the trust's assets. If inflation pushes up the prices of these assets, you'll get the same percentage of the higher prices. Moreover the trust can be more flexible in its investment policies than you could be, perhaps, when your capital was tied up in real estate that you couldn't sell without paying taxes. Still further, your heirs can be drawing income immediately from the unitrust after you die—perhaps with lower estate and inheritance taxes, certainly with lower costs for will probate and administration.

Contrast all these benefits with what would probably happen if, instead of giving your property to charity, you sold it and reinvested the proceeds. If your original cost basis was negligible, you might owe Uncle Sam 25 percent or more of the proceeds in capital gains taxes. With only 75 percent available to reinvest, your prospects for future income would be trimmed accordingly.

Aside from the monetary benefits of a unitrust, there are the intangible benefits: the satisfaction of contributing generously to a worthy cause, and perhaps of being such an important donor that the charity will honor you in various ways. Maybe you'll find that it names something after you, so that you'll be remembered long after you're gone. Such considerations might warm your family's heart in years to come.

REMEMBER THESE HIGH POINTS:

When you buy property, make clear in the documents that you're buying as an investment.

Don't buy and sell too often in too short a time.

Keep sales transactions to a minimum by trading wherever possible.

Mortgage notes can often be used at face value in exchanges.

If you're temporarily short of cash, taking a repurchase option when you exchange is a money-getting technique.

Leaseback arrangements can be good tax shelters.

You can trade with someone even though he may be short of cash.

When you want to make a sizable donation to charity, consider giving property instead of money. There are tax advantages.

XXII *On Your Way*

You have finished this book. What has it done for you?

Perhaps you've already found it the best investment of your life. It can be, if you're putting into practice the simple but powerful money-making methods it explains.

Or maybe you don't know yet what the book can do for you, because you haven't started to use it. Why wait? Golden opportunities in real estate are out there for the taking, no matter whether you live in a huge city or a tiny village, no matter how fat or slender your bankroll. This book tells you where to look, how to recognize the big profit opportunities when you see them, what to do to cash in on them.

Detailed examples have shown how people like you put these wealth-building principles into practice. If you too will apply the knowledge in this book, you can get results.

It takes some work, of course. But the work is fun—because you're creating things. You're creating better places for people to live. You're creating financial ideas that will make money for you and for everyone else involved. Making money is fun too.

Your only barrier is inertia. Most of us have an inborn reluctance to bestir ourselves. Professor William James of Harvard used to say that the average person uses only one-tenth of his brains and energy. Anyone who makes a real effort gets much further than seemed possible.

If you've read all these chapters just nodding your head in understanding but not getting started on your own investment program, you should turn back now to Chapter II or Chapter III and follow their directions in mustering your financial resources or hunting for good buys. Get started! That's the hardest single step. Most of us sit still and promise ourselves we'll do something tomorrow. Once we get out of our chairs and into action, everything is easier.

Remember the old proverb? "Well begun is half-done." So begin!

Do something—anything—to start your muscles moving and your brain working. It's rather like warming up for a football game. Some players rehearse a few signals. Others run around, or throw a ball. Others push against each other to get the feel of contact. So do whatever is easiest to get yourself started. Pick up the phone and chat with someone who's active in real estate. Or pick up the paper and study the real estate ads.

Then immediately, while you're in the mood, start looking at real estate. Look again tomorrow. Whenever you're with other people, seize opportunities to steer the conversation toward real estate. You'll find that almost everyone is interested in discussing it. Let people know that you're looking around for real estate bargains; soon you'll be tuned to the grapevine and you'll hear of promising opportunities. Then you'll be on your way for sure.

Review this book early and often. Don't be satisfied with an occasional glance. Whenever there's a problem that puzzles you, look in the table of contents and you'll almost certainly see keys to a solution. Before each step in the investment process—hunting, analyzing, negotiating, borrowing or lending, figuring profits and taxes, deciding when and how to sell or exchange—turn back and review the sections of this book that show you the money-making angles connected with that particular phase.

Even on your third or fourth reading of a chapter, you'll probably find information you've forgotten or minimized. Reviews will advance you easily toward the point at which you'll use all this knowledge automatically, with no conscious effort.

I wrote this book out of a sincere desire to help you. It will give me great happiness to know that the book is helping you achieve your goal of financial independence. The principles in this volume work when you put them to work.

We may never meet in person, but in this book we have met. We are friends. Let's keep moving ahead together. Good hunting and God bless you!

REMEMBER THESE HIGH POINTS:

Opportunities for small investors in real estate are everywhere.
Your biggest barrier is inertia. Make yourself get started!
As you go along, review pertinent chapters of this book.

Index